Praise for Catching Tadpoles

Occasionally hilarious, often terrifying, sometimes gossipy, always engaging, Catching Tadpoles *is a brilliant account of a child growing up in a brutal, unfair system, and at the cusp of adulthood saying: no way, not me, damn their eyes.* – Richard Poplack, author of *Ja, No, Man: Growing Up White in Apartheid-Era South Africa*

Ronnie Kasrils gives us the first 21 years of his life with all the elements that have made him beloved of freedom fighters and book readers alike: his dash, his cunning, his humour, his humanity and – most of all – his irrepressible joie de vivre. He comes of age, he comes to political consciousness and he brings his early worlds – from Jewish Yeoville to Bohemian Joburg – to life. Unputdownable. – **Mark Gevisser**, author of *Lost and Found in Johannesburg: A Memoir*

Catching Tadpoles *is beautiful because Kasrils is impossible; disarmed but more dangerous with pen than a rusting Makarov.* – **Ashwin Desai**, author of *Reverse Sweep: South African Cricket since Apartheid*

I love his story. It is like mine: trauma, tension, fear, fun and belief in something. His was right; mine was never left. I now call him a friend, a patriot en 'n bietjie mal. – **Evita Bezuidenhout**, performer, author, satirist and social activist

The vivid details in these memories are captivating, and from them emerge a coherent narrative of an extraordinary life fully lived. It's a hugely enjoyable read and reveals a life which South Africans young and old – and others – have so much to learn from. – **Victoria Brittain**, author and journalist

In this new work, we get closer to the boykie who grew up whitish to become the man we have come to respect for his steadfast political and existential courage, for his integrity, for his wit and humour, for his fierce commitment to apparently lost causes, for his ability to think and act and engage beyond the limitations of self and of tribe and political expediency and interest. All of the foregoing — and then to be a true writer as well! From this apparent contradiction, he has forged a dialectic for decency. – **Breyten Breytenbach**, poet, painter and author of several books including The True Confessions of an Albino Terrorist and Dog Heart: A Memoir

Radiant and rumbustious, Ronnie wears his youthful heart on his sleeve ... a powerful read. – **Albie Sachs**, activist and a former judge on the Constitutional Court of South Africa

Kasrils' conscience, his questioning mind and a sense of justice predestined his collision with racial domination and apartheid. A decade of teenaged youthful rebellion was crystallised into active participation in the national liberation struggle by the Sharpeville Massacre of March 1960. Once he had connected the dots, he committed himself, heart and soul, to the struggle to liberate South Africa from racial oppression. In these pages, Kasrils shares with us the social milieu, family and societal values that shaped the mature liberation fighter. – **Z. Pallo Jordan**, Letters to My Comrades: Interventions and Excursions

As a young black female author, I am enthralled at how Ronnie managed to use his voice and other resources available to him in order to serve the world and rally for justice. I am immensely captured by the image of a young Ronnie Kasrils who feels so intensely and believes wholeheartedly. That is the kind of young South African that our ancestors wished to pave a way for. We are each called to view and partake actively in our societies with a potent combination of optimism and the relentless activism of a young heart that is on fire. – **Zanele Njapha**, author of An Eye for Love

Kasrils is irreverent and irrepressible – the original rebel without a pause. – **Zapiro**, cartoonist and author of several books, including *WTF: Capturing Zuma – A Cartoonist's Tale*

In this delightful book, Ronnie Kasrils lifts the veil on the formative years of a revolutionary activist. It is a fascinating read and a rich account of a white boy coming of age in apartheid South Africa. It provides the clues of how this remarkable South African first began to explore the vision of a new and free South Africa. – **Luli Callinicos**, historian and author of *The World that made Mandela* and *Oliver Tambo: Beyond the Engeli Mountains*

Here's the boykie before he becomes a Bolshevik. This is Ronnie, not yet Kasrils the ANC guerrilla, anti-apartheid fighter, underground operative. A white Yeoville boyhood lovingly recalled. In its unpretentious way it challenges the fashionable identity politics of our times. We're more, it gently reminds us, than the early identities into which we're nurtured. And yet ... somehow, always marked by them too. A childhood and adolescence recounted with Kasrils's eye for detail and an empathetic memory. – **Jeremy Cronin**, author of *More Than a Casual Contact*

Many South Africans have wondered what influenced Ronnie Kasrils as a child to have empathy for the underdog and ultimately take on the apartheid state as one of the founding members of Umkhonto we Sizwe in Natal in 1961. The answers lie in Kasrils's beautifully written narrative of his formative years, which portrays in vivid detail the origins of his early politicisation. A revolutionary had been born in the belly of white apartheid South Africa, who would rise up in defiance of one of the world's most unjust systems. Catching Tadpoles *is an illuminating read which unpacks how it came to be that a few whites, often of Jewish extraction, developed the courage to reject everything they were taught.* – **Shannon Ebrahim**, Group Foreign Editor for Independent Media, South Africa

This fine book illustrates that Kasrils's rebel child is father to the revolutionary man. – **Mongane Wally Serote**, author of *Yakhal'Inkomo*.

Catching Tapoles *is a delicious artistic achievement by Ronnie Kasrils on multiple levels: the aesthetic quality of the writing is enviably masterful; the meditation on the psychological quandary of reliable memory is philosophically rich; and the narrative of how a young white boy came to recognise the humanity of all of his fellow citizens regardless of racialised identities – with the concomitant moral and political duties that that awakening brings – will re-inscribe much needed hope into our discourse, making the case again for the possibility of cross-class solidarity in the continued struggle for an anti-racist South Africa.*
– **Eusebius McKaiser**, talk radio host and author of *A Bantu in My Bathroom! Debating Race, Sexuality and Other Uncomfortable South Africa*

Catching Tadpoles

Catching Tadpoles

The Shaping of a Young Rebel

A Memoir

Ronnie Kasrils

First published by Jacana Media (Pty) Ltd in 2019

10 Orange Street
Sunnyside
Auckland Park 2092
South Africa
+2711 628 3200
www.jacana.co.za

© Ronnie Kasrils, 2019

All rights reserved.

ISBN 978-1-4314-2935-6

Also available as an ebook.

Cover design by publicide
All photographs are from the Kasrils family collection unless otherwise indicated.
Layout by Alexandra Turner
Editing by Alison Lowry
Proofreading by Lara Jacob
Index by Megan Mance
Set in MrsEaves 11/15pt
Printed by ABC Press
Job no. 003544

See a complete list of Jacana titles at www.jacana.co.za

*To my mother and father, Izzy and René Kasrils,
and my grandparents,
Sarah and Nathan Kasrils; and Clara and Abe Cohen
And to Nanny Poppy Molefe who also brought me up
In loving memory*

Across the road, tadpoles are dancing
On the quarter thumbnail
Of the moon. They can't see,
Not yet.

— JAMES WRIGHT (FROM SMALL FROGS KILLED ON THE HIGHWAY)

For whatever reason, one lone moment [in early childhood] has been selected and stamped in our brains as the first day our life experiences became worthy of mentally filing away and cataloguing. In a sense, they're our cognitive birthday.

— BILL BRIGGS[1]

If you live to 18, you will have enough to write about for the rest of your life.

— JULIE GURNER[2]

Contents

Preface xv
Acknowledgements xix
Prologue xxiii

PART ONE: 1938–1946
1 Albyn Court, Raymond Street 3
2 The Other Side of the Fence 16
3 Who Killed Jesus? 27

PART TWO: 1946–1951
4 Yeoville Boys 45
5 Dancing with the Sachs Sisters 66
6 Once a Zionist 78

PART THREE: 1951–1956
7 Six of the Best 91
8 Poppy 106
9 Growing Pains 112

10 Liberty, Equality, Fraternity............................. 121
11 Girls, Pinball and High Treason........................... 133

PART FOUR: 1957–1958
12 A Short Walk with July.................................. 145
13 Uncertain Justice 156
14 Assault and Robbery.................................... 167
15 Rigging the Market..................................... 175
16 Rock 'n Roll 181
17 Back of the Moon...................................... 192
18 Patsy.. 200

PART FIVE: 1959–1960
19 Cousin Joel's Library 211
20 Water's Edge.. 218
21 Hidden Persuaders..................................... 231
22 Sharpeville 245
23 Crossroads 251

Afterword 259
Notes... 269
Appendix 283
Index 287

Preface

IT WAS MY PUBLISHERS WHO CAME up with the idea for this 'coming of age' book. Three previous memoirs had been published, covering my life from the age of 20, when I became involved in the South African liberation struggle in 1960.

'Now's the time to deal with those formative years,' they suggested. 'Readers want to know what made a young white boy like you give up privilege and join the liberation struggle. What was life like in the South Africa of the 1940s and 1950s? That will fascinate both whites who did not take your route and blacks, both young and old, but particularly the "born frees",[3] who want to understand why someone like you would give up your privileges for, effectively, their sake.' There's a universal message there, they pointed out.

The suggestion appealed to me. I had been answering those very questions innumerable times in South Africa and abroad. Reminiscing about the past had become second nature. I needed to work on a way of dealing with the tricky issue of memory, however, so as to convince the reader that I was not producing a work of romantic fiction, filled with narcissistic boasts and fantasies.

I had a vivid recall for the key turning points of my life and no sooner was the suggestion made than I began to plunge into the task before me. Plunge being the operative term for in fact I took to it like a duck to water, as I enjoy passing time in a swimming pool, where meditation comes very easily to me. It was there that the metaphor of catching tadpoles came to mind, not only because of my childhood fascination with the impish creatures, but because in the environment of the pool I found that striving to get hold of fleeting memories and slippery images of the past was akin to catching those eccentric amphibians-to-be with one's bare hands.

To write this book, I have relied heavily on memory, backed up by research where possible, to enable me to be sure of certain times, places and events. I haven't been challenged in the other three books as to the fallibility or otherwise of my memory, which is surprising since memory is notoriously unreliable. There was one exception in a review of *Armed and Dangerous* where I was scoffed at for claiming that at the age of seven I was able to ask my mother whether the way black people were being treated in South Africa was akin to the suffering of the Jews in Europe. I write about that particular moment in greater detail in this book. In addition I have read treatises both on memory and the cognitive reasoning of a seven-year-old; I have also talked to young people today and have questioned adults about their memory, and I have no lingering doubt: I stand by my claim of having had the ability to raise such a question at that tender age.

There is a telling anecdote attributed to John Lennon which illustrates and supports my contention. When he was five years old, apparently his mother told him happiness was the key to life. Later at school he was asked what he wanted to be when he grew up. He responded that he wanted to be happy. He was told that he didn't understand the question. He told them they didn't understand life.

To be clear, I am not writing history, but rather recording my impressions of the past as a child, teenager and young adult. A memoir, by dint of the definition, is about memory and personal experiences.

There is no way a writer can recall exact dialogue from the past, and it is often better to summarise narrative than use inverted commas signifying direct speech. Yet there are times when an exchange of words can be dramatised through direct dialogue and this is where I believe a compact between writer and reader can be created to accept an account that is clearly a reconstruction of events for the better telling of the story.

One of the initial things I did before actual writing commenced was to try and recollect my very first memories. This proved to be a fascinating experiment. How far back in my memory could I go? Bill Briggs refers to that first memory stamped in our brain as one's 'cognitive birthday'.

It was out of early memories that I began to build and string together the events that make up this memoir. As the story gained traction and after I had navigated early childhood, my power of recollection improved.

Psychiatrists have had a great interest in studying and analysing memory. They explain that memory becomes reinforced when we begin to speak; and that most people's memories become more meaningful from when they are about five years old. It is from around that age that this memoir commences, apart from the first few chapters where I recount my family origins.

I found that I am at my best in recounting events and experiences, remembering people's faces and mannerisms, when I relax and meditate. This can be extremely fulfilling but also a torture. The torture factor arises when there is so much buzzing around in one's mind that sleep becomes impossible. When this occurs I creep off to my computer and my wife Amina, who is a light sleeper guesses – correctly – that the tadpoles are biting once more.

Acknowledgements

WHEN AT THE AGE OF 24 YOU find yourself on the run from the police with a flight into exile for 27 years, there is not much of your past personal record that survives. This memoir could not have flourished without the invaluable assistance of family and friends in helping to prod my mind, when they didn't even know it, and in providing a treasure trove of photographs, many of which capture the personalities I write about and which adorn the pages of this book.

My mother provided me with many family photographs, as did my sister Hilary Jaffe and various relatives, most particularly my niece Michelle Jaffe, who has a superb collection and went out of her way to assist me. My appreciation to Michelle and her brother Ian Jaffe; Judy and Hymie Feinberg; Lynne Marks; the late Joel Tobias and son George; and Marlen Dyne. Special thanks to Ian Jaffe for assisting in the research for my maternal grandparents' Latvian background; and to both him and Lynne Marks regarding my paternal grandparents' Lithuanian background. Additional thanks to Judy Feinberg for trying to obtain information about her uncle Joe Sher and the majestic racehorse Danny Boy whom he owned in the 1940s. Thanks to Lynne Leister of the National Horseracing Authority for her assistance in this respect as well.

Acknowledgements are due to old school friends Bobby Fussell, David Mackenzie (Mac) and Peter Louis for reinforcing my memory about our days at King Edward VII School (KES) and the photographs provided; and to Megan Ellish of the King Edward Education Trust. Gratitude to KES headmaster, Mr David Lovatt, for the permission so gracefully extended. It needs to be noted that KES no longer practises the corporal punishment of my day, and has transformed along with the guidelines of a democratic South Africa. A scholarship fund is being established to take in a learner from Yeoville Boys, my former primary school, which nowadays caters for almost a totally black African community.

Former KES Old Boy Grenville Middleton connects both with schooldays and early career at Alpha Film Studios and my thanks to him for his reminiscences and photographs. Thanks to Salim Valli for his thoughts and reading matter on education and corporal punishment. Particular appreciation to Larry Salomon, who has provided memorable photographs from his extraordinary collection, including the one on the cover of this book. (Worth visiting is his twelve-part video *History of South Africa* uploaded on You Tube – see https://www.youtube.com/my_videos?o=U.) Thanks to Professor Ian Edwards who discovered the photograph of me with the black eye and some other pictures in the files of the Durban security police. Gratitude to my dear friend Vladimir Shubin for assisting me with the Russian translation of my grandfather Nathan Kasrils' documents; and to Karina Simonson at the Vilna Gaon Jewish State Museum in Vilnius, Lithuania for her co-operation. My indebtedness to Moray Hathorn and Jessica Ferreira at Webber Wentzel Attorneys; and Jenny Friedman Attorneys for their invaluable assistance, although thwarted, owing to lack of court records, in the search for guilty verdicts and sentences in relation to the Western Main Reef share saga. I rely heavily on my archivist at the Wits Historical Papers Research Archive, Gabriele Mohale, a devoted and engaging professional.

It is difficult to put into words my deep appreciation to my dear friend Victoria Brittain for her endless encouragement and the time she finds in her unimaginable busy life to comment on my writing. Thanks to my dear friends Hillary and Tony Hamburger, clinical psychologists of note, for their affinity with the Yeoville and Hillbrow era we were privileged

Acknowledgements

to share, for their encouragement and the sounding-board they provided concerning my questions about children's ability to remember.

I always joke about being BBC as far as modern technology is concerned and I am referring here to having been Born Before Computers. My gratitude to Cassim Boorany for his invaluable assistance and patience in all the computer problems and requirements I plagued him with.

I am lucky that my son Andrew lives down the road and thankful for his stimulating encouragement.

I am very fortunate that my writing life is in the hands of Bridget Impey and Maggie Davey, who publish what they like. It is an honour that they like what I write. Amina and I had the pleasure of attending their wedding party at the end of 2018 and I was asked to be one of the guests who proposed blessings. Mine was in the style of a four-stanza limerick which ended as follows:

Hail dear Davey and Impey
stern foes of izimpimpi
upholding truth
against the uncouth
power in pen and inkey.

Thanks to their hard-working team, including Megan Mance, Lara Jacob, Alexandra Turner and Kelsey Matus for the dedication and professionalism in every aspect of production, including the photographic selection, copyright and proofreading. My highest praise for the skilful work of my editor Alison Lowry. She is a supreme make-up artist, using delicate cosmetic techniques to smooth over my flaws and blemishes, subtly enhancing the complexion of the subject to pass muster in the light of day, and adroitly reconstructing when necessary. For her my unbounded admiration.

I'm grateful to all those who played a role in helping me surmount many problems. My wife Eleanor through 48 years; and my present wife Amina, who has proved to be such a comfort to me.

I am the grandfather of a most beautiful little girl named Leilani Eleanor, daughter of my son Andrew and his wife Stella Olawumi. My hope is that Leilani's generation and those to come will inherit a better world from us. May their clear bright eyes sparkle with wonderment for our beautiful universe and be spared the barbarism we have seen. To achieve that dream means we human beings have to work for it and pass on to them the flame of purity and hope.

Prologue

I WAS WITH MY GRANDMA CLARA when I first saw a tadpole. We were picnicking near a pool and I was already doing the doggy paddle. It was summer and the water was tepid with just a slight sandy colouring but otherwise very clear. I would laugh and cry 'I'm a doggy, woof! woof!' and wonder what else I would be.

I was astonished by the quirky black blob with a powerful tail that eluded my groping hands. Grandma helped me catch it with a net and we took it home in a jam jar. She had pointed to the jelly-like mush floating on the water and told me that was where the tadpole had spawned from froggie eggs. I put the jar on a shelf in my bedroom and fed the tadpole on pieces of grass. Over the coming days I watched it begin to transform into what would become a frog. When we finally put the emergent creature into a garden pond I asked Gran whether the frog would remember having once been a tadpole.

She shook her head and laughed. 'It's like the chicken and the egg,' she said. 'The chicken doesn't remember being in the egg. When you are old like me you will remember being a child. If you didn't have that memory you wouldn't have any history. Never forget from where you come and who you are.'

I was mischievous and contrary. 'I'm a wiggly tadpole,' I replied.

'To grow up to be a frog?' she said in mock astonishment.

'Yes, a big green one,' I answered, puffing out my cheeks and trying to frighten her.

'Well,' she said, 'if you try hard enough you can be anything you want.' From then on she often called me her tadpole.

PART ONE

1938–1946

First memories get beyond the presentations of everyday life – of clothing, career and status – and reveal something distinctly personal and unique about you ... something about our families or environment. But all of it has something that has been so resilient that it has withstood many years of other memories and experiences without erasure. For some it will be fun, for others, very painful – but for everyone, it's personal.

– JULIE GURNER[4]

CHAPTER 1

Albyn Court, Raymond Street

As I swim Grandma floats into view, arms outstretched, beckoning to me. Within the quivering lightness of water I inhale and exhale. Ear-drums beat as in an echo chamber. I hear her calling to me in a teasing way, 'Come, come, Ron-a-la, my little tadpole.'

Dark fluffy hair, translucent skin, protective gaze fixed on me. I surge through the shimmering pool with powerful frog-like kicks propelling my body forward with the butterfly stroke.

I love being with her. With her and my mother René, who says my *bobba* (grandma) Clara Cohen never told a lie in her life. Grandma smells of lavender and wears floral dresses. She died in 1946, which was an eventful year for me, aged eight in rumbustious Johannesburg. The city was my womb. A city which grew out of a rip-roaring mining camp when gold was discovered in 1886[5] – also the year of Grandma's birth.

Impoverished rural African farmers, transformed into a proletariat, drawn to sell their labour power in the mines and factories, referred to the city as '*Gauteng maboneng*' – the place of gold with the lights – or simply as 'e*Goli*'.[6] They could have been speaking for the European and Asian fortune seekers who flocked there, or for that matter the white Afrikaner miners who lost their farms after the Boer War. Everything and everyone was in a state of transformation and flux. My grandmother used to click her tongue when reading the newspapers, saying the city had not outgrown the gold rush mentality. Her husband, my *zeder* (grandpa) Abraham Cohen, commercial traveller and inveterate gambler, would sidle out of the room when she did that, thinking she was referring to the likes of him.

I was delivered into this world at the Florence Nightingale Maternity Home in 1938 when the city was a mere half-a-century old. Jean-Paul Sartre writes somewhere that one is 'thrown into the world' and although my mother would be shocked by such a description, and by all accounts my birth was quick and smooth, my birthplace was a stone's throw from Johannesburg's infamous city prison on Hillbrow ridge called The Fort. I realised much later that the cries of newborn infants must have accompanied the screams of black prisoners on the rack, and that being thrown into the world was an apt description. Gerard Sekota's paintings immortalised those convicts in red shirts and khaki shorts breaking rocks.

I grew up on the borderline of Bellevue-Yeoville, boisterous twin suburbs filled with Jewish immigrants. Bobba Clara and Zeder Abe Cohen lived around the corner from us. Abe was a corpulent character filled with *joie de vivre* while Clara was demure and reserved. Both were from Latvia – she from the port of Libau and he from Salant near Riga – but met in South Africa. My father, Izzy Kasrils, was from Vilna (now Vilnius), Lithuania. Jews from those territories under Russian rule were collectively referred to as Litvaks. That was around the turn of the century as they sought economic opportunities and an escape from the dreaded pogroms that periodically descended on their necks. They yearned for change. They were lucky to have left before the Second World War when most Jewish communities were wiped out by the Nazis – 204 with names approximating to Kasrils[7] and thousands more with the name of Cohen – along with tens of millions of anti-fascists, gypsies, homosexuals, the physically and mentally disabled, prisoners of war, and countless communities in the territories overrun by barbaric aggression, bombings and total war. The total dead on all sides was estimated at 85 million, of which 27 million were soldiers and citizens of the Soviet Union and six million were Jews. A relative who managed to escape from their birthplace, Libau, reported how 5000 of the Jewish inhabitants were shot in public spectacles in the town square and on the beach every Sunday. German soldiers from all around would descend like tourists to watch the spectacle – until there were no Jews left.[8] Fortunately, Grandma's family had emigrated to South Africa by then.

Grandma told me how as *kindele* (children) in the Russian Empire they had run in terror from Cossacks on horseback galloping through the shtetl with sabres swinging. A relative had a scar across his back – a token he never ever talked about as he ascended the ladder of opportunity in South Africa. I only realised much later in life that they were mute about the days they had been treated like serfs. What self-respecting petty bourgeois with a newly acquired status would want to interrogate that ugly Rorschach stain from the past? Best let it sink without trace in the primordial soup. They spoke with the remnants of an East European tongue for both she and her husband traversed between Yiddish, German, Russian and – with only the slightest of accents – English. It was when they lapsed into Yiddish that the characteristics of their mother tongue came to the fore and both amused and enchanted me. As such families anglicised, the terms *bobba* and *zeder* lapsed to be replaced by the words grandma and grandpa. The more orthodox Jewish families retained the Yiddish terms of endearment. They always addressed me as Ron-a-la. My parents always referred to me as Ronald.

I peer through the cool eeriness of the water, trying to grasp at memories as indistinct and slippery as tadpoles hiding in blind recesses. The suction tips of my mind grapple for long-lost chimera floating twixt flotsam and jetsam within the pool of my brain.

My mother looks after Grandma in her closing days. *I care for you now that you have no teeth as you cared for me when I had no teeth.* I vacate my bedroom to share with my sister Hilary while Granny Clara sinks beneath the waves of my eiderdown. The aroma of medication hits me like a blast of chlorine when the door is ajar, countered by the scent of lavender wafting in its wake. The room aired with fragrant herbs to soothe the patient has a whiff of citronella to keep the mosquitoes at bay.

Gran Clara and Grandpa Abe – I called him Gramps – were the same age. They met and wed in their late teens in South Africa. The wedding photograph showed them in the formal attire of the times – she in bridal dress, he with a Charlie Chaplin countenance and moustache in top hat and tails. How did a small slightly built man become so corpulent, I want to know. 'I drank too much beer,' he explains with a belly laugh. Granny Clara butts in to say it was because he sat around playing cards every night, never exercised and consumed too much *shmaltz*. That was before she became so ill. Ahead of her inevitable end I was whisked off to relatives to alleviate the burden on my mother. A cousin I temporarily lodged with, Judy Feinberg née Cohen, tells me I was an excitable little boy who used to run out of their home in the middle of a freezing winter in response to the ice-cream man's bell with my tickey coin (equivalent to three pennies) for an ice lolly. A grand-aunt amused at my antics at a family event referred to me as 'a little gangster'; another haughtily contradicted her by asserting 'There are no hoodlums in our family.' My mother chimed in to make the peace but could not resist telling them what a good boy I was, how I had recently removed a banana skin from a pavement so that people should not slip and hurt themselves.

Abe Cohen would laughingly claim that in years gone by the family name had been Zaga-Kahn, shortened to Cohen, but since he was something of a joker no one took him seriously until it was proven long after he had died by a distant American relative who was compiling a family tree.[9]

Clara and Abe had two children, my mother René and her younger brother Solly. The parents ran a delicatessen store in Hillbrow while the two offspring attended the oddly named Jewish Government School in downtown Doornfontein – another of the first ports of call for immigrant Jews arriving in the big city. They remembered the white miners' rebellion of 1922 (The Rand Revolt) against the employment of cheap black labour which threatened their livelihoods. They were sent home from school when General Smuts began the aerial and artillery bombardment of workers' strongholds in neighbouring Braamfontein and along the Rand, doing the dirty work on behalf of the mining magnates greedy for greater profits. Smuts had been a distinguished guerrilla fighter against the British. Now he was tantamount to what the Boers called a 'turncoat' – someone who changed sides.

In marked contrast I recall stories of the Cohens' pet monkey Pepe, who they ultimately gave to the Johannesburg Zoo, where they often visited him on Sundays. Whenever there was what we referred to as a 'monkey's wedding' – bright sunshine during rainfall – my mother would become sentimental about Pepe, remembering how there had been a monkey's wedding the day they presented him to the zoo. I would imagine Pepe in a bow-tie and tuxedo and his bride in a white wedding dress. And when we saw chimps dressed up that way on the cinema screen my belief was confirmed.

The Cohens first stayed in a semi-detached house in the working-class suburb of Belgravia, which was another of the initial stops for Jewish immigrants. René and Solly's first couple of years at school was at a Catholic convent a block from their front door. My mother vividly recalled a tragic occasion when the two of them had gone to play with the boy next door on a day when his parents were out. In his excitement he showed them his father's revolver which went off with a loud bang – the poor lad dropped to the floor stone dead. The siblings went screaming into the street.

Years later, after I returned from exile, I took my mother for a drive in search of the house she grew up in. We unsuccessfully criss-crossed the streets of Belgravia for a while and just when I was thinking of giving up her intuition kicked in and she told me to turn a certain corner. And there it was – the Catholic school and, opposite from it, the semi-detached houses, including the one where the little boy had accidentally shot himself. Almost 90 years later René remembered him. His name was Alfie, she said sadly.

I swim as effortlessly as I can, musing over the thought that I was a mother's boy for sure. Even up to the age of six or seven I would sneak into my parents' bed, snuggling up against her warm deeply breathing body, her arm lying lightly around my father. I never ever dreamed that they might engage in sexual intercourse. Oh no, not my parents. Strange how he used to stroke her thigh at family picnics, I used to wonder, although no one else seemed to notice.

My father Izzy, short for Isadore, was born in July 1900 in Lithuania and was six months old when their Baltic liner berthed in Cape Town. As a commercial traveller he was often on the road so I was much closer to my mother and only managed to draw closer to him later. René was as full of beans as her father, who attributed this to being tickled with a goose feather when she was born. When my mum was in a swinging mood at a party she would wiggle her hips on the dance floor and declare that she was Riga René. She could switch roles and loved to mimic Carmen Miranda, the Brazilian bombshell with the ornamental fruit piled high on the head: '*I, Yi, Yi, Yi, Yi, I like you very much, I, Yi, Yi, Yi. Yi, I like you grand*' – looking straight into my eyes.

She liked dressing my sister according to the fashion of the time as a Shirley Temple look-alike, and sang to us songs like 'The Good Ship Lollipop'. She was adorable. The kind of mother every child wanted. She had a wide repertoire, from 'Bei Mir Bist Du Schön' (To Me, You Are Beautiful), originally a Yiddish tune, to the Russian 'Song of the Volga Boatmen' – 'Yo ho heave oh – pull hard once more – yo ho heave oh'. Her favourites, though, were The Andrew Sisters and especially their early calypso hit about American sailors in Trinidad where both mother and daughter worked 'for the Yankee dollar'. When I told her years later that the lyrics could have been taken as a reference to prostitution she was gobsmacked.

My mother also owned a banjo, somewhat battered, which she would haul out on family picnics and accompany herself singing some of her favourite ditties. We loved her strumming and we'd all sing along – Grandma Clara, Grandpa Abe, my dad, my sister and me:

Oh! Susanna, now don't you cry for me.
For I come from Alabama
with my banjo on my knee.[10]

She would pause to slap her thigh and we'd all beam as she took up the next lines:

It rained all night the day I left;
The weather was so dry.
The sun so hot I froze to death.
Susanna don't you cry.

My sister and I would scream with delight. The expressive way my mother sang it, rolling her eyes and her shoulders, hid the sadness of the song. The phrase '*the sun so hot I froze to death*' beguiled me more for the strange juxtaposition than concern for the person who froze to death. The magic of words like that simply carried me away as if by an ocean current and remained with my mother's smile forever.

We lived in apartment number 7 on the 2nd floor of Albyn Court, 22 Raymond Street, Yeoville. It was a fine but modest apartment block built in the art deco style of the 1930s, with pressed steel ceilings imported from England and wooden pine flooring, the beauty of which was hidden under inexpensive practical carpeting to keep the rooms warm in winter. There were nine apartments – eight occupied by Litvaks and one by a Jewish Scot from Glasgow, name of Jock 'the shnoz' Silver, on account of his large nose, who was a racecourse bookie. The rest of the tenants were either shopkeepers or travelling salesmen – commercial travellers to give them the professional-sounding title.

Yeoville of my childhood was something of a Jewish shtetl, well captured in many a reminiscence, according to Chandrea Serebro, who writes: 'Yeoville. What started out advertised as a "sanitarium for the rich" where the air was clearer because it was ... high on the ridge overlooking ... the smoky mining town of Johannesburg ... soon became a hive of multi-culturalism with a distinctly Jewish flavour. While the wealthier target markets looked for greener pastures elsewhere, the eastern European immigrant Jews settled into Yeoville, quickly turning it into the shtetl of Johannesburg, with the smells of freshly baked challah wafting out on a Friday and the sounds of a new Jewish world in the making. "It was a dynamic hub of Jewish life with an open community," Isaac Resnik explains, that was as diverse as it was accepting of differences.'[11]

My father worked for a low-budget candy factory in Doornfontein. Grandpa was a salesman for a men's clothing firm, which was more prestigious than the factory that employed my father. They plied their trade by motoring from country town to country town at a time when many roads were gravel or sand. Their clients called them 'travellers'.

I bump my head against the side of the pool which sets my recollections off on another tangent.

It was the Dutch stranger Henk van Ghent emerging from the

watery ripples who set me on a roundabout track for the memories I was searching for. Henk was a raucous visitor who, on account of his dandy sartorial appearance, had earned the nickname 'The Gent from Ghent'. He was given to telling tales that had even my reticent father smiling. It was evening and my father and his pals had been arguing as usual about the controversies of that day's racehorse meeting. They attended every Saturday (the Jewish sabbath) throughout the year; my father's nominal religious affiliation hardly interfered with his and Grandpa Abe's primary addiction to the 'gee-gees', as they called the horses. Second to the horses came poker. Synagogue barely featured. That was a place for bar mitzvah[12] boys and the orthodoxy who walked to shul on the sabbath. It was only on the most holy of days that the likes of them would put in a subdued appearance.

Probably their generation had had enough of the claustrophobic stranglehold of religion in Czarist Russia where in their villages they were under the rigid control of the medieval-type rabbi in his frock-coat and fur hat. Life in South Africa gave them individual freedom, a novelty which they exercised to the full, ready to ignore the strictures in the absence of a village rabbi dictating to them. In that sense they were free spirits. When my father was a schoolboy playing football on Saturdays, he had to creep out of the house with his sporting gear as he was forbidden to engage in games on the sabbath. There were a few things they did not do – one was eat pork – but I suspect that was more psychological than religious adherence.

On this particular evening Henk was holding forth. Every time he ended an anecdote, he dropped his gentleman's veneer and brayed like a donkey for a juicy carrot. Midway through his guffaws he would remember the patient, my grandmother, down the passageway and cup his mouth with his hand in apology at the thought of disturbing her. It was that comical expression that was etched in my mind, on cue to resurface from my subterranean reservoir. I have forgotten what the gambling fables were about that day, but I was drawn to the adult company by a statement Henk made, which he articulated with great force.

'They tell me,' Henk affirmed in a hoarse voice, 'that the natives better keep off the streets on December 16th – you call it Dingaan's Day?' At first everyone thought he was referring to the Dingaan's Day Handicap, a big event on the summer racing calendar, but soon realised he had shifted from the gee-gees to politics.

In full stride Henk continued: 'Because the Afrikaners will skin them alive. Ja, they are still looking for revenge.' He nodded sagely. 'They got it at Blood River, but I hear they want it a second time.' He had big bulging eyes like Popeye, and as his peepers panned round the table, his formidable gaze held his audience. 'As it is said here,' he tapped on the table with an index finger, 'your Boers want to finally put the kaffir in his place because they say that General Smuts is too soft on them.' He peered around for approval. The 'K' word was not used in our household. However, since Henk was seemingly paraphrasing what the Afrikaner Boers were saying he was not contradicted, although he certainly appeared to relish the idea of a blood-fest. He repeated in Afrikaans for good measure in his warbling Dutch accent, '"*Die kaffir in sy plek*"?', making it sound like a question. Then he gave his hoarse laugh and peered around seeking agreement.

Even a child like I knew what that meant – whether you approved or not. The underdogs who needed to be kept in their place – *in sy plek* – did the dirty work in the kitchens, in the mines, factories and fields, and in the streets where you would see black labourers sweeping up the white man's litter and being cursed, even by children, and sustaining blows for no apparent reason.

'Will they fight back?' asked Henk rhetorically, for indeed an African miners' strike in 1946, which had grounded my father from using the country roads, had been ruthlessly suppressed.

Sam Lazerson, our next-door neighbour, born with six fingers on each hand and consequently called 'Six Finger Sam', who had sauntered into the flat uninvited, wasn't perturbed about the prospect of black resistance: 'That'll be the frosty Friday!' he sneered. Sam revelled in sayings like that. Another was swearing on his mother's or father's lives when he felt it necessary to underline that what he was saying was nothing but the truth. Those such as he would swear on their parents' graves after they died. I felt those oaths were insensitive, tantamount to needlessly tempting fate, and they would shake me rigid.

My father was a more thoughtful man, given to speaking in an understated way. 'Well, Sam,' he said, in response to Sam's dismissal of black resistance, 'maybe they'll give us a shock one day.' Then he added, 'After all, every black man carries one of these in his pocket.' He held aloft a box of Lion matches which he rattled for emphasis before perching it on the table.

Sam Lazerson's face reddened, and he muttered: 'Just let those shwartzes try. We'll send in the Marines.'

My grandfather, who was by no means a liberal, always seemed to oppose Six Finger Sam, on principle. 'Tell us, Sam, will you be serving in the Reserves?' he snapped.

Ignoring the talk, my mother cheerfully began to serve food and refreshments, whch distracted Henk from his topic. He always raved about the Yiddish cuisine, which he was unaccustomed to, and particularly my mother's *gefilte* fish, which she served with red horseradish, called *khren* in Russian, which tickled the nose and drew tears from the eyes. '*Magtag Mama*! This stuff is hot. Has a kick in it like the finest old Dutch *ginivere*, our national drink,' he said, wiping away tears.

That's when I was drawn to the table. Earlier my father would have gone through the ritual of carefully placing his sizeable racing binoculars in a drawer and his grey fedora on the hat rack, above which was a photograph of the family hero Danny Boy winning the South African Derby at Turffontein.[13] That race had netted both him and Grandad Abe a welcome pot and made up for the great disappointment of the decade when a horse Sam Lazerson had backed, Cape Heath, pipped Danny Boy in a photo finish that had them arguing for ages. They had little time for Sam for he was a know-all who clearly irritated them. He gave them 'the needle' – a favourite term in their circle.

The mood was good and high with whiskey and soda flowing, although my dad was a sparse drinker. He was content merely to dispense carbonated water for his whiskey-drinking guests – all of whom were members of the cosmopolitan horseracing fraternity, which boasted a big following in South Africa – from a fashionable glass-bottled soda siphon. Fred May, a burly man with sad eyes, along with Jock Silver, he of the big nose, neighbour and racecourse bookie, smoking a cigar, made up the party. The presence of some Gentiles lay in the fact that unlike most of the Jews of the neighbourhood, my father had friends such as Mr May. Fred had a fine baritone voice and after a triumphal race meet he would sing the Irish classic 'Danny Boy' they played on our gramophone. Essentially the song is about a parting with a loved one, implying death, but it was intoned in celebratory mood despite my fast-ailing grandmother in her room down the passage.

Jock Silver would sing along in a Scots accent:

'Oh, Danny boy, the pipes, the pipes are calling
From glen to glen, and down the mountain side.
The summer's gone, and all the roses falling ... '[14]

Henk, it emerged, was a Dutch colonial who, having quit Indonesia after the war and on his way back to the Netherlands, had decided to settle in South Africa, where he became a commercial traveller and card-playing buddy of my grandpa. Jock Silver coined the sobriquet 'Henk the Gent' or 'Henk the Gent from Ghent'.

Henk thought he should change the mood and distance himself from what the Boers were up to by declaring, 'You know, we Hollanders don't approve of the goings-on here. But it is said that the Afrikaner Party is bound to win the next elections.' Fred May, a Smuts man through and through, disagreed. 'Jannie Smuts is a wily man, he knows the politics game, been around since before the days of the Union. He will remain in power, you can bet on that.'

At the offer of a bet Abe Cohen weighed in: 'Ahh, here's two shmakeroos, Freddie boy,' said he, slapping down two pound notes. 'I tell you, boychik, Smuts has had his day. You can smell it on the road, in the dorps, at the *klabberjas*[15] tables. The farmers want change.'

Fred reached for his wallet. 'I'll give you evens on that, Kepkela.'

Kepkela was my grandfather's nickname. Every time he won a round of poker or backed a winning horse he tapped his head to show how clever he was. 'I've got the *kep*,' he'd brag (Yiddish for *kop*, meaning a wise head). 'Kepkela Cohen, that's me.' His other totem was the champion jockey Cocky Feldman, a Jewish jockey and a rarity at that. 'Ride him, Cocky!' the Jewish punters would yell as he galloped the winner down the home straight. 'Give more mit da stick!' – and sometimes in an undertone to themselves they'd add: 'Show the *goyim*!'[16] Off course, 'Ride him, Cocky!' was Kepkela Cohen's war-cry as he slapped the winning hand down in a poker game.

'I'm with Fred, count me in for ten bob,' announced Six Finger Sam in an aside, busy filing his nails, with pedantic attention to his extra pinkies. Abe Cohen was unwelcoming, a dismissive sneer on his lips, his voice thick with sarcasm: 'Mazel Tov! Hail the big punter! Put your money where your mouth is, Rockefeller, we don't bet with fresh air.'

'I'll hold the stakes,' offered Jock the Shnoz, pocketing the four singles and holding out a hand to Sam Lazerson, who ignored the remark and the outstretched hand, concentrating on his fingernails.

Abe had a particular distaste for Sam Lazerson and his assertiveness. What particularly *needled* him, and Sam never gave him the opportunity to forget, was the fateful night at a hot poker game when my grandad thought he had won a fat pot with a full house – three nines and a pair of fives. But the triumphant cry of 'Ride him, Cocky!' was dashed when Six Finger Sam produced a royal flush. What made the issue far worse was the framed hand of cards – 10, Jack, Queen, King and Ace of Hearts – mounted behind glass adorning the Lazerson sitting room wall with the title: 'My Royal Flush – Samuel Lazerson'; place and date; and, to rub salt into the wound, the neatly typed wording: 'beating Abe Cohen's full house. £60 pot! Mazel Tov Sammy boy!!' I had seen that irritating object many times because Sam's son Ivor was my best friend and I was often in their home.

Sam Lazerson was apparently from Odessa. Abe Cohen said it was the city of *ganefs* – rogues and thieves. Whatever the background, they had settled in Yeoville, which Sam liked to refer to as 'Jewville' just as Johannesburg with its growing Jewish population was referred to as 'Jewburg', although the Jewish population was a minority, some 10% of Johannesburg's half million at that time. They were go-getters and punched above their weight. Sam was one of the first of their group to move out of the suburb, migrating to the more salubrious northern parts of the city, putting on airs and graces about that fact. What came to our attention through the grapevine was his sneering about Abe Cohen as a *peruvnik* – a coarse type. After hearing of that my mother was irate and vowed she would never allow him to darken our doorstep again.

There they were, an unusual mix of Gentile and Jew, with the party drawing to a close. This was sensed by that most sensible man Fred May, perhaps a trifle perturbed by the loud voice of the Dutch newcomer whom he had introduced into the circle. 'Afore we depart, may I thank Izzy and René, on behalf of Henk and myself, for their kind hospitality,' he said in his very smooth English. 'Hoping Mrs Cohen's health improves.' My grandfather's jaw trembled at the thought of his falling rose, and Fred May moved to change the atmosphere by raising his glass: 'Let us charge our glasses in salute of the finest three-year-old in this country – Danny Boy.'

'*L'Chaim*!' (To life) everyone chorused. I found it astonishing that they would use the Yiddish or Hebrew salutation in relation to an animal. It sounded strange to me and I am sure the devout would have been scandalised by such sacrilege. There was a ripple of applause around the table as glasses were raised, punctuated by Grandpa's irrepressible war-cry: 'Ride him, Cocky!'

CHAPTER 2

The Other Side of the Fence

WHEN I ASKED MY FATHER LATER about the significance of December 16th, he explained it was because on that day in 1838, exactly a century before I was born, the Zulu king Dingaan had ambushed the Voortrekker leader Piet Retief and slain him and his band. Ever since the Afrikaner had wanted revenge. After Retief had been killed reinforcements under Andries Pretorius had defeated the Zulus at the Battle of Ncome – which the Boers named Blood River because of the colour of the swirling water during the massacre.[17]

Spears were no match for the musket, he told me. And matches? I might have asked, but that would have come later when I was a bit older. The threat of a black uprising came up sporadically at the card table but only when there was rioting in the townships. My family was as frightened as most whites. My father's way of calming my mother's fears was to tell her that the African people were too disunited along tribal lines to effectively challenge law and order. They needed to let off steam now and again, he would tell her, don't worry. The reaction of people like Sam Lazerson and Jock Silver, on the other hand, was fully in support of the police, to the point of supporting the mowing down of people with machine-guns. Well, at least that was the way they expressed themselves when the emotions were high. My father would scoff and say they were full of hot air.

I reach the end of a length of the pool, tumble and turn, and roll over into a leisurely backstroke, which is the best way to relax. I look up where wispy cirrus clouds streak across an enigmatic sky and count the strokes so that I don't forget where I am to avoid bumping my head at the other end. I search for tadpoles and trigger mechanisms where the tricky sunlight reflects and refracts.

I recall a time when I took off from our apartment, without a word to our maid Poppy, and decided that I was off to visit Granny. Poppy was general factotum, who cooked and cleaned the apartment and my nanny on whose back I had often slept as an infant attached by a wrap-around blanket African style. Black surrogate mother for white infants with no thought yet of colour, class or race.

Granny Clara is just one block away. It's a cozy semi-detached cottage with hydrangeas in abundance in soft mauve and pink hues. The white gravelled pathway crunches underfoot as I knock on her door. There she is, my darling diminutive grandmother, smelling of lavender, an apron around her waist. She has been busy making pot-pourri, capturing the scents of summer from her garden as family gifts for Hanukkah, the coming Jewish festival of lights. She greets me in a Yiddishe momma way by gently massaging my cheek. 'Ron-a-la,' she says fondly, and then: 'How's my little tadpole?' It is as though she hasn't seen me in ages, even though every Friday evening for as long as I can remember she and Grandpa are at our shabbat table. The table is always draped in a fine white cloth with two silver candle-sticks on it, my mother lighting the candles at sunset and reciting a sabbath prayer. Grandma brings the snow white braided *kitka* bread she's baked – the glossy brown crust brushed with egg white.

Grandma pours me a glass of milk and gives me some cookies and I seem to be with her for hours. My mother arrives in a state because when she had got home she found I had disappeared. I can't understand what the fuss is about. Granny knows how to calm her down. Having cut some flowers, bound the stalks with twine, popped the bouquet into my hand, and gestured in a surprisingly English way with a Yiddish mix, which showed how powerful the urge for anglicisation was, she cried: 'Chrysanthe-Mums for Mum, Ron-a-la!'

'Mumm! Mumm! Mumm!' I echo.

I yank back as though rowing a boat, and pick up speed, my feet beating the water, the images swishing before me in blurred focus. Such an English phrase. How did a sedate Litvak mama, with a fair amount of German, acquire such language and name her daughter René with a French accent? I pause at the end of a length for breath and to adjust my swimming goggles, which have misted over.

My overnight bag is packed and my mother ushers me into my room where my dear Gran lies buried beneath my eiderdown. She stares at me with sad eyes but manages a faint smile as I kiss her on her forehead. I am taken to stay at Uncle Solly's; my sister at some other relative. My father comes to see me from time to time. Every time he departs I cry and at my aunt Minnie's home, where I also stay for a while, I am made to feel like a sissy by her youngest son. Mervyn Barkman is a champion on the playing fields of King Edward School (KES); he has learned no manners there, but instead been grounded in arrogance. Cruel to his mother, he berates her as a 'penny-pinching Jewess' when on returning from school he finds no biscuits for tea. I can't believe my ears.

I change from backstroke to crawl.

The year 1946, the time of Grandma's death, was Danny Boy's best year, probably the height of the era. It was 'a mug's game', my father would tell me in an effort to play down his enthusiasm for the horses, hoping to set me on the straight and narrow. He would tap his nose and explain that he only placed bets because 'insiders' tipped him off whenever there was a 'hot-shot – a sure thing'. Now that's a story you often hear told but in my father's case he had impeccable sources – the Real Deal. A relative – Judy's Uncle Joe Sher – was none other than the proud owner of that rising star of the racetrack, our beloved Danny Boy. Our living room was adorned with framed black-and-white photographs of the stately steed galloping past the winning post. But it was not only from Danny Boy that my father augmented his income. The fact that he was known to be circumspect and reliable, could keep his lip buttoned, meant that owners and trainers alike, even prominent jockeys like Cocky Feldman, used him to lay their bets in small amounts at various bookmakers so as to keep the odds favourable for as long as possible and enable them to make a killing. In those days jockeys and trainers had no share in the winning stakes, which went exclusively to the horse's owner. They worked for a set wage, and scrambled to lay bets – not unlike commercial travellers, who worked for commission.

Danny Boy's trainer was a man with the Runyonesque name of Jumbo Goldstein. The horse was stabled at his brother's farm outside Germiston. Jumbo's brother was Abe Goldstein, whose son Ezra was a few years younger than me. In time he became a respected judge. Ezra's son, Warren Goldstein, became the country's Chief Rabbi in 2005. I wondered whether he had ever heard of Cocky Feldman or realised that the family fortune derived from that unlikely source. Balzac wrote that every great fortune comes from a great crime. The priesthood and politicians, along with the captains of industry, mining magnates and land barons benefited enormously through inglorious ways.

As iconic as Danny Boy was in our family, so, too, was Cocky Feldman. The day I saw him in the flesh stands out in my mind as a magical milestone. From all the talk I had imagined that Cocky was a gnarled old-timer, but he was no such thing. There he was, astride his magnificent mount, looking down and listening attentively to Jumbo Goldstein. They had come back into the stable area after a training session. I had fed carrots to Danny Boy in the paddock many a time so my eyes were drawn to the rider, although you couldn't really distinguish the one from the other. A young, handsome fellow, with dark Jewish features and assertive self-confidence, Cocky held the reins with strong hands. He sat so immaculately high from the ground that he looked to me like a god on a throne. He had a swagger about him, hence the nickname Cocky. After he had dismounted and Danny Boy was getting a rubdown, my father stood chatting with him. 'Is he hot, Cocky? Will he be hot on the day?' Dad enquired. 'Mr Kasrils,' Cocky answered politely, 'as hot as Bobba's horseradish!' and they laughed.

Afterwards I remember Jumbo Goldstein saying to my father that there was no jockey more fearless than Cocky H. Feldman – not even his chief rival, Tiger Wright. Cocky was the champion jockey for the 1946/47 season with 137 wins, easily outstripping Tiger Wright's 87.[18] There was particular pride in Cocky Feldman among the Jewish horseracing fraternity because he showed that a Jew could triumph in a Gentile's world – a world still reeling from the Nazi atrocities. A world where Jews, like blacks, could not be members of the Gentiles-only golf clubs, although all the caddies were black. Jewish would-be golfers had to start their own clubs.

Born in 1938 and living through the war years meant that fear of the Nazis and anti-Semitism lurked in the shadows even thousands of miles away from Europe. The war, its fears, victories and defeats, and the fate of the Jews, was a regular topic of conversation – the latter issue discussed in hushed tones and not for the children's ears.

Not that I understood very much at all – and racial politics in South Africa was not a conscious awareness for me yet. Take, for instance, the fact that my father hardly ever joined us on the beach when we went to Durban or Muizenberg for summer holidays – this was when the hot tips proved right and the commissions from business were generous. I could never understand why he wore a gown and hat over his bathing suit when everyone else was soaking up the sun. I learned from my mother years later that he avoided tanning his swarthy complexion in case he was mistaken for a 'non-white' when they went to the whites-only cinema and cause embarrassment. René generally saw the funny side of things and she giggled like a schoolgirl when she told me this.

It was when I became confused about the anomalies that abounded around us that my mother invariably sought to comfort me. I must have been an extremely sensitive child. Once, when I was about five years old, one moment I was supremely happy motoring with my sister in a small boat around a beachfront pond and the next my heart sank like a stone as I noticed a black man and his small son peering from behind a fence at the white kids having so much fun. I suffered for the deprivation of the young black boy as much as for the father, who must have felt so utterly emasculated. When I scrambled out of the boat my mother sensed my unhappiness but I had no words to explain. Was it because I was self-conscious and embarrassed about enjoying myself while they could only look on? Was it because while I could be happy they could only feel dejected and I felt it was unfair that they could not be happy like me? I was a capricious child and was happy to enjoy the boat ride in the evenings when there were no black people around. But not during the day. That was my first involvement in a boycott of sorts. From where did I derive such sensitivity? Could a tender mother who was always playing with me and my sister to make up for our father's absence – tickling our feet for which Hilary and I hung out of bed expectantly at night, waiting for the frolics and the goodnight cuddles – have been the primary source?

My mother had a palpable sense of what was unjust. She was always ready to recite poems from her schooldays, one of which was a passionate rendition of a Victorian melodrama entitled *Guilty or not Guilty?* It was about an orphaned waif arraigned before the courts for the crime of stealing bread for her starving siblings and it touched me deeply. We never went hungry as children but there were occasions when my parents were hard up. My mother strove to get us to understand that there were hungry people, especially children, not only in the black townships but in Europe after the war. Eat up, come on, finish your food, just think of all those starving children in Europe, she would say. I could never make the connection. On one occasion when resources were low she dished out on a dinner plate each for my sister and me one solitary meatball apiece. We looked up at her in astonishment – is that all, Mum? And she broke into a song that Lena Horne had made famous: '*One meatball, just one meatball, you get no bread with one meatball.*' We thought she had gone cuckoo. She explained it was a song composed during the American Depression years and the hardships people had to endure. After which she doled out large helpings of mashed potato and peas smothered in gravy. It was delicious.

My mother enjoyed playing jokes like that on us – 'pulling our legs'. The family favourite was mince-meat, usually presented my favourite way as cottage pie. When she needed to be thrifty we had more frugal meals such as mince on toast. To make it more interesting she would spice the mince with a pinch of chili powder. In cafés this was called 'spicy mince' but, teasing us, she would call the dish 'spicy mice' and then ask us what letter she had omitted.

At sleep time she used to play that delicious game beloved by children with our toes –

This little piggy went to market,
This little piggy stayed at home,
This little piggy had roast beef,
This little piggy had none
And THIS little piggy ... (holding the pinky)
   ... *ran wee-wee-we all the way home* (running her fingers up our legs to joyful laughter).

When Grandma had a turn, looking after us when our parents were out, she substituted little tadpoles for the little piggies.

I cut through the water, racing after that particular moment that concerned perhaps the most important lesson I learned in my life. A lesson I learned from my mother's lips and which came through a circuitous route.

Somehow the memory of Henk the Gent with his talk about the Zulus and Blood River led from one thing to another. It led to visions of a dramatic downtown encounter witnessed by my mother and I which invoked what I imagined Henk's forecast about blood running in the streets was all about.

My pulse beat accelerates, stroke after stroke through the water, as I relive the horror that gave rise to my mother's words of wisdom that followed the incident, and I sense that I am tapping that particular tadpole.

It started on a day in 1946 when she took me for a treat to the movies in downtown Johannesburg – perhaps as a break from being stuck at home caring for Granny Clara. Fancy art deco cinema houses they were (we used the word 'bioscope' in those days): Metro, 20th Century Fox, the Plaza, Empire, Colosseum and His Majesty's. We would catch the B-2 tram from Rockey Street, corner of De La Rey, the latter named after a famous Boer general who my paternal grandfather in fact knew – and alight near the Rissik Street post office. One moment I was anticipating the joy of a Hollywood film with ice-cream, the next all hell broke loose. My mother yanked my arm to get us out of the way of a bunch of cursing white hooligans furiously swinging punches at a man who was reeling under the blows. The man wore a smart jacket and slacks and a pair of fashionable black-and-white shoes. These I noticed before he sank into the gutter, blood streaming from his head. I remember the flash of a bronze knuckle-duster striking his temple with a sickening crunch while kicks and blows thudded into his body. The thugs' faces were ugly and vicious, filled with primitive hate. White pedestrians scattered. I noted older boys from the Yeoville hood, tough guys I looked up to, scurrying out of the way like rabbits. A smartly dressed woman shouted: 'Stop! Stop! You're killing him!' and they jeered at her – 'Kaffir-loving bitch!' as they slunk away after stamping the man's fine hat flat and kicking it into the gutter.

What had this person done to merit such a beating? We heard a guy muttering – 'The native ought to have got out of the way. He was taking up the pavement, this is a white man's town. The native must know his place. How dare he think he can become a white man by changing from animal skins into western clothing?'

By the time my mother and I turned the corner I was sobbing. 'Aw, Ma, let's go home. I don't want to go to the bio anymore.' My mother must have persisted, probably to get both her mind and mine off the nightmare, and we went anyway. I think the movie was *Road to Rio*, featuring Bob Hope and Bing Crosby with the Andrews Sisters – so it appealed to us both.

That night, much to my shame, I peed in my bed. The shame was even worse when the older boys at Albyn Court teased me: the sheets drying on our balcony exposed me as a *pisher* – a kid who pisses his pants. *Aw, Ma, why were my sheets hung out?*

That afternoon my mother took me to her favourite sanctuary, where fine ladies sat politely drinking tea, in the quiet of an upmarket department store called Anstey's. She knew how I loved the egg mayonnaise sandwiches with grated lettuce there and, most of all, their strawberry milkshakes. But first she asked the waitress for two cups of water, to which she added a teaspoon of sugar, stirring vigorously. I well knew the routine. Gulp down the contents. It was her tried and trusted remedy, no doubt handed down from her mother, to counter a shock.

Eureka! I had caught the tadpole. Grasped it out of the blue – out of the sugar water as I propelled myself forward through the water with burst of speed and energy. That's it! I must have just turned seven. That was the turning point – the memory of the Allied flags on display. A link in the convoluted chain was Gerald Coyan of Albyn Court apartment 9, calling me a *pisher*. His father Jack had come home from serving in the war at the end of 1945 and they hung a string of paper flags from their balcony in celebration. The same paper buntings with the victorious Allied flags – America, Australia, British, Canada, France, New Zealand, South Africa and the Soviet Union – were strung up in celebration all over downtown Johannesburg, including in Anstey's tea lounge.

The chain of incidents led to the frightful incident and my asking my mother within the week: 'Are black people being treated the way us Jews were treated in Germany?'

I had seen the gruesome scenes on the overseas newsreels in the cinemas. Despite my mother pushing me below my seat to obscure my view, I managed to peer between the seats and see on the screen images of emaciated victims in the concentration camps and the piles of corpses. The prospect of a victorious Hitler arriving in Yeoville to round up Jews had me looking for hiding places in my bedroom, just in case. The choices were the closet or under the bed behind my white porcelain chamber pot with the blue rim. If only I could make myself invisible. By daylight I was braver and along with other kids would march around the school playground holding our forefingers horizontally under our noses, ridiculing Hitler's silly moustache, arms raised in mock salute, jeering: *'Heil Hitler, Go to hell, Let your arsehole burn as well!'* We linked arms in the neighbourhood and marched around the streets, gathering more and more children in a long line, chanting: 'In 1944 the Germans went to war, They had no guns so they shot with their bums in 1944.'

I see my mother's dear face, her pensive expression, her eyes closed in thought, searching for what to say. 'Ronald –' the words come out slow and clear '– people were starved in those death camps and thrown into the gas chambers, so it's not like that over here. But …' and there is a long pause '… it starts with the bad things we often see here, and the way black people are spoken to, cursed with horrible language, and beaten like we saw the other day. That's how it starts. We must be kind to people. We must speak politely and we must treat others as we would like them to treat us.' She stares into my eyes, reaching deep into me, to be sure I understand.[19]

My god, how I underestimated that dear soul. Fifty years later at the launch of my memoir *Armed and Dangerous*[20] she told an enquiring journalist who wanted to know about childhood influences that I was a kind boy, always caring for stray animals, bringing home injured birds and homeless kittens. In my stupidity I was utterly embarrassed. Until I read the letter written by the incarcerated socialist Rosa Luxemburg during the First World War, from her prison cell in Breslau, weeping for beasts of burden delivering supplies being mercilessly beaten by their driver within her sight – reflecting my own dismay over suffering.[21]

Turning point? René kept my mind open. She helped me maintain the natural empathy that I believe all children have for those who suffer; for any form of cruelty, be it to animals or people. My friends like Ivor, many of whom were far cleverer than me at school, would have asked similar questions, but in most cases they were told, for I heard it not only when Sam Lazerson spoke to Ivor in sweeping generalisations but elsewhere too: 'Don't worry yourself about the shwartzes. They are used to it. Live and let live, keep out of trouble and look after yourself.' And with that Slam! Clang! Grunge! The mind snaps shuts. Questions end. Empathy with others wanes. Nothing but your own ego dominates. Children are self-centred for a start.

My mother kept my mind open – ventilated. She was a simple woman, without much formal higher education, certainly no matriculant, for she went to work as a shop assistant and in a post office when she was quite young. From her, and my father, came no easy generalisations but instead an instinctive reliance on normative thinking; applying standards of behaviour – a value system to weigh up right and wrong. I often think how much my mother would have gained from more advanced schooling but in those days even among Jewish families higher education was not regarded as necessary for a woman. Yet René could reason and analyse life with an intuitive clarity that all too many among the highly educated could not match.

That was the first turning point in my life and probably the avenue to all else. For of course other lessons came if you had an open mind. Came with the tadpoles that I grapple with as I plough my furrow through the water.

The secret of trapping liquid moments long past is all about embracing the context in which they whirl. Tadpoles look like wriggling spermatozoa viewed through a microscope. Wired to mate with the female egg after a frenetic swim with a myriad rivals on a life and death race from ejaculation into vagina to fallopian tube. Quite the relevant analogy. The drama of birth. Suck in another breath and cut through aquamarine. Aim for the fallopian. Those miniature amphibians sneak in and out of the popping bubbles birthing into sublime images or morph into anxious nerve-lines in a forest of tangled seaweed.

CHAPTER 3

Who Killed Jesus?

WHEN MY FATHER WAS GROWING up, my grandfather Nathan, the jeweller, must have been fairly affluent, because after some years in a working-class area called Mayfair, they moved to an upmarket suburb of Johannesburg called Kensington. Izzy attended the nearby Jeppe Boys High and appears to have been quite bright at school, although he never went further than matric. He told me stories about Johannesburg's early period, events that he had personally witnessed. One such event concerned the notorious Foster gang – bank robbers who hid out at a cave in Kensington in 1914 as the police were closing in on them. My dad slipped away from school to witness the final showdown. Rather than give themselves up the gang committed suicide.[22] Coincidentally, General Koos de la Rey, whom my grandfather Nathan had supported during the Boer War, died at around the same time from a gunshot fired by a soldier manning a roadblock that had been set up to catch the Foster gang. The driver of De la Rey's vehicle, which was taking him to meet other Boer War veterans who were considering siding with the Germans at the outbreak of the First World War, refused to halt when ordered to do so. Nathan Kasrils would have been saddened by De la Rey's sticky end.

My father had recollections of the 1922 white mine workers' strike resisting the employment of cheap black labour at their expense and of actually witnessing a striking miner being shot down in cold blood. The man had bared his chest at a barricade and had challenged government soldiers to shoot him or join the miners. As a commercial traveller Izzy witnessed flying columns of armed Afrikaner miners on horseback reliving the Boer War while attacking black mine workers who were still at work. Once he was caught out on the road near Benoni, a miners' stronghold on the East Rand, when government planes began bombing their positions.

It struck me that Johannesburg was a violent place where much blood had flowed. In time I realised that gold was at the heart of everything. The entire economic value chain flowed from it, as did all relationships both bitter and sweet, triumphant and tragic. Vast fortunes were made by the dominant magnates while the mining industry sucked the life out of millions of toilers; it polluted the air, water, soil, vegetation, livestock and population on its doorstep for generations to come, well into the new democratic era where even the government had a *laissez-faire* attitude.

My father's work as a commercial traveller meant he was up at dawn and home late at night and sometimes away for most of the week. His route was along the busy Main Reef Road – the spinal route east and west of Johannesburg where the gold vein ran deep in the earth. He also attended to customers along the other major tributary road north along Louis Botha Avenue to Pretoria and beyond. His customers were generally proprietors of corner cafés, hard-working Greeks and Portuguese and Lebanese; and trading stores run by Chinese and Muslim families serving the African townships and low-cost neighbourhoods of Asians, coloureds and so-called poor whites.

I would accompany him for the odd day during school holidays from when I was about ten years old, helping to carry his sample cases of boiled sweets, liquorice all-sorts, toffees, chocolates, chewing gum and the preposterously named 'nigger balls' coated in black which sold at four for a penny. The pride and joy, Crispettes' flagship line, were the mock-up packets of red-tipped candy cigarettes which children sucked at and pretended to smoke. Inside each pack was a collectable card of rugby or cricket stars, of which I – as an insider – naturally had the full collections neatly mounted in special albums. That did much for my street credibility, which I needed as I was one of the smallest and skinniest boys on the block.

Crispettes Candy was owned by the Pratt family and run by my father's boss Stewart Pratt. My father said they were decent people who allowed black people access to their Magaliesberg farm land for picnicking. David Pratt, doyen of the family, who ran the farm, was to carry out an abortive individualistic assassination attack on Prime Minister Hendrik Verwoerd in 1960 after the Sharpeville massacre. That attempt put paid to my father's work because afterwards the factory was sold off.[23] Fortunately, he found employment elsewhere at a firm called the Anglo-French Sweetworks. In the coincidental twists one so often encountered in South Africa I later developed a close friendship with the daughter of the family, who ran the company, Sonia Bunting, a staunch communist.[24]

My father would doff his hat as we entered a store. 'Good day, Mr Ismail' – 'And Good day to you, Mr Kasrils. Do sit down. Come have some tea. And what would you like, sonny? A cooldrink, I am sure.'

The young boy would sip his lime cordial through a straw on the veranda and watch the young African kids, patronisingly called *piccanins*, kick a makeshift football of old rags tied expertly together with twine, possibly an old tennis ball at its core so that it had a bit of a bounce. He would marvel at the tricks and dexterity as the barefoot urchins kicked up the red dust.

As I swim I distinctly recall the rag-ball rolling near my feet and kicking it back to lusty shouts of approval. The electric hum of connectivity throbs within from fingertips to toes as I work my way through the water.

On a later occasion I took along an old football and presented it to those kids, who were overjoyed. I kicked the ball around with them while my father was doing his business. They hailed me as '*umlungu*' (white man) in a very friendly way. Travelling home in my father's lime-green 1947 Plymouth I felt all warm and rosy. A feeling of calm satisfaction.

I churn through the water, seeking more answers from the tadpoles.

I was proud of my father. Proud because of the mutual respect between him and his customers, people who would be regarded by my Hebrew tribe as 'the other', who you ought not to trust and in fact looked down upon – less so then than in contemporary times. My young mind sensed the mutual respect and civility between people from strange and different cultures, although I could never have articulated this. But the school of tadpoles communicate and I have no doubt whatsoever in my reminiscence why I felt so content as my dad drove steadily home in heavy traffic.

Izzy was a careful driver, who often struggled not only with tiredness at the end of an exhausting day but because of the smoker's cough he battled with even as he lit up another fag. He was encouraged to change from plain to filter-tip by my mom, who did her share of the smoking too, but then the wily tobacco companies produced king size. A working man could never win. One year around that time my father got dreadfully ill with double pneumonia and nearly died. In intensive care in hospital his temperature rose to 105°F. He was the first patient they tried out the miracle new drug streptomycin on, which had been developed during the war. Fortunately, he survived. My mother was at his bedside for several nights and barely slept. She came home when the worst was over, as wan as the dough used to make *kitka*, and collapsed in her bed. Izzy convalesced for six weeks at the Goldstein horse ranch and my mother said it was owing to his proximity to 'Dr Danny Boy' that he recovered. I remember her chiding him over the way he had scolded a redhead night nurse at the height of his fever in hospital, shouting, 'Keep that witch away from me, she's making me drink *skokiaan*!'[25]

I inherited my dad's bronchial complaint, even though I did not smoke for many years as an adult. It has come to strike me that it was not only cigarettes but the toxic dust of the mine dumps blowing over Johannesburg that affected his health. He had initially grown up in Mayfair on the side of the town closer to the mine dumps and the African townships, which bore the brunt of the toxic waste and the contaminated groundwater.

Although we drove home mostly in silence, punctuated by my dad's coughing fits, I asked him about his customers and mentioned how kind they were. When I asked him where they were from he became animated. He appeared to have liked Geography and History at school and he spoke about his Lithuanian background, where that country was situated compared to Mr Walid from Lebanon, Mr Stephanos from Greece, Mr Lee from Hong Kong and Mr Ismail from Gujarat state in India. How come all of them were in South Africa, I asked. Then he would give me a brief history lesson about poverty in those countries and the lure of gold in South Africa. He would also speak a bit about his work. A man was lucky to get a good job, but the pay was never equal to the labour you put in, and above all a worker deserved a fair day's wage for a fair day's work. Then without elaborating he would add that it didn't matter who you were. Your labour needed to be respected and fairly rewarded. But his thoughts of labour and capital never went further than that.

Izzy never spoke much politics. He never read much either, although he did read the *Star* newspaper every evening when he got home. But later in life when I met the secretary of his union, the Commercial Travellers Union (CTU), I was told that my father was a socialist. The man who was telling me this knew what he was talking about for he was a leading communist, a fellow Litvak orphaned during the Russian Revolution and adopted for a while as a mascot by the Red Army. His name was Eli Weinberg, a man well known and adored by black South Africans. He served a long jail term in South Africa. I met him in exile years later, long after my father had died aged 63 soon after I had fled the country. I asked Eli why he considered my father a socialist. The tadpoles are being netted very easily now. 'Because,' Eli explained, 'he was stable, solid and consistent when it came to union affairs and our negotiation with the bosses.' Most of the travellers blew hot and cold, they were highly individualistic given their solitary work, at one moment all wanting to come out on strike but at another deflating like a burst balloon, he told me. Izzy Kasrils stuck to his guns. He was a man of principle and therefore was well respected.

Out of the blue a tadpole presents itself to me. I suddenly recall my mother reporting to me that Eli's wife Violet had attended my father's funeral on his behalf because at the time Eli was under house arrest.

What I came to realise about both my parents and what they taught me at such a young age was that they never generalised but attempted, without much formal education, to apply normative judgements in their opinions. My father had more savvy than my mother, could relate to world politics and events, but both had an innate grasp of the general principles of life.

They were good parents, both of them, and I was very fortunate to have enjoyed a happy childhood. There were the low points, crying and squabbling, harsh exchanges, but the happy glow predominates. My father was rational in discussion but he had a short fuse and he did not tolerate fools. That was when his temper and impatience showed, flaming up with my mother and grandfather but also those who gave him the needle like Six Finger Sam. Looking back I believe I am a mixture of both my mother's and father's good and weak points; certainly I have my mother's smile and sociability, and on the negative side the quick temper of my father.

Possibly my earliest memory – really a fragment of one which had no connection – was bliss when I could have been maybe three years old. I was with my father in a park full of children playing merrily on the swings. I set my eyes on a gigantic slide, my arms outstretched, longing to embrace it. My father helped me up a flight of steps to the very top so that I could see all over the park and look down the steep chute. He was anxious that I might fall off, so much so that he stood right beside me. I looked into his face for reassurance because I was standing on the top rung of the ladder, which was as high as he was tall. He gestured to me to let go of the sides of the slide and I slid down – on and on and on to the very end. Wow! I felt so big. I remember him smiling proudly too.

At that very early age came the first parental warning about dangers in the big world outside our communal circle. Never ever take sweets from strangers! There was no explanation as to why not so I thought some evil persons went around with the aim of poisoning children. Time stopped with such thoughts and the mind went blank as though one was up against a massive wall. A condition I came to associate with bewilderment when one was at a complete loss to understand the outside world and you could feel the cold hands of the unknown gripping your heart. I would experience a nagging, almost painful urge bordering on paranoia to be informed so as to understand where I fitted in. That urge never ceased. Not even into adolescence. It lasted into adulthood.

There was another fragment of memory which also stuck in my mind.

My sister Hilary was taking ballet lessons, the fashionable thing for little girls then and now. I would get *shlepped* along by my mother. On spotting a boy in the class one day I couldn't restrain myself from shouting out that he was a sissy. I might have been as young as three years old. I am able to estimate that age because my sister, three years older than me, became very ill in her seventh year, which put paid to her ballet classes. My embarrassing remark shows that the macho madness was taking hold at a vulnerable age.

My mother joked with me from when I was very young and was inclined to repeat many stories which may have become exaggerated or distorted in my mind. I have a birthmark on my upper right thigh which looks like a speckled hen's egg. That was something I must have asked about at a very tender age. She told me that when she was heavily pregnant Uncle Solly had playfully placed a boiled egg down the back of her dress and it had rolled out on her thigh at that exact point.

Experts are divided on how far back our first memories of childhood go and how accurate they may be. Some psychoanalysts argue that it is possible to retain memories from as young as two, while others are of the view that four or five is necessary for a linking narrative, owing to the crucial role of speech, but that does not mean that memory is accurate.[26] Apart from disconnected fragments of earlier recollection, my memory appears to go back to when I started primary school at age six. In trying to catch those tadpoles I have followed up on clues through reference to family relatives, photographs and that search engine called Google.

I turn onto my back, somewhat disturbed by memory of my rudeness in ballet school, and ease myself into a comfortable floating position in search of other tadpoles: head thrust back, toes sticking out of the water, arms akimbo, palms pushing ever so gently downwards. I am totally relaxed, weightless, suspended as though in a timeless bubble.

It was not as though my father had no prejudices – what white person in South Africa could claim that? One day, excited, with half a crown in my hand, the silver coin given to me by my grandfather as extra pocket money after a big win at the races, I was about to rush off to the Rockey Street shops when my dad stopped me in my tracks, a scowl on his face, my mind uncomprehending: 'Put that in your pocket,' he ordered. 'A native will cut your throat for money like that!' He only spanked me once, a story my mother loved to recount. Apparently, as my father had me over his knee, ready to administer the punishment, he sneezed. 'God bless you, Daddy' was my spontaneous utterance, according to Mum, which had him bursting into laughter and that was that.

The hiding was earned by my first experiment at arson. I was playing with matches – 'Thou shalt not do that' being an 11th commandment – and my bedroom curtains caught alight. They were lace, split into four separate panels and luckily only one panel caught fire. Although I was in a state of panic, I managed to beat the flames out. But what to do with the damage? I came up with a swift answer of stuffing the evidence into the bottom of the family laundry basket, intending to smuggle it out of the house at a convenient time. I rearranged the undamaged lace trio to cover for the absentee. I had sadly miscalculated, however, for laundry day was the following day and on her discovery of the burned curtain in the basket a worried Poppy immediately reported her findings to my mother. René hit the roof! Telling me I could have burned the place down, she said I was going to have to answer to my dad. My father had a temper all right, which tended to flare up when he found my mother was overspending or when he disagreed with my grandfather about the way he had played a hand of poker or had spread too many bets at the races or when he had the needle for someone or other.

The worst times were when he had the needle in for something my mother had done, so that they didn't speak for days. Those were the lowest points of my childhood and I would get terribly distressed, begging them to speak to one another. But my father never descended to the level of some of the neighbours, such as when Sam Lazerson almost came to blows with a neighbour who owed him money. Sam picked on the wrong man, who spent much time in the gym. His busty wife Fay had to come to his rescue by getting between the two gentlemen. This was a very public event in the forecourt of Albyn Court and Fay did not endear herself to the servants by yelling to the would-be pugilists: 'Stop behaving like kaffirs!' Sam's opponent scoffed afterwards: 'That coward had to rely on his wife's huge tits to save him from a hiding.'

Among the domestic workers who witnessed the event was our

maid Poppy Molefe, a vibrant young woman from whom I learned to speak a little of her native Setstwana; and, along with my sister Hilary, how to dance and sing. Thursdays was generally the day that domestic servants were given the afternoon off. On Thursdays Poppy would dress fashionably in flared skirt, tight sweater and chic beret, and head for a mysterious place called Sophiatown – one of the rare places where black and brown people, and the occasional whites, could chill out with music and dames at illegal booze outlets called shebeens. I often wondered who Sophia was and why she was so important as to have a town named after her. As Poppy transformed in front of our eyes from kitchen maid to swinging diva she would practise a few dance steps in key with her expectant mood. She taught us how to sing 'Chattanooga Choo-Choo' and 'Alexander's Ragtime Band'. She would whirl around, clicking her fingers and swaying her hips like a movie star. I hugged her and told her that when I grew up I would marry her. This shocked her but she also laughed and admonished me: 'Eish, Baasie Ronnie, you are a skelm! You mustn't talk like that!'

It was some years after Gran Clara's demise that my paternal grandmother, long widowed, came to stay in our apartment. Her three adult offspring took it in turns to look after her. Grandma Sarah was well into her 70s by then, had iron grey hair and prickly whiskers on her chin that scratched when we gave her an obligatory peck. She was short-tempered, untalkative and irascible. My sister and I irritated her immensely. Whenever I hovered around thinking of a trick to test her mood she would emit long sighs of irritation. When she complained to my father in Yiddish the two would counter one another with the single Russian word 'Nu?' – which I later discovered from Russian friends was an expression with myriad meanings, all roughly translated as 'So?' as in 'So what?' or 'So what can be done about it?' She could have been responding 'Nu?' as in 'Well, you have to decide' or 'Don't ask me'. In a more neutral vein the word could even be used as a form of greeting: 'Nu?' or 'So how are you today?'

As it turned out the poor woman was entering a lingering stage of dementia. My father and his two sisters – my aunts Minnie and Betty, the former born in Lithuania – had been taking turns at looking after her. Aunt Betty, youngest of the three, remembered her mother as a gay young woman with what she described as hair the colour of a golden sovereign. She would shake her head in sorrow and say how unkind life could be as one grew old. Gran Sarah died aged 80 in a retirement home. I seldom saw my father weeping but at her funeral, which I attended – I was ten – he found it difficult to hold back the tears.

I never met his father Nathan, who died soon after I came into this world. I learned from my mother that when he was told a boy had been born he was delighted that the family name would be carried on. From what I have made out Nathan was a most interesting man. Born in Vilna in 1861, he travelled to South Africa in the early 1880s, according to the earliest document in my father's possession, by the lure of riches in the hotly contested Kimberley diamond fields. He went back and forth to Vilna several times and married Sarah, who gave birth to my aunt Minnie in 1895, with a later trip home resulting in the birth of my father Isadore, before returning to South Africa in 1900 some months before their arrival.

I often used to study a family photograph. Nathan Kasrils seated formally at the centre, with a grey moustache, in a three-piece suit, neat and compact, looking sombrely into the camera. At his side Sarah sits, looking more formidable than I ever would have imagined – like most Lithuanians of the time she was short and grew stocky with age. They are surrounded by their three children: the eldest daughter Minnie, with her husband, Harry Barkman, a journalist with the *Star* newspaper, who hailed from Australia where he had been a devastating cricketer, a bowler of repute. He looks tall and stately. Minnie, like her sister Betty, has their mother's build. Minnie is prim while Betty is a sweetie with a mischievous smile. She is married to the affable George Tobias, who runs a music salon in Cape Town, and was the lead violinist in that city's prestigious orchestra. My father and mother are newlyweds. Izzy wears a fashionable sports jacket, has well-groomed dark hair with a side parting – a very handsome slightly built man, given to scowling when irritated, not unlike Humphrey Bogart. René leans on his shoulder, elegant in a stylish chiffon dress, and is very beautiful indeed, with the most engaging of smiles and a fine figure. Think of the actress Claudette

Colbert and that was my radiant mother. The adults line up behind the old folk while the grandchildren with impish grins sit cross-legged in the foreground. A colourist had given the women rosy cheeks and the garden background appropriate colour. The portrait is set up in what looks like a fine locality, presumably in upmarket Kensington for Nathan had made some money as a diamond dealer. By the time I was born he had lost a modest fortune in a stock exchange crash with little inheritance for his wife and offspring. The sisters invested their inheritance in the share market and my mother used to joke with them about the bulls and bears and the stocking exchange.

Nathan Kasrils was a young man when he first sought his fortune in the South African diamond fields. He grew to loathe Cecil John Rhodes and consequently British imperialism. He clearly hid this from the British. He received a naturalisation certificate from the colonial secretary of the Cape Colony dated 25 November 1889, granting him 'the same rights and obligations of a natural-born British subject in the colony'. This meant he had resided in the territory for some years and possibly arrived in 1884. A discharge certificate from the British Kimberley Rifles attests to the fact that he was enrolled with them from 1890 to 1893 and that his conduct was held to have been 'very good for the whole period' and that 'he was attentive to duty'. On 20 September 1902 he received a testament from the Royal Naval Dock Command in Cape Town to the effect that 'he has been employed in the intelligence department of this office from December 20, 1901 up to this date, during which time he has performed his duties to my entire satisfaction'.[27] That would have entailed that he operated for them during the Boer War. There are official Russian documents allowing him passage back and forth to that country. His full name in Russian lettering is recorded and spelt as 'Nathaniel Azemov Kasriels'. The middle name 'Azemov' was likely his father's given name. The surname could have been interpreted as Kasrils in South African immigration records. Kasrils is an uncommon name and I have never met anybody outside my own family who has it. Shalom Aleichem, the famous Lithuanian author who emigrated to America, where his books were first published, writes about characters in a Jewish village called Kasrilevka. I wondered whether my grandfather had ancestry linked to the place but have been told it was a fictional village. Variation of the name Kasriels was not uncommon for Lithuanian, Latvian, Polish and German Jews.

From one of my cousins, Joel Tobias, I learned years later, in a letter from Israel, to where he had emigrated, the extraordinary revelation that Nathan Kasrils had been operating as an agent for the Boers. Joel had seen a letter – a testimonial, in fact – written by the Boer guerrilla leader Koos de la Rey to the effect that Nathan was 'a good sharpshooter and spy' *('n goeie skerpskutter en spioen)*.[28] He must have had a very strong nerve and clearly operated skilfully in his deception, given the positive references he received from the British. One false move and he could have been summarily executed as a Boer spy.

Nathan knew how to live on his wits, and his wife aided and abetted him. Joel said that Sarah would bake bread – diamonds secreted within – so that he could smuggle gems to Russia. That was how they had managed to establish a jewellery business in Johannesburg. No doubt a letter of good standing from the Intelligence section of the Cape Town Docks Command stood him in good stead on his trips abroad. He was regarded as one of their 'assets' which in intelligence agency terms is regarded as being of value. One of his tasks in those busy docks appears to have related to acting as an interpreter for Jewish immigrants arriving from Central and Eastern Europe, but my conjecture is that the British must have expected him to be on the lookout for pro-Boer spies from Russia.

It was consequence of Nathan's trips home to Lithuania that my father and his elder sister Minnie were born. Back in South Africa, at an opportune time, he sent for them. There was the story about how as a babe in arms on the train to the Baltic port of embarkation for South Africa my father was left in the care of Minnie while mother Sarah was napping. A strange woman gave Minnie money to go and buy sweets and assured her she would look after the baby. When Sarah discovered my father was gone she gave Minnie a thrashing. They found the vagrant, my father in her arms, begging in the harbour. Such are the miracles of the tadpoles – spermatozoa in this case – that had he not been found I would not have seen the light of day. And perhaps that was where the 'Never take sweets from strangers!' came from.

It was from Aunt Minnie that I heard how difficult it was in their Lithuanian village where by the age of four she had to carry out countless chores and how hard her daily duties were after rising early in the freezing temperatures to clean out the kitchen stove which warmed the house. The task covered her in ash.

Nathan had taken a temporary job as an interpreter on the ships in Cape Town, and hadn't received a letter in time that his wife and two children would soon be arriving. He was pleasantly shocked to be summoned to translate for them.

My mother is talking to me, and it is the very day before I begin primary school, so I am just a couple of months past my sixth birthday. 'Ronald,' she says earnestly, clutching me by the hand, 'if they tell you that Jews killed Jesus, you tell them, it was not the Jews it was the Romans.'

We had just been shopping for final items of my school uniform in Rockey Street, Yeoville, just around the corner from where we lived. We had turned into Raymond Street (if I retraced my steps, I swear I could point out the very spot) where I stood gazing up into her dark brown eyes. Normally her eyes were alive with warmth, but now they were bathed in anxiety. 'Who were the Romans, Mommy?' I asked. I knew Jesus because his effigy was on a cross at the church around the corner from where we lived. The crucified body used to spook me every time I walked by. I would shut my eyes and look away.

Try as I might, stroke after stroke, the rhythmic inhalation and exhalation of air in and out of my lungs, length upon length of the pool, I can't recall her reply. She might have said something like 'That evil man Nero, who fiddled while Rome burned' since she went to the cinema so often.

Never mind the Romans, or even the Nazis – what arguably put far more fear into our lives than either of those was the poliomyelitis epidemic that broke out at the end of 1945. It lasted into the summer of 1946 (to reappear in 1948 and sporadically up to 1956), during which my mother forbade me from visiting the local Yeoville public swimming pool where I had learned to swim at an early age. We were discouraged from attending public gatherings in parks and cinemas and school almost shut down, but the authorities refrained from declaring that kind of emergency for fear of sowing greater panic. Something like 1500 cases of the dreaded infantile paralysis were reported in 1946, with 150 deaths of mainly young white children from the more privileged homes. The epidemic bamboozled white South Africa as there were fewer reported cases among the black population, which was invariably blamed as the source of disease.

Cholera, typhoid, dysentery and TB clearly broke out in slum-like conditions lacking proper sanitation but it was soon observed that the majority of polio victims came from middle-class white homes where the standards of hygiene were at the highest level. Since the blame could not be put on the African population, the villains were said to be flies. Reports from the medical and municipal services urged an all-out war against flies on a par with the recent wartime propaganda against the Nazi menace which threatened the British Empire. Fly-traps, sprays and sticky flypaper became the norm in white homes. The fly-swatter was the infantry weapon of choice and we children outdid one another for the number of kills we chalked up – almost like the wartime Spitfire pilots.

I totally misjudge my tumble-turn at the end of the pool, hopelessly breaking rhythm. Swallowing water, spluttering and coughing, I recall the day when an enormous, ugly blue-bottle fly I had squashed into a messy pulp with my swatter, part of it still twitching, stuck to my leg. In horror I observed the gory mess dribbling down my leg, imagining the polio germs seeping through my pores into my bloodstream. I had visions of ending up in an iron lung, a monstrous looking industrial contraption which assisted the stricken to breathe. Terrified, I ran to my mother who, with an anguished expression, wiped the wretched fly off with antiseptic and then proceeded to flush virtually my whole leg in the ointment. That was the last time I engaged in a fly-swatting crusade.

The battle royal against the fly, however, did not abate. The household fruit and vegetables were flushed in a pink solution of potassium permanganate – Condy's crystals – guaranteed, according to the media, to eradicate all germs. Poppy, like all domestic servants, was expected to wash her hands in the solution every morning when she reported for

TOP: *Kasrils family, Johannesburg, 1934. Centre in hat, Nathan and left, wife Sarah, extreme left Aunt Minnie, second from far right her husband Harry Barkman (all seated); Standing: second left Izzy Kasrils, René, her mother Clara Cohen, Aunt Betty Tobias*
Front row, children from left: Stanley Barkman, the two smallest children in the middle, Marion and Joel Tobias. All others are Goldberg relatives.

BOTTOM LEFT: *My grandma, Clara Goldberg, later Cohen, Libau, Latvia, aged 14, 1899*

BOTTOM RIGHT: *Cohen family – Abe and Clara, René and Solly*

TOP: *Card game – Grandpa Abe Cohen, second from the right with Goldberg inlaws. René and Solly foreground, Johannesburg, 1912*

BOTTOM LEFT: *René's first job at the post office, 1924, aged 16*

BOTTOM RIGHT: *René playing banjo.*

TOP LEFT: *René and Clara Cohen, 1935*
TOP RIGHT: *René and her cousin Molly, Durban*
BOTTOM LEFT: *René at 20*
BOTTOM RIGHT: *René Cohen (left) and chums, Durban, 1918, aged 18*

TOP LEFT: *René, aged 18*
TOP RIGHT: *René Cohen, aged 18, and Izzy Kasrils, aged 20, 1920*
MIDDLE: *Newlyweds, 1934*
BOTTOM LEFT: *Izzy and René, front passenger, courting days, 1933*
BOTTOM RIGHT: *Izzy and René on honeymoon, Cape Town, 1934*

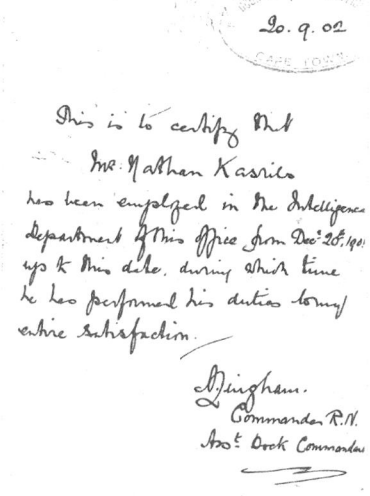

TOP LEFT: *Izzy and René on honeymoon, Cape Town, 1934*
TOP RIGHT: *René and Gran Clara, sea side, 1935*
BOTTOM LEFT: *Newlyweds. Izzy and René Kasrils, 1934*
BOTTOM RIGHT: *Nathan Kasrils good conduct letter, Intelligence Department, Cape Town docks, 20 Sept 1902*

Nº 61674

CAPE OF GOOD HOPE.

LETTERS OF NATURALIZATION UNDER ACTS No. 2 OF 1883 AND No. 35 OF 1889.

BY HIS EXCELLENCY *Lieutenant General Henry Augustus Smyth, Companion of the Most Distinguished Order of Saint Michael and Saint George, Senior Officer in command of Her Majesty's Forces in the Colony of the Cape of Good Hope in South Africa administering the Government of the said Colony and the Territories and Dependencies thereof and Acting as Her Majesty's High Commissioner &c &c*

Whereas *Nahtan Kasrils,* a Native of *Wilner,* in *Russia,* and now residing at *Kimberley,* in *the Colony of the Cape of Good Hope,* has addressed to the Colonial Secretary of the said Colony an application dated the *5th* day of *November,* 1889, setting forth that his present age is *28* years, that he is a *Jeweller,* by occupation, that he has resided in the said Colony *for four years,* and praying for Letters of Naturalization in terms of the Acts No. 2 of 1883 and No. 35 of 1889.

And whereas proof has been furnished to the satisfaction of the Colonial Secretary as to the fitness of such applicant for the grant to him of Letters of Naturalization:

ABOVE AND OPPOSITE: *Nathan Kasrils certificate of naturalisation, Cape Colony.*
5 November 1889

And whereas the said *Nahtan Kasids* has made and subscribed a Declaration of Allegiance to Her Majesty the Queen, in the manner provided by the Sixth Section of Act No. 2 of 1883:

Now, therefore, these presents, being Letters of Naturalization issued under the said Act, are to certify to all whom it may concern, that the said

Nahtan Kasids

shall henceforth to all intents and purposes whatsoever, be deemed, taken, and esteemed to be entitled to all political and other rights, powers, and privileges, and be subject to all obligations to which a natural-born British subject is entitled or subject in this Colony.

Given under my hand and the Public Seal of the Colony of the Cape of Good Hope, this 25th day of November, in the year of our Lord One Thousand Eight Hundred and Eighty Nine.

H. A. Smyth, Lieutenant-General, Officer Administering the Government.

By command of His Excellency the Officer Administering the Government in Council,

Colonial Secretary.

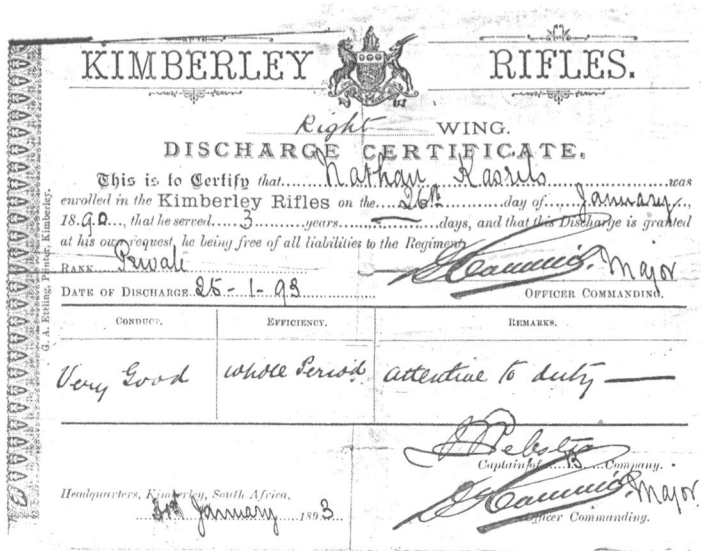

TOP: *Nathan Kasrils discharge certificate, 26 January 1890. Kimberley Rifles*

BOTTOM LEFT: *Durban beach 1937. René with Hilary, centre. Izzy and Grandpa Abe Cohen right*

BOTTOM RIGHT: *Izzy with Hilary, 1938*

work. I wore a small camphor bag on a string around my neck because it was said to ward off germs. The epidemic came close to home when my mother's cousin, wife of the district surgeon Jack Friedman, telephoned with terrible news that their little boy had contracted polio and was confined to an iron lung. My mother was aghast; she felt she had tempted fate by lighting up three cigarettes with a single match between herself and two chums – considered to be unlucky by soldiers in the wartime trenches as it was said to invite sniper fire. She was distraught and after that news even more terrified for my sister and my safety.

White housewives were made to feel extremely guilty by the media and the Department of Health statements which laid the blame on unsanitary conditions in the home. Matters got even worse when a boy I played with who lived on the Yeoville border with Berea died after contracting polio. This was a lamentable tragedy and we all felt devastated because he was very popular, but at the same time there was a feeling that death was stalking every one of us.

The war against flies continued until some wise commentator observed that where flies were most numerous, in the African townships and even some white working-class suburbs where the bucket system instead of water-borne toilets persisted, there were far fewer polio cases. What emerged was that it was precisely those homes where cleanliness was a feature that the epidemic struck more often – the reason being that the young children who were washing their hands day and night, and being forbidden to play in the dirt, had not built up the resistance to deal with the infection, unlike township kids. In the same way I suppose they had no resistance to the pervasive racist brainwashing rife in society.

PART TWO

1946–1951

Dear Teachers
I am a survivor of a concentration camp. My eyes saw what no person should witness. Gas chambers built by learned engineers. Children poisoned by educated physicians. Infants killed by trained nurses. Women and babies shot and burned by high school and college graduates. So I am suspicious of education. My request is: help your students become more human. Your efforts must never produce learned monsters, skilled psychopaths, or educated Eichmanns. Reading, writing, and arithmetic are important only if they serve to make our children more human.

– HAIM G. GINOTT (1922-1973: SURVIVOR OF THE EUROPEAN HOLOCAUST AND EDUCATOR)

CHAPTER 4

Yeoville Boys

You can take the boykie out of Yeoville, but not Yeoville out of the boykie.

– LOCAL SAYING

I HAD ALREADY COMMENCED PRIMARY school at the beginning of 1944 when I turned six. My parents enrolled me at Yeoville Boys, a short walk from where we lived. I never had to blame the Romans for the death of Jesus because there was no such accusation. On rare occasions as I grew older I did get into the odd punch-up arising from some stupid playground dispute when I was called a 'bloody Yid' and I would instinctively swing a blow or two and receive a couple in return. I was small for my age until my teens, when I had a late growth spurt, and learned earlier on to go on the offensive with a 'first strike' at my opponent when the occasion demanded. There was nothing as effective as hitting a bully smack in the face to stop him in his tracks.

My father introduced me to the art of boxing and enrolled me in such a school to better defend myself. I almost joined a boxing school run by the famous Toweel family which was near the Benoni horse racetrack.

The idea was that whenever he attended races there my dad would drop me off for a boxing lesson but because of the distance it didn't prove convenient. That was a pity because I would have met the up-and-coming South African bantamweight champion and son of the family, Vic Toweel, who later became world champion. What a disaster it was when my hero Vic lost his title to the Australian Jimmy Carruthers.[29] Whenever I sported a black eye I gained in street credibility and I sensed my father was proud of me, although my mother would get very upset and end up remonstrating with him that I was too young to be engaging in the sport. She didn't mind me having some weights around at home and a chest expander, which I used to build up my body. I was quite disciplined in this, and along with my bedtime prayers half an hour's nightly exercise became a ritual.

It was vital not to show you were afraid of anybody. The word in Afrikaans for being afraid, of being a 'scaredy-cat' or 'chicken', was *bang* or a *bangbroek*. If you backed away from a threat of any kind, you were laughed at and called a *bangbroek*, by children and even some teachers, from primary to high school. If you wanted to challenge somebody to a fight, you'd throw down the gauntlet by demanding 'Are you *bang*?' Alternatively, you could lay down a threat by declaring, 'I'll *donner* you!' (I'll thrash you) This was all part of the makings of macho males, a legacy I would guess from Joburg's ingrained mining camp mentality.

There was a mild-mannered, gangling boy in my class, who was short-sighted and wore spectacles. He was often bullied in the playground and I took to defending him. His name was Kasril Herman, which drew me to his side, although I never discovered how he came to have such a name and, unaccountably, we never discussed it. One day we were riding in a bus on a school outing and the vehicle was having trouble pulling up a steep hill. An obstreperous boy with strong shoulders and a perpetual scowl began rousing everybody to push the seat in front of them in a forward direction, as though that would help the bus gain momentum. Kasril Herman was slow in responding, resulting in The Scowl pummelling him roughly into action. In two ticks I sprang to his defence. I jumped into the aisle and gave The Scowl a solid punch on the nose. He retaliated at once, striking me under an eye. We both landed an additional punch each, then stopped in our tracks blinking at one another, and sat down. That was that. All done and dusted, as the saying goes. Each of us would be sporting black eyes next morning. No complaints, no grudges. In point of fact an exchange of blows would invariably create mutual respect and the brawlers would become on polite nodding terms.

To square off against bigger boys I had to overcome their height advantage. I found a training manual and discovered the secret lay in what is called 'the southpaw position'. This meant learning to switch from the natural right-hander's stance to the southpaw position, natural to left-handers, with right foot and hand forward. This meant I kept my left hand in a defensive position near my face, allowing me to lead with strong right jabs. I found this confused my opponents, and created greater confusion if I kept switching stances. I exercised my left hand until it became almost as powerful as my right. Right foot forward, I would move close in to the big boys, with a combo of two quick right jabs to the face, followed by a left cross into the body and then my big punch from close in, right hook to the side of the head or uppercut to the jaw. That right from the southpaw position only had to travel a short distance and consequently the blow was much more powerful. Being of shorter stature, and crouching from underneath their guard, my taller opponents never saw those blows coming. The added advantage was that most boxers are used to fighting right-handed opponents owing to the fact that southpaws are so rare. So they were unaccustomed to the left-handed stance. It earned for me at the boxing club the nickname Southpaw Ronnie. I loved that name for I felt it gave me a roguish image and street cred. I used that strategy in many a street brawl so that as I grew older I was not picked on. My father, who wanted me to be able to look after myself, was extremely proud.

I once had an unfortunate accident in the school playground (nothing to do with self-defence). For some strange reason I climbed up a ladder at playtime, my pockets full of marbles I had won during break. When the bell rang I jumped to the ground. A protruding nail on the ladder gouged a lump of flesh from above my left knee and I was carried to the classroom in a shocked state, where the wound was temporarily bandaged. My mother was summoned and I was rushed to the doctor, who cleaned up and stitched the wound while I screamed my head off since no one at school could hear me. There were no apologies from the school and neither did my parents lodge a complaint or seek financial redress for pain and suffering from the carelessness of leaving a ladder in the school playground in that state. There was a touching aspect to this episode. As I tumbled to the ground most of the marbles scattered, including prize cat's eyes and smokies in beautiful colours that were much sought after. When I got back to school after a few days my schoolmates handed every last marble back to me. It was a special act of kindness and solidarity that really impressed me because the battle to win *marlies*, as we called marbles, off each other was possibly the fiercest of all individualistic competitions at school.

We would create castles of four to twelve marbles, and even more, stacked in a pile. The greater number of marbles forming a castle required the boy shying his marble to stand further back. If he hit the castle, he won the marbles. Boys lined up in the shying line waiting their turn and you sat behind your castle keeping all the marbles that missed. Larger marbles were called goons and had a higher value, as did ironies. Where on earth that game came from no one seemed to know but it was played in all the schools. Our teacher said clay and stone marbles were found in Egyptian pharaohs' tombs and games with marbles were also played by native American Indians. Cast from ceramic or glass, they became universally popular among school-age boys in the early 20th century.

Yeoville Boys was a small redbrick school with a tarmac playground but there was a sandy area where we played marbles. There was another very South African game called *kennetjie*, which also required a sandy field. We tended to play that on the sports field after school because a fair-sized space was required. We imagined the game came from the Voortrekkers since the name had an Afrikaans ring. It was played with two hard sticks, one about 30-cm long and the other half that size. A shallow furrow was dug in the ground and the short stick placed horizontally across. Then you 'bucked' down over it with your backside to those fielding and you struck it as hard as you could with the larger stick. If it was caught, you were out and the next player took your place. If the fielders missed catching the stick, they tried to throw it back into the furrow. The defender would try to hit the stick while it was in the air. There was a system of scoring points. Some of us would get totally absorbed into the game right to sunset. It was a great way of honing one's eye to hand co-ordination. I am sure that was where my friend Springbok cricketer Ali Bacher honed his skills for he was a Yeoville champ at both *kennetjie* and marbles.

There was a view that the focus on sport and games in South African schools was detrimental to learning. This undermines the importance of skills development, team and confidence building, and sheer fun. I was probably one of those far too preoccupied with such pastimes until nearly the very end of my schooling when I suddenly developed a latent passion for study. I confess that I was one of those, probably the majority, who was impressed with those boys who excelled at sports and looked down on those who were studious. It took me quite some time into adulthood to realise that it was those with a developed intellect and thirst for knowledge who were in fact easily the most interesting in society. And I by no means equate that with those who made the most money.

The majority of the pupils at my school were Jewish, with a minority of Christian children, many of whom were working class. We were taught in English and the school, like the suburb, was whites only, which was the norm throughout South Africa and unquestioningly accepted as the natural order of things. Although whites might have had a vague fear of being under threat from the vast majority of the Africans they lorded over, the thought that things might in any way change was as ludicrous as the idea that man might one day land on the moon.

We collectively recited the multiplication table up to the 12th numeral by rote, which served me well my entire life in preference to a calculator.

One of my teachers asked us to select stories from our books at home and tell them in class. I chose to relate something I liked from a compendium. It was about a cruel ruler on another planet called The Highty Tighty Mighty, who separated his subjects according to big and small noses, round and square heads, large and small feet and so on in order to exploit them by the divide and rule principle. In the end he gets his come-uppance. The teacher asked why I had made the choice and I told her because it was so funny. I am sure I was too young to have had any cognitive motive.

We were introduced to exciting fiction such as Enid Blyton's *The Famous Five*, the Hardy Boys' adventures and a German classic banned by the Nazis called *Emil and the Detectives* – banned possibly because the boys concerned solved a robbery which the Weimer police could not. Our teacher read a chapter of *Emil* to us every Friday but, alas, before she got to the end the book disappeared from her desk drawer. The literature we read was designed almost exclusively for boys and helped to affect our feelings of primacy over girls. In contrast to the heroic exploits of the Hardy Boys, young females were encouraged to read the Nancy Drew schoolgirl detective novels, which my sister loved and so did I. I read all the titles in the series with as great a devotion as I did the Hardy Boys. I believe this gave me a healthy respect for what young girls like Nancy Drew could achieve. A highlight of the week was the arrival at the newsagent in Raleigh Street, which continued into Rockey, of British Boys' Own papers. I had on order both the *Wizard* and *Champion* with beguiling stories such as *Roy of the Rovers*, RAF hero pilots such as *Biggles*, *Tom Brown's School Days*, and Scotland Yard mysteries. There was a unique mix of both British and American comic culture - something that stood me in good stead as an adult playing the board game Trivial Pursuit.

Boys started off with *Superman* and *Batman* comics but *Captain Marvel* (the earlier initial 1940s version) was my favourite. This little boy would cry out the magic word '*Shazam!*' and a lightning bolt would strike him from the heavens to transform him into Captain Marvel, an indestructible masculine superhero.[30] If only I had such powers, I mused, as did countless other kids, imagining how I would fight off all that was evil, from Hitler to arch-criminals and baddies galore.[31] There seemed to be a drought as far as girls' comics were concerned. My sister liked Dagwood and Archie comics because they featured Blondie, Betty and Veronica, and DC comics which featured Wonder Woman but I can't recall anything from Britain for girls.

Comics tend to be dismissed as kids' stuff but at their inception in the 1930s they were read by many adults and especially became popular as they contributed to the war effort in depicting the role of a mythical superhero in defeating fascism. Many of the originators of the genre were Jews who had arrived as immigrants from Europe.

Besides that, comics are a great way to learn to read. The Coyan family at number 9 Albyn Court all read comics, parents and sons, even at the dinner table, which I was forbidden to do at home. I never ever saw my parents reading a single comic.

I graduated to the *Classic Comic* series with their romantic artwork and storylines, such as *The Last of the Mohicans, A Tale of Two Cities, Don Quixote, Uncle Tom's Cabin, Les Miserables* and so on. These comics stimulated my imagination and gave me a thirst for the real thing – especially Charles Dickens – when I reached my teens. The motto of Alexandre Dumas's *Three Musketeers*, 'One for All and All for One', captivated me. Later, when I was in my teens and *Mad Magazine* began publishing, my mind flipped with it and I began to view many things in its masterful irreverence and anarchic style. One of my favourite comic strips was that magazine's 'Spy versus Spy' series, although I could never have imagined that over half a century later I would find myself in such mirror image fiascoes in my real life as a minister of South Africa's bizarre spying fraternity.

Collecting comics became a way of life. I would join other kids at Saturday morning matinées at the local 'bughouse' where we not only flocked to see the latest Western but also had the chance to swap comics. Several hundred children would yell 'Half time!' when our cowboy hero took time off from *donnering* crooks to kiss his leading lady. One got one's money worth on those Saturday mornings with a supporting programme featuring Tom and Jerry cartoons, *The Three Stooges* and *Captain Marvel* adventures. Joy was unbounded until the newsreels, which had the ability to produce howls of fear whenever Hitler and Nazi goose-stepping Storm Troopers appeared. As the war came to a close and scenes of advancing Allied soldiers dominated – guns blazing, cannons roaring, tanks rumbling, planes dropping bombs – the cheering was deafening. At times the cinema's manager tried to subdue us and patrolled the aisles with a swishing cane in hand. He was usually inebriated and we realised his bark was worse than his bite and ignored him.

I clearly had compassion for the underdog or the lonely, particularly anyone I perceived as being left out on the margins. Another regular cinema goer was a young adult, dark and sun baked, who always wore the same clothes – grey trousers and a black blazer, with unbuttoned shirt. He was always first in the queue on Saturday mornings. He would shun the better seats and make a beeline for the worst seat in the house – front row, the extreme aisle seat in the corner side of screen. That choice of seat baffled me. It reminded me of the African father and his child locked out of the playground, yet this man was able to enter the whites-only cinema. Clearly something of not belonging led him to isolate himself. I was frustrated because I was still too young to work at the reason. I tried to befriend him but this was almost impossible. He could barely understand English and spoke only Yiddish. Someone told me he was an orphan out of Germany, so probably had no family; he worked as a gravedigger at the Jewish cemetery. The Chevrah Kadisha (the Jewish burial society and charitable fund), who must have given him the job, should have seen to his education.

You never saw beggars in Yeoville. One day I was running to the newsagent to buy comics and passed a dejected African man in an old army coat, limping along with the use of a crutch. Coming back I came across him leaning against a wall and wiping his brow with a handkerchief. He had taken off his old hat and put it on the ground. To his obvious surprise, I popped a few pennies into it. He was taken aback and cried out after me, '*Dankie, baasie!*' I waved back in acknowledgement and he waved back with his handkerchief and then dabbed his eyes. I could hear a voice in my head telling me I should have given him more since I had several coins in my pocket, but I was too shy to turn around and go back. So I ran right around the block to find him hobbling my way. As I came closer, I noticed how deeply furrowed his brow was, his scraggy grey beard, his eyes squinting at me in curiosity. I gestured that I wanted to give him some more money and he cupped his rough hands, bowing his head, and received my few copper pennies.

'Bless you, *nkosi wam*, God bless you, *baasie*.'

I was aware that he had called me his 'lord' in Zulu, which gave me mixed feelings; on the one hand I was pleased that the small change I gave him made some kind of difference to his day but on the other I felt upset that I was regarded as so superior to him. I myself was so overcome with emotion that I fished out the last two coins from my pocket – a couple of silver tickeys which added up to 6p, the price of a bioscope ticket. When I popped these into his big palms, hands that had seen so much hardship, he cried, 'Hallelujah! Hallelujah! God bless you!' The tiny silver coins gleaming in the sunlight in stark contrast to the palms of his hands looked like the milk teeth of a child. They were so minute and inconsequential yet gave him such abundant joy. As shy as I was, I felt it was polite to exchange some words with him and the first thought that came into my mind was to ask him where he got the army coat from. He told me he had been a soldier for General Smuts in the war and that he had been taken prisoner by the Germans at Tobruk. I almost cried, telling him he was a good man and thanking him for fighting the Germans. How unfair life was, I thought. Here was a man who had actually fought the Germans and must have been extremely lucky to have survived imprisonment. Why had he been so discarded in our country? Here he was, in a predominantly Jewish neighbourhood; surely he deserved a red carpet to be rolled out for him, if only the people knew. If only they knew – what a laugh! Even at that age I knew they would have just ignored him, not even up to inviting him into the kitchen and offering him a bowl of soup, never mind a job. That night in my prayers I asked God to look after him.

Words fascinated me and, for that reason, I loved jokes. The first joke I ever picked up, probably in Grade One at school, I practised on Gramps. Brothers Ikey and Mikey lived on the upper block of a building. Their father had forgotten his car keys and shouted up to Ikey, who was on the balcony: 'Throw down my key.' So he threw down his brother Mikey. My grandad roared with laughter but I needed to know that he understood the joke. 'Do you get it?' I enquired, which made him roar even louder.

I took to improving my vocabulary and soon I was reading a page of a dictionary nightly. When our teacher wrote on the blackboard a paragraph in which the adjective 'nice' was repeatedly used and told us to find different descriptive words I threw myself eagerly into the challenge. It was that kind of teaching creativity rather than learning by rote that got through to bored pupils. It certainly stimulated in me an aspiration to write but first we had to master simple tasks such as spelling and rules of grammar, which could be very taxing and difficult to follow if you failed to concentrate.

Concentration could be a problem with me. When boredom set in I would daydream a great deal. And yawn. 'Oh dearie me, I have just been swallowed by a whale,' a corpulent teacher called Mrs Sieve intoned sarcastically, drilling into me with her beady eyes, her double chin quivering. She was new, a relief teacher when our regular kind old lady took ill. For some reason Mrs Sieve took an aversion to me. She was a very large lady with spectacles that gave her an owlish look. She wore a frumpy old dress, with no waist, to try and hide her corpulence. Instead of shoes she wore large open-toed sandals which reminded me of the Romans I had by then seen in a film. This was the first personality clash I experienced in my life and it was most unpleasant. I managed to survive.

Despite her attempts to humiliate me my schooling began well, owing more to a talent to run fast than erudition. Sports were held in high regard and earned for me the necessary self-respect to withstand the derisory remarks that Mrs Sieve aimed at me. For games of all kinds we were split into four houses: St Andrew's, St David's, St Edward's and St Patrick's, with the respective distinguishing colours of blue, yellow, red and green – representative of the countries of Britain. I was allocated to St Patrick's and for sports day my mother sewed green ribbon strips down the sides of my running shorts. Sporting a large green rosette on my vest I won two races for my year, although one was just a novelty sack race; the other the 40-yard dash. On receiving my second prize from a city councillor, who was Irish, he asked what kind of a St Patrick I was. I caused him to laugh by replying 'A Jewish one, sir.'

There were downsides to my success. When I got back to Albyn Court with my friend Ivor we encountered his father, who asked him, without acknowledging my presence, whether he had beaten me. I remember feeling affronted and stealing quietly away, feeling sorry for Ivor who of course had to give a negative answer which disappointed his father.

The following day was a worse experience, for clearly with my mind on the previous day's excitement I messed up a spelling test by writing various letters back to front. Maybe I was a tad dyslexic. Whatever the reason Mrs Sieve got in a rage and sent me off to the headmaster to show him my work. At least he did not treat me like the village idiot and in fact congratulated me on my performance the day before. Mrs Sieve struck back with a vengeance. We were in an arts-and-craft class under her domain and with my mind miles away – possibly preoccupied with Granny Clara's illness – I absentmindedly trimmed the hairs off a paintbrush. After the materials had been collected the whole class froze as she bellowed out: 'Who's given this paintbrush a haircut?' She held up the offending object as though it was a tool of the devil. For a moment my mind was blank until the awful fact dawned on me that I was the culprit. I stood up, probably trembling and pale faced. She hauled me before the class, demanding an explanation. I stood there silently for I had no explanation to offer. 'Cat caught your tongue?' Mrs Sieve screamed. She promptly marched me back to the headmaster's office, evidence in hand. He gave me two raps across the knuckles with a ruler while she looked on. I was given a curt note for my parents demanding payment for the paintbrush. My mother always took my side in such matters and I believe both my folks understood that I was going through an uneasy period due to my grandmother's illness.

My mother had sensed that Mrs Sieve had an attitude towards me and she went to complain to the headmaster, who called the teacher in. I don't know what happened but after that Mrs Sieve stopped her campaign of trying to humiliate me in class. Thankfully the regular teacher recovered and Mrs Sieve disappeared. One negative aspect was that for years into adulthood I had an antagonism towards obese people and had to work hard to eradicate the prejudice.

Fortunately, for the rest of my time in primary school I had decent teachers and happy memories. This was particularly the case on sports days for I continued to win all the races I entered except in the last year when Sam Lazerson bought his son spiked shoes, a rarity for primary school, and Ivor managed to beat me into second place in the 100 yards. I had asked my father whether I could have spiked shoes but he said it was too soon. I felt it was because of the price but I wasn't bothered.

Yeoville Boys Primary was a well-integrated school with devoted teaching staff. A new head, Mr Leitch, returned from the war to take command in 1946 and at school assemblies he often made the point that we were living in a new era in a world where freedom had been preserved. That the black people beyond our horizon, thousands of whom had served in the army as stretcher-bearers and labourers, were certainly not the recipients of that victory did not appear relevant. They received a khaki overcoat and a bicycle for their war effort while white ex-servicemen were rewarded with decent housing and the chance of a free university education if requested. We learned some geography and history, all carefully prescribed by the education authorities to turn us into obedient citizens. The problem was we learned everything by rote in preference to a dialectical question-and-answer approach which would have helped us to analyse the subject matter and develop our ability to reason things out. In Geography we learned basic facts about the towns, mountains and game parks of the country and its mineral wealth. As for those who dug the gold out of the bowels of the earth, who had lost their land to white conquest, we heard next to nothing. In History we had to memorise names and dates about the English Royal family. We sang 'God Save the King' at assembly and stood to attention in the cinema while the British national anthem was played. There were always some whites who walked out in disgust when the anthem started and we realised they were the Afrikaner nationalists still fighting the Boer War.

In 1947 the Royal family paid a visit to South Africa and we schoolboys were marched down to Louis Botha Avenue, paper Union Jack flags in hand, to wave at the passing cavalcade. As we awaited their arrival a boy began singing a vulgar song: '*Do you ken John Peel with his balls of steel; and a chisel up his arse ...*' None of the predominantly Jewish boys could match such a ditty and our parents would have been panic-stricken if we had been so publicly anti-Royal. Gentile boys seemed to know many vulgarities such as that, and I soon became infatuated with them. I started mastering a wide repertoire. Excitement arose as the Royal party of King George, his wife Elizabeth, and their two daughters, Elizabeth and Margaret, drove sedately past, waving in a genteel manner. We responded with ear-splitting cheers. They looked incredibly pale to me.

Apart from love of the Royals, at school we imbibed the fact that the country had been empty save for wild animals until the arrival of the Dutch at the Cape and the alleged simultaneous movement into the country from the north across the Limpopo River by what was termed the 'Bantu tribes'.

One of the more unusual boys who joined us for a few months at Yeoville Boys was a concentration camp survivor whose name, if I remember correctly, was David Magid. He showed me the scar on his wrist where the tattooed concentration camp number had been removed. He told me that he had survived because his mother had hidden him in a stack of hair; otherwise he would have ended up in the gas chamber. He said what was almost as bad as the fear of death was being terribly cold and hungry. He recounted how they had been freed by Russians who gave them blankets and food and that they were so grateful they'd kissed the liberators' hands. Some prisoners died because they ate too much too quickly.

One day when the school toilets were blocked and there was an awful stench David became terribly upset. When I tried to console him, he said he was reminded of the overpowering odour of those terrible days. That and the acrid smell from the crematorium. I was prompted to ask him what they did for toilet paper in the camp. He explained that the guards would occasionally give them newspapers to tear into pieces, one piece a day, if you were lucky, but I didn't press him for more information because he seemed embarrassed. They used buckets to relieve themselves at night and foul-smelling ablution blocks during the day. That was military-type 'long drop' camp design with no flushing water. Pieces of soiled newsprint found flying in the wind would be eagerly pounced on to be read for any information they contained – even adverts. It was rare to get David to talk but he did confide in me in a detached way. Before I could get to really know him, however, he transferred to another school. I used to fill his pockets with sweets I filched from my father's sample case.

The mention of toilet paper reminds me of an occasion when three Afrikaans boys knocked on our door in Yeoville to ask if they could use the toilet. My mother readily agreed. After they had gone on their way she discovered that they had filched the toilet roll and one to spare, plus some items of disinfectant and a toilet brush. It did not bother her. She simply reflected on how poverty-stricken the boys must be.

The only time we Jewish boys were made to feel different was when it came to Bible reading. Although perhaps it was the Christian boys who were made to feel different. The Jews were in a group that studied the Old Testament and the Christian boys in a group that studied the New Testament. So we missed the explanation about the Romans and Jesus. On Jewish holidays we did not go to school and most of us spent the day in the Orthodox synagogue nearby. I remember walking home with Ivor from the shul past the school and distinctly feeling very sorry for the Gentile boys, not because they had to attend classes but because we believed that as the 'chosen race' the Lord God preferred us.

What I remember most about Yeoville Boys was how we excelled in football. Whatever the rivalry between Ivor and myself, we both played for the school team, which won the championship in 1949 and 1950 for under 11s and under 12s respectively. We were very proud of our yellow-and-blue football jerseys. Ivor's position was at left back while I played at centre forward. Our captain was Brian Henning, a gifted all-round sportsman, who went on to become, along with his bevy of brothers, a leading professional golfer. At inside right was Yudel Bacher, whose younger brother Ali became South Africa's cricket captain. Yeoville was a hothouse of sporting talent and an example of the role environment could play. The school encouraged various sporting disciplines and outside of the formal activities the outdoor life was a great inducement for further competition and rivalry as we played in the streets and the nearby open spaces on the ridges and koppies. In our revelry, we would fail to notice the dramatic thunderstorms rolling in, the sky pierced by forked lightning, and we would scamper home, drenched to the bone by the fierce summer rains.

The football match I remember most was against Norwood Primary, played at their home ground Patterson Park on a very rainy afternoon. In those days we played with a leather ball which became very heavy as it soaked up the mud. We beat them 15-1 and I scored seven goals. Opposite me was the one good player opposing us and that was their captain, Graham Bales, who was a good head taller than me. He had a powerful kick and because we were the better team most of the game was played in their half, with him taking the place kicks instead of the goalkeeper. Despite the heaviness of the ball, he managed to kick almost to the halfway line and it was my fate to have to head it down. Every time I did so I felt a ferocious pain in my neck, almost like whiplash. Reading newspaper reports these days about professional footballers suffering early dementia as a result of heading the old leather ball makes me think of that game, where I stood my ground every time the ball came rocketing towards me. I did not have the good sense to duck in case I was regarded as a sissy boy. Instead I must have had millions of grey cells killed off every time that ball struck my head. Graham Bales went on to become a leading professional football player in South Africa.

One year our school team was entered into a knockout tournament which included the schools of Johannesburg's working-class southern suburbs. I came to realise how tough the boys from that background were. We managed to reach the quarter-finals but lost 3-1 to a team that was not more skilful but certainly much tougher. I do remember scoring a very fine goal, though, owing to the presence of my father. The school was near Turffontein racecourse from where he'd slipped away to watch our match. It was an uphill battle for us and we could just not penetrate their defence. Our left half, a boy called Berty Hopkins, had a throw-in on the halfway line. He had been constantly feeding our captain and best player Brian Henning on the left wing, who was good enough to dribble down that flank but kept getting blocked by a couple of big defenders from crossing to me in the penalty area – a fox in the box, if I say so myself, from where I scored a great many of our goals. Suddenly there was my dad on the scene, encouraging Hopkins to change tactics by pointing to me coming over from centre field where there was a big gap. I will never forget that image of my dad standing next to Hopkins with a decisive finger pointing my way. I collected the ball and moved very quickly towards goal, thumping the ball past a surprised goalkeeper before the defenders could recover. A memory like that lasts a lifetime. Indelibly printed on my mind. It still gives me such a surge of excitement and a wonderful memory of my father. I fancy I can still see the startled look on the goalkeeper's face, but that surely must be imagination.

I often went to football games with my pals and we unreservedly supported Rangers in their black-and-white striped shirts. We were attracted to them because their goalkeeper was a flamboyant Jew called Lubbe Snoiman, who wore a bright yellow jersey. I was ill at home when Rangers played Boksburg in a Transvaal soccer cup final in 1946, Ivor promising to bring me back a commemorative programme. Rangers won the game two goals to one.

The first time I attended a rugby Test match was alongside my pal Ivor in 1949 when we were all of 11 years old. We walked all the way from Yeoville over the ridge to the huge Ellis Park stadium in Doornfontein, leaving home early to be sure of getting into the ground and finding a seat. There was a huge buzz as robust spectators shouted in Afrikaans their support for the Springboks. It was the first time we saw Afrikaners en masse: busy grilling boerewors outside the ground, and swigging brandy and Coke and Castle or Lion beer. They appeared to be burly people full of confidence in their Springbok regalia, waving all manner of flags, from that of the Union to those of the old Boer republics, in honour of which they would shout with gusto the war-cry '*Vrystaat*!'

We sat between burly, bearded, highveld farmers wearing short pants and thick jerseys in the freezing cold, swigging their bottles of beers and munching naartjies. They had a huge disdain for wine. A conversation, usually in Afrikaans, might have gone something like this:

'Hey, boet, have you heard the one about the *larnie rooinek* showing off his knowledge about this and that wine? Van der Merwe gets pissed off with him and *sommer* asks what's his opinion of *noil reeb*? The *rooinek sommer* says, Oh I believe that's the new cabernet, still have to try it, old chap. *Voetsek, jou bliksem!* that's Lion Beer spelt backwards, Van der Merwe answers and gives him a *klap*.'

One of my most abiding memories was seeing the young Irish winger Tony O'Reilly, representing the visiting British Lions, scoring a fabulous try in which he ran the length of the field. The Afrikaans spectators were so impressed they dubbed him *Die Rooi Haas* (the red hare), owing to the flaming colour of his hair and his speed.

One of the favourite players was Okey Geffen, who was in fact a distant relative of Ivor's. We had been to his home in Regent Street, Yeoville, to get his autograph. He was a big man who played flank forward and took the penalty kicks. In those days the rugby ball would not be slanted in the direction of the goalposts but placed upright. Apparently, he had honed his skills in a German prisoner of war camp where a fellow inmate was a rugby coach. His accuracy was decisive; it won the Springboks the match against their rivals that day and the rest of the series – the touring All Blacks from New Zealand. Geffen was highly popular with the fans, who regarded him as providing the Bokke, as the Springboks were affectionately called, with the luck of the Jews.

Ivor didn't like the Afrikaners. Like his father he called them 'Dutchmen'. He said they were ugly, not realising that as farming people in origin they were yet to acquire the svelte figures and sophisticated demeanour of the urban middle class.

There was strict racial segregation at all sports events, whether rugby, cricket or football. The most inferior part of the ground was reserved for so-called non-whites in a corner enclosure where the view was poorest. The behaviour of South Africa's underclass infuriated the privileged whites because the black spectators were most demonstrative in their support for any overseas team. Whether it was a try in rugby, a goal in soccer or a six hit by an opposing cricketer, they went ballistic with joy. So unrestrained was this that at times black spectators ran onto the field in celebration of an opposition's success. We were witness to police baton charges as well as irate white spectators hurling empty beer bottles into the black enclosure. The missiles often fell short, hitting white spectators instead. The newspapers were full of photographs of stricken whites receiving treatment from first aid attendants. There were never photographs of injured black spectators struck by police batons or bottles.

In 1949 the Australian cricket team toured South Africa with all-time celebrities such as Ray Lindwall and Keith Miller. A Battle of Britain pilot, Miller was my favourite. Because there was always talk about the pressures sportsmen faced he famously said: 'I'll tell you what pressure is. Pressure is a Messerschmitt up your arse. Cricket is not.' That served as a reminder that sport, all too often unduly elevated, was not the be-all and end-all of life.

I had the rare distinction of forecasting the results in a *Star* newspaper competition and won a book by J.H. Fingleton of Bradman's last tour to

England in 1948 signed by all the players on the South African tour. Gramps said I had the luck of the Irish and he often asked me to pick out winners from his race card. We would do that by picking numbers from a hat. That luck has followed me down the years, an intuition for a racehorse or a lucky number at the roulette table on odd occasions when I feel the itch to take a chance. Something of the *sangoma*, African friends say. I laugh dismissively. Grandpa himself benefited from good fortune. He once won £10 000 on the Irish sweepstake and was generous enough to send my mom on a sea cruise and treated the whole family to a seaside holiday.

There was another game that helped me identify the time I went to war with Adolf Hitler. It was 1946 or 1947 that a German family moved into our suburb and were virtually neighbours of ours since they lived on the Raymond Street corner diagonally across the road from Albyn Court. I began playing with a boy a few years older than me called Stephen Pearls. He was affectionately called 'Bubi' by his mother, which in southern German meant 'small boy'. His father was a professor who always appeared to keep to the shadows. They lived in a large house with a garage off Muller Street. My introduction to Bubi was when I saw him painting a Union Jack on the exterior door of their garage but only in red and blue. I stopped to watch and told him that he was leaving out the white lines. This surprised him but after checking with his mother he came back and thanked me. I saw him on and off after that and invited him to play in a scratch football game in the local park. I was invited into his home for tea and cake and at Easter that year witnessed him and his sister Renata eagerly searching in the garden for hard-boiled eggs his mother had painted in vivid colours, some with stripes, some with polka dots. I learned that the family were in South Africa for a short while on the way to America. At some stage I learned that they were German.

One day we were playing in their garden watering the flowers when suddenly we spotted Gerald Coyan, my neighbour from Albyn Court, trying to shoot a bird perched high up a tree with a pellet gun. Observing this, Bubi turned the hosepipe on him and shouted, 'Don't be so cruel!' Gerald was incensed. Pointing his gun at Bubi from across the fence, motioning as though he was going to shoot, he screamed out: 'What do you know about cruelty, you bloody German? We'll get you, you bastard!' Another voice piped up: 'The only good German's a dead German!'

When I told my mother that Bubi was German and asked whether I should continue to play with him, she said not all Germans were bad Germans, and that one of her relatives had escaped being rounded up because a German family had helped him. I continued to visit Bubi. He was a bright and interesting boy; and his mother was very kind to me. I remember the occasion when he pointed out spectacular photographs of a rugby match in the Sunday newspapers. A player in a striped jersey was literally flying through the air, rugby ball in hand, in the act of scoring a try. I had never seen anything like that before as at that point had not been to any rugby match and it literally took my breath away.

Things changed between Bubi and me shortly after our excitement over the rugby photographs. Hanging around his home I noticed on the inside of the garage door, the one with the Union Jack painted on the outside, what appeared to be a similar Union Jack. But it was quite easy to discern that actually a swastika had first been painted, and then rather clumsily – perhaps on second thoughts – turned into a Union Jack. Well, what did that really mean, I could have thought. Not so much depicted as a sign of allegiance, but rather simply out of habit of a child growing up in Nazi Germany? The situation became ominous, however, when one day we were playing inside the house and Bubi and I sneaked into his father's study. He rifled through some drawers and took out a photo album. Grinning, he pointed out photographs of his father in overalls with a group of men, some of whom were in uniform. He pointed to the central figure and to my astonishment it was none other than Adolf Hitler. Bubi giggled. I was stunned. I tried to grab the album and we started wrestling until we fell to the ground. His mother rushed in and behind her, to my dread, was the professor, white faced, screaming at his son in German, grabbing the album from him. I jumped up and ran as though my life depended on it. As I exited their gate I picked up a stone and threw it onto their galvanised iron roof where it clattered noisily like a machine-gun going off – rat-tat-tat-tat!

I was badly in need of reinforcements. Everybody appeared to be at work apart from the children. Ivor was at home with a cold and he was the first person I wanted to consult. Surprisingly his father was home too. I struggled to get out the story of Professor Pearls and Hitler in a photograph together. For once Ivor had nothing to say, perhaps because he was not well. His father gawked at me, took a long draw on his cigar, said nothing and shuffled away.

Next I spotted Gerald Coyan coming home from school – or rather I heard him long before I saw him. Gerald was in the Athlone School cadet band and used to practise on his bugle while walking home. He took me seriously all right and we waited for his elder brother Leonard, who was also in the school band and a few minutes behind Gerald. They loathed Germans and had heard lots of stories about the war from their father, who had served with the South African Armed Forces in North Africa and Italy. They were ready for anything, including going and confronting the Pearls family immediately in their militaristic cadet uniforms to spook them. That worried me, especially since I thought the older brother Leonard was a bit crazy. The two brothers used to fight a lot with each other and Leonard would gnaw at his wrist and grunt as he sought to close in on his younger brother. They thought of waiting for their father but to my dismay then decided to go and spy on the enemy then and there. I had no alternative but to follow in their footsteps, but I felt uneasy about turning on Bubi. And I was terrified of being accosted by the professor. We bucked down behind a hedge and peered through it but saw nobody. Leonard picked up a large stone and, like I had done, threw it onto the roof – rat-tat- tat-tat – and we ran like blazes.

I was telling my mother and father about the Hitler photograph that evening when Jack Coyan and his sons arrived at our door. There was a big consultation, with my father suggesting he would talk to his friend Fred May who had contacts with the government. Gerald and Leonard said they would go and spy out the house since it was dark but their father told them not to be stupid. Then the adults got into a conversation about something else entirely and I followed the two brothers, who were drifting off, thinking that they were getting up to something. Sure enough they decided to go back and throw stones on the German family's roof which I thought was a good idea. We picked up some good-sized missiles and again crept up to the Pearls' home. Suddenly we stopped in our tracks. There was a large man sitting on a chair outside the front door of the house. He seemed to have a stick and a torch and was clearly keeping watch.

'Crumbs!' I heard Gerald mutter. 'We'd better split.'

'Wait!' hissed brother Leonard. 'He's asleep. Let 'em have it.' He threw his stones onto the roof and so did Gerald. The sound on the galvanised iron roof was like a military battle. In my haste to clear off with them I totally misfired my lone stone, which bounced off the Union Jack Bubi had painted on the garage door.

Fred May agreed to check on Professor Pearls. The furore soon died down, however. It seemed the professor was *persona grata* as far as the Smuts government was concerned and anyway the family were soon off to the United States of America. In retrospect Professor Pearls must have been one of those German wartime scientists who both the Americans and the Russians had enlisted into Cold War service. Mr Coyan said that Pearls was not a German name and that it must have been used to hide the professor's true identity.

Was it 1946 or 1947, when I was seven or eight? Western Province lost the Currie Cup final to Northern Transvaal in 1946 but defeated Transvaal in 1947. The photos my one-time friend Stephen Pearls had shown me could have been from either of those years.

The irony of those times. On the one side of the road the Pearls family out of a vanquished Nazi Germany. On the other side, almost at the same time, lived a family with Stalin's portrait in their living room.

CHAPTER 5

Dancing with the Sachs Sisters

WITH MY MOTHER WORKING AT a city department store and nanny Poppy Molefe having little control over me, I generally played out in the streets after school. There were few vehicles about and the streets were rather safe so we neighbourhood kids, as white children, experienced a splendid degree of freedom of movement. We organised scratch sports games on the streets, competed in marathon races up to the Yeoville water tower on the ridge and back to our start at Albyn Court, or played cowboys and Indians on the nearby koppies to which we had free and easy access. We explored every nook and cranny, although it wasn't difficult to locate a landmark at the highest point of the ridge. This was a monument to Indian soldiers who fought on the British side and had perished in the Anglo-Boer War (renamed The South African War) and it became a sacred spot to us. The inscription was to those of Christian, Hindu, Muslim and Zoroastrian faiths. The latter reference was puzzling but cleared up when I looked it up in the dictionary. It was a pre-Islamic religion of ancient Persia that worshipped fire. The fire aspect was fascinating to me and the name brought to mind a movie series at the Yeoville bioscope called

The Mark of Zorro. I never worked out whether he might have been a Zoroastrian but the eponymous Zorro was a masked Mexican outlaw skilled in all manner of weapons from daggers and swords to guns and whips. He would carve his trademark Z on the face of the 'baddies' he vanquished. I re-christened our gang's name from the 'Albanians' to the 'Zorro Gang' and then simply 'Z-Boys', with our array of weapons from pea-shooters and catties to the more feared pellet guns.

It was our Geography teacher who explained that the spine running east to west across Johannesburg, the White Waters Ridge (Witwatersrand), was not only a geological feature connected to the gold reef running below ground for 300 km, but the watershed between the Indian and Atlantic oceans. On visits we would relieve ourselves by peeing either side of the ridge and contribute to the run-off into both oceans. It was a favourite place, with a magnificent scenic view looking out across the city's southern suburbs and northwards over Yeoville and beyond to Houghton and through the haze to the distant Magaliesberg range.

I was one of the more restless boys in a suburb that pulsated with energy and I organised the Zorro Gang to compete with several others in the neighbourhood. In season we organised acorn fights since there were many beautiful oak trees that lined the streets producing a profusion of the green missiles we would fire from our home-made catties. We used water-pistols as well and soon some among us acquired pellet guns, which we used in battles held on the koppies that undoubtedly prepared many a youngster for recruitment into the racist army in later years. I would use the Boer War monument as the rendezvous point and headquarters of my gang. I acquired a Red Rider air-gun, joining the armed elite, and I became a crack shot. We had a rule not to fire at one another's faces for fear of being blinded. The pellets bounced off our bodies with a painful sting like that of a bee which we certainly strove to avoid. There were loads of interesting things going on.

Several houses kept poultry in their back yards and there were some people who bred pigeons. On the Frances Street side of Albyn Court, a German Jewish family had a chicken business. This required that the poultry be slaughtered by a *shoichet* to make them kosher. When we saw this religious man arrive with his little bag of special knives we kids dropped whatever we were doing to go and observe the antics. Headless chickens would run about for up to a minute. Rudy, a young boy of the household, had the task of catching them for the *shoichet* – cheered on by us. There was an occasion when a chicken actually flew over the fence and ran about headless in Raymond Street pursued by a posse of boys and dogs. I produced a hand-written news-sheet called the *Albyn Court Courier* and one of my proudest stories was headlined 'Last Run of the Headless Chicken'. I wrote the stories in pencil with headlines in red crayon accompanied by pencil drawings. There was one copy only, written in a school notebook, which circulated by hand. I kept it going for several months and many an adult reader forecast that I would grow up to be a journalist.

I was blissfully unaware that I was being scrutinised by three sisters who lived across the road from the Pearls family. I was shy of girls and pretended not to notice them. But everyone was aware that the Sachs family had moved in and they were clearly Jewish. You could spot Litvaks a mile away. I had seen my father talking on a street corner to their father, a stocky man with a warm smile. He was a real worker for he wore overalls and carried a toolbox. My father said he was Solomon Sachs from Lithuania. His daughters called me over one day as I was walking back home from my war on the koppies and offered me a glass of home-made lemonade. I was very thirsty and could not resist. The eldest introduced herself as Bella. She had long dark hair with a bold parting in the middle, was extraordinarily beautiful and must have been all of 16. The middle one's name was Minky, and she was tall and skinny, quite attractive but not nearly as beautiful as Bella, I thought. The youngest one, my age, was small and scrawny, very plain with a sharp nose and mousey hair, name of Faygie. Once they had got me to relax they took me into the parlour and said they wanted me to dance with Faygie. I told them that I had no idea how to dance except for the few wiggling motions Poppie had taught me. They laughed and Bella said they were going to teach me a more formal way of dancing like people did at weddings. Minky sat down at a piano while Bella showed me how to hold Faygie. Minky began to play and they soon got Faygie and I to dance in time to what turned out to be a foxtrot, which Bella said was the easiest dance of all and the best way to start. 'One – two – three together ... One – two – three together,' she called out and it wasn't long before I was able to accompany and even lead Faygie, who was well ahead of me in the routine. She was extremely docile; in fact I can't remember her ever opening her mouth. She obediently followed everything her sisters told her to do. The sisters soon had a hold over me all right for I enjoyed the lemonade and, much to my astonishment, I enjoyed the dance routines too. I dutifully reported to them once a week from then on and before long had mastered the waltz, the Charlton, rumba, samba and finally, to great acclaim from Bella, with whom I had fallen hopelessly in love, the tango. I always left before Mr Sachs came home, not to avoid him but because he got back late. When I did bump into him, which was rare, he gave me a very warm greeting. His wife looked like a very wizened Faygie. She spent her time cooking, sewing, attending to her vegetable garden and to her ducks and hens in the yard. I was taken aback one day when I observed her pinching her nose and expertly flicking the snot to the ground. I was no snob but I had never seen a woman behaving that way and knew nothing of the personal habits of peasants.

It was not only the dance routines that were edifying for me. For a start, where our sitting room was full of photographs of Danny Boy their parlour was lined with photographic portraits of Joseph Stalin and what I realised later must have been the Soviet leadership. Stalin's features were well known to even a ten-year-old like me but I learned much about him from the stories the girls told. To them he was superior to even a movie star like Errol Flynn who, if you believed Hollywood, defeated the Japanese single-handed. For such fiction they had open scorn. They regaled me with stories about Stalin's childhood, leadership as a Bolshevik, and how he was the genius who had led the Red Army and Soviet people in the defeat of Hitler. There was a story about how he had escaped from jail by dumping a bucket of shit over the head of a guard, grabbing his keys and pistol and making good his escape with his comrades. They all laughed when Bella used the word 'shit', glancing at me for my reaction, and then they laughed again because I turned red in the face. I heard about the Cold War from their lips and got regular updates about the darkening international situation. America was the villain, had used the atomic bomb on the defeated Japanese people as a warning to the Russians, and aimed to use nuclear power to enslave the world. They appeared to know from radio news when the next nuclear detonation was to take place and had me in shivers in case it all went wrong and the world caught fire. They believed that a test was planned to drop the bomb on a ship filled with sheep and if it missed and landed in the sea that would be 'overs cadovers' for us all because the sea would catch fire.

But an even worse prospect, apparently, was the coming general election in South Africa. They said if the Afrikaner National Party won, not only the African people but the Jews as well would be in deep trouble. This was because the Nats, as the apartheid party was called, was nothing more than a fascist, anti-Semitic organisation that had supported Hitler and had hoped he would win the war. Within months, on 26 May 1948, the forecast of Henk the Gent came true, Fred May lost his bet, the white electorate had voted the apartheid party into power, and the Sachs daughters were in tears. I had become attached to them and certainly learned a great deal from my encounters with them – and far more than the dance routines.

To most English speakers the bookish General Smuts, Oom Jannnie, as he was affectionately called, appeared mild mannered. By contrast, his successor as prime minister, Dr Malan of the Afrikaner National Party, looked mean and vengeful. One of Malan's right-hand men, Dr Verwoerd, came across as an avuncular professor but appeared to live up to the concerns of the Sachs sisters, who talked about how he had studied philosophy in Germany and was a believer in racist doctrine. He was the architect of apartheid. Where the Sachs sisters picked up their information was beyond me but I trusted them completely.

George Formby, the famous English singer and comedian, was touring South Africa at that time and performing to some mixed audiences. Dr Malan, the very week of winning the election, apparently phoned Formby's manager, who also happened to be his wife, and requested that they only play to segregated audiences. The Sachs sisters clearly had good connections because they learned that she had given him the brush-off by simply responding with the words 'Piss off, you stupid little man.' When they told me that we all laughed uproariously, even if I blushed in embarrassment.

I began to think the girls were connected to the Communist Party for rumour had it that they knew everything that was going on. I wondered whether it was their father who was a member. As Malan and his party moved to outlaw the Communist Party there were demonstrations against the move. For the first time direct politics appeared to enter our home with my mother expressing fears about the fate of two of her cousins – both married sisters – who were members of the Communist Party. One cousin was Jacqueline Arenstein, who lived in Durban. The other cousin, Charlotte Lowenstein, lived in Johannesburg and had participated in support for the 1946 mine workers' strike. I knew both of them as my 'aunts' and noted how similar they looked to my mother – quite exquisite Semitic beauties.

Around this time a slogan mysteriously appeared on the prominent wall of the Yeoville playing fields – venue of our football matches – in bold black letters: AN ATTACK ON COMMUNISM IS AN ATTACK ON YOU. There was an initial buzz of interest and all the talk was about who could have been responsible. An attempt by the police to have the slogan scrubbed off failed; the paint must have had some substance in it that burned the lettering deeply into the rough-hewed surface of the wall. The offending slogan which initially was scrubbed and made fainter kept re-emerging in all its glory, which made the message even more intriguing. It remained there for years. The rebellious words became ingrained in my mind and I kept thinking about those who were responsible. Their daring impressed me. Why should they risk punishment, I wondered, realising from all the talk about how the police would hunt them down, that they had done something for an ideal and not for themselves. Most of all I pondered about the meaning of the message itself, although I wasn't sure why an attack on communism should relate to me personally. Why should it be an attack on me, since I was not a communist? If the Sachs family was communist, then of course they could be a target of such an attack. The newspapers were full of reports about how the Nats were going to annihilate the communists. Britain, and for that matter the Americans, were also sworn enemies of communism (as the Sachs girls had told me), but my mother's cousins were kind and decent and I did not see them as wicked people; certainly not wicked like Dr Malan and his party. What I did know was that they stood up for black people and it was all too clear how appalling the treatment of black people was. Was it that communists stood for the African people and wanted to eliminate their suffering? I felt I could go along with that. I resolved to speak to my mother's cousins when I had a chance.

We had an important football match coming up and quite a few after that and I became lost in that challenge. I did have a chance to ask the Sachs sisters what they thought of the slogan and they clearly supported it but I doubted that they had been responsible. Communism stands for a better life for all people, Bella explained over a glass of lemon tea. It was winter and they had a Russian-style samovar from which they filled endless hot cups which they called Russian tea. Bella would hold a sugar-lump in her mouth and sip the tea through it, which I thought was ultra-sophisticated and very Russian. I so admired her teeth, which were gleaming white. She had lucid eyes, and smiled confidently when she spoke, which always reassured me that she was telling the truth. It's better for people to live as equals, she said, sharing the wealth of society, without some being super rich and others being desperately poor. If you have equality, you will do away with wars. That's why, she explained, when the oppressors like the Americans and British, or the South African government and the Nazis before them, attacked communism, they were attacking the interests of ordinary people who deserved better. I was amazed that a young woman still in her teens and not so much older than me could speak with such confidence and about ideas that I'd never dreamed of and certainly hadn't heard expressed in my own home. I didn't know any black people so couldn't check whether they thought that way, although it seemed that they must. But there were signs beginning to speak of a different outlook to that we picked up in our schools and from our friends.

One afternoon Gerald Coyan and I were kicking a football around a yard in Yeoville when it soared over a fence into the street. There was an African man passing and we waited for him to kick it back to us. He couldn't resist skilfully toeing it about, lofting it onto his head, nodding it from head to toe and back. Gerald grew impatient.

'Hey, boy!' he yelled. 'Kick that back!'

The man was instantly angry. 'Don't call me boy. I'm no boy of yours!' Then, kicking the ball back, he waved his finger at Gerald and said: 'Just you wait, *umfaan*...' – we all knew that word meant 'boy' – '... just you wait. In 20 years this country is going to change beyond recognition. Show respect. And when you are big, teach better manners to your children.' His prediction about change was correct, at a time when even top professors of politics would have dismissed such an idea as preposterous. His timing was 20 years premature but, historically speaking, that is no time at all. It struck me that his might be the voice of the communists. As for the slogan on the wall, it would be a little over a decade before I actually met the people who had painted it up.[32]

Mind you, that was not the end of my early communist education. Ivor and I often went to the movies together. After Churchill's Fulton speech in 1946 about an Iron Curtain coming down across Europe we were inundated with Cold War films, of which *Animal Farm* had been the first. We saw a film called *Pickup on South Street*, featuring Richard Widmark, which was about the tracking down of a communist spy ring in the United States by the FBI and concluded with the hero beating up a red agent. Ivor, increasingly the 'wise-guy' like his father, exasperated me all the way home going on about how the Yanks hated the 'commies' and knew how to deal with them. I could only think of my mother's cousins and how I would be prepared to defend them for their beliefs.

Then there was a lengthy documentary about the Second World War which was put on one evening at the Yeoville Boys School hall for the public at large. It was heavily slanted to favour the Americans and the British as the key powers, ignoring their alliance with the Soviet Union, that had defeated the Germans. It could not avoid the Eastern Front and the retreat of the Germans from Soviet territory but attributed this to the harsh winter weather. Sequences of German troops slogging through adverse climatic conditions was accompanied by a commentator repeating the words 'mud, sleet, snow and more mud'. The Germans had not been defeated by Soviet forces but by 'Generals November, December and January'. Most of the attention was given to the opening of the Second Front in Normandy and Montgomery's victories in the African desert.

As we filed out of the hall there was a flurry of activity and voices raised in an argument.

'It was not General January but General Zhukov who defeated the Nazis!' Solomon Sachs was admonishing the organiser of the film show, a pompous looking member of the British Legion. An irate Bella, who was at her father's side, added that even Churchill had stated after the Battle of Stalingrad that it was the Red Army that had ripped the guts out of the Nazi army.

All this occurred around 1953, which was in fact the last time I saw the Sachs family for they moved out of the suburb soon afterwards. The sisters were extremely depressed when I visited them for the last time. Julius and Ethel Rosenberg had been executed in New York by the electric chair, having been found guilty of spying for the Soviet Union. There were huge protests in New York against their execution because it was widely believed, according to Bella, that they were framed on trumped-up charges by the FBI for political reasons. (The later declassification of security documents reinforced that view.)

The relentless propaganda around the Cold War disturbed me. In the movie houses, especially, it was inescapable. In the warm-up to the main feature, newsreels such as *Movietone News* and a series called *The March of Time* relayed the latest confrontations from around the world. Apart from Russian spies providing the Soviet Union with the atomic bomb, we were held spellbound by pictures of the Korean War, where the battle for the free world was said to be taking place. We saw Stalin and Mao Zedong shaking hands with the North Korean leader, all beaming in delight but clearly up to no good; the Vietnamese in battle with the French, who were in danger because of the Chinese yellow hordes gathering in the background; the Persian leader Mossadegh having the temerity to nationalise Western oil interests; Nasser overthrowing King Farouk and set to nationalise the Suez Canal. All of these frightening developments were accompanied by loud martial music and a chilling voice warning that Armageddon was almost upon us.

My sister's schoolteacher, Mrs Hurley, had a son who was a fighter pilot with the South African Squadron in Korea called the Cheetahs. She visited our home once a week to give me and Hilary extra lessons in Maths and would stay for supper. She was a burly, loudmouthed woman more petrified about her precious son falling into North Korean hands than getting killed. My parents showed her sympathy but I believe we all got worn down by her relentless invective against what she called the 'yellow devils' threatening our freedom. The South African news playing in the cinemas parroted what we saw on the American and British newsreels, with regular coverage of the Cheetah Squadron in contrast to benign sequences of Dr Malan opening flower shows and the South African Parliament. While we were treated to sequences of North Korean bombing of South Korea, the destruction of North Korean towns by American bombing was withheld. The one local event that the English press did project was that of the Springbok Legion of ex-servicemen marching against the government. I was aware of this because one of their number was cousin Stan Barkman, who had served with South African forces during the war. The government warned that the Springbok Legion was simply a front for the communists and, similar to what was taking place in America, provided evidence to show that members of the local Communist Party had played a significant role in establishing the organisation during the war to protect servicemen's rights.[33] As ever, anti-Semitic sentiments were never far away. When newsreels featured developments in Israel loud voices, usually at the rear of the cinema, would shout out 'Down with the Jews!' and these were not people sympathetic to the Arabs. When we queued for the trams in town and crowds bustled to get on board it was not uncommon for someone to sarcastically bark out, 'Give way for the Jews.'

It was not only political views that intrigued me. One day an affable family moved into Albyn Court. The father was an exceptionally handsome man we came to call Uncle Philip, a commercial traveller and follower of the gee-gees so he became very friendly with my father and grandad. He was married to an attractive woman named Thora, who had converted to the Jewish faith. I became very close to their son Eddie, a couple of years older than me, and his feisty sister Valerie, who was fun to be with. When Uncle Philip won at the horseraces he would slip me a ten-bob note, probably because he was benefiting from my father's tips. Thora was very beautiful and before marriage had modelled dresswear and underclothing. She was a good cook and I was always welcome at their table. It was from them that I heard interesting phrases such as Valerie commenting that 'the way to a man's heart is through his stomach', a tactic she seemingly had learned from her mother. I even used to accompany the family to watch Valerie, a promising ballet dancer, performing in the eisteddfods.

The siblings loved aping adults and knew all the card games from rummy to pontoon and poker. We bet with sweets like polo mints or matches to see who would come out top. Valerie was a bit of a flirt and when we played 'spin the bottle' at parties she loved being the one on the receiving end of an innocent kiss on the cheek. She really helped me overcome my shyness with girls. Their company was very enjoyable and they were also very funny. They had numerous names for the toilet, such as 'the joint', 'the throne room' and 'the gas chamber' and if anyone farted Valerie would almost wet her pants with laughter, which would encourage us all to try and emulate that first emission. Gerald Coyan had an amusing trick of giving you his finger to pull. As you did so he would emit a fart. A sharp pull, at his instigation, would result in an instant eruption; a long, slow pull would extract a wheezy, spluttering phenomenon. Girls found all this more hilarious than boys did.

Ivor liked to ferret around in Eddie's bedroom – I hated his slyness in this – and one day, after finding a school form which identified our friend as 'English medium', he pointed knowingly to the words as though they meant that Eddie was not fully Jewish. What the form was referring to, as I later discovered, was Eddie's language group as he was about to go up to high school ahead of us. Even though a Gentile woman might convert to Judaism, and in the process learn far more about the religion than those born into it, most Jews appeared to regard them as not being true Jews – *shiksa* was the disparaging term used for them and for black domestic workers alike.

Eddie was an extremely thoughtful boy. He wanted to be an accountant and he was very good at maths. He talked to me about the law of averages. We spun a coin 100 times and he carefully recorded the number of times it came down heads or tails. When we got to the 100 that turned out almost evens. He decided to write a letter to the *Star* newspaper about this as they had a children's column about unusual facts. His report was published and he received half a crown for his effort. I was so astonished that I spent days trying to think of how I might emulate him. I counted in the telephone directory the number of times the names Brown, Black, White, Green and Grey occurred (I seem to remember that Brown was the most common and Black the least) but they didn't even respond to me. I was desperate to get something published in the newspaper and wrote several letters to the editor, even the one about the headless chicken in Raymond Street – all without success.

Eddie also knew a great deal about cricket. I used to creep out of my bedroom at 5 am to listen with him to crackly radio commentaries from Australia when the 1952–53 touring South African cricket team of our heroes Jackie McGlew and Roy McLean were on tour down under, which, to our delight and beyond expectations, managed to draw the tests 2–2 with one drawn. It was an outstanding accomplishment for South Africa and we were overjoyed. While we all knew and worshipped players like Bradman, Hutton, Ray Lindwall and Keith Miller, we knew next to nothing about the West Indian team. Eddie was so well informed that he could reel off the names of past and present West Indies players, including those he called the three W's (Worrell, Walcott and Weekes), and George Headley, who was nicknamed the Black Bradman. I was so impressed that I covered my entire cricket bat in black tape.

Eddie came to watch me play for a Yeoville Boys cricket team on a very rain-soaked pitch one afternoon. Before I went in to bat he advised me to step out of the crease and turn the spin bowler's balls into full tosses, because allowing the ball to bounce would have been tricky to play. I made 14 runs out of a total of 28. We skittled our opponents out for 14. Not a fantastic achievement but for me the greatest innings I've ever played, thanks to Eddie.

I really enjoyed being with that family and was shattered when the parents separated. Thora demanded the separation for a trial period owing to her husband's apparent dallying with younger women, who were greatly attracted to him for his looks and his charm. He went to live on his own in a hotel in town with worse tragedy to follow. After a heavy night of drinking, as my mother later explained to me, and having accidentally taken an overdose of sleeping pills, Uncle Philip died.

CHAPTER 6

Once a Zionist

THE CRICKET GAME EDDIE HAD COME to watch me play in was at the Yeoville fields where the communist slogan was still prominent. A few years earlier, in 1948, there was another symbol that came to occupy my attention and symbolise my hopes and dreams that year and for some time thereafter.

It came in the form of a blue-and-white collection box and it caught the imagination of children and adults alike. On it was a map of Israel based on the entire territory of biblical Palestine and the initials JNF, for Jewish National Fund, superimposed. At card games it was always prominently displayed and the players filled it with coins. It appeared on the counters in most Yeoville shops. With friends I set up a stall selling off our second-hand toys on the steps of Albyn Court, the takings being deposited in the box. It was our way of contributing to what we understood was Israel's very survival. We certainly did not comprehend that the JNF was buying up all possible land in the territory once known as Palestine for exclusive Jewish use. From the time of its establishment in the early 20th century the JNF, in co-operation with the Zionist movement and all Israeli governments since 1948, achieved legal control over 93% of Israeli land being reserved in law for the development and settlement of 'Jews' only. Neither were we aware of its overall agenda as one of the handmaidens of the Zionist state, including aiding and abetting the ethnic cleansing of the Palestinian people and conquest of further territory by the Israeli Defence Force.[34]

I had first heard of a place called Palestine from Granny Clara, who had friends there, before she died in 1946. She received letters from them and gave me the stamps from the envelopes for my collection. I remember the British Protectorate logo. Neither she nor anyone in the family seemed to have any desire to emigrate there, however. I remember her saying that it was so hot there that you could fry an egg on the pavement. I actually tried that out once but failed miserably. It seemed it could be done but only on the bonnet of a car on an extremely hot day in a desert. It appeared that Palestine, like South Africa before the Dutch landed, was an empty land. For us the Zionist phrase 'A land without people for a people without land' had powerful appeal. Refugees from the concentration camps of Europe had a pressing need for a place where they could be incorporated and settle. If there were people in Palestine, they were the British, who needed to go home, and Arabs, who had plenty of land elsewhere in Arabia where they came from. We had learned from the Bible that Israel was the land promised by God to the Jews. It was as simple as that. The Jews had a right to return to the biblical land after having been expelled by the Romans over two thousand years ago. At last Israel had been reborn but at that fateful hour its very existence was challenged, or so we understood, by an invasion from the Arab states that surrounded it.[35] If David was to defeat Goliath, then everyone had to rally to the cause of Israel's very survival.

For as long as I could remember we had been singing its anthem of hope, *Hatikvah*, at bar mitzvahs and weddings. Now that Israel had been created we could sing that song with renewed vigour. Jews were no longer weak people who could be trampled upon. After the experience of the Nazis it was inspirational that Jews could stand up for their dignity and fight back. And it showed anti-Semites that we were no longer easy targets to be bullied without retaliating. It was not only the few individuals among us like Cocky Feldman and Okey Geffin who had courage and beat Gentiles at their own game.

Although my family were by no means ardent Zionists, my mother made sure that the JNF collection box was regularly filled and replaced. The JNF ran a campaign mainly for us children to plant trees in Israel so that the desert should bloom. In return for donating a shilling we received a certificate for a tree planted in our name to create a South African forest there, covering, without our knowledge, the Palestinian village of Lubya, whose inhabitants had been driven out in 1948 and their homes and property flattened to the ground.[36] In time I had three such certificates framed and stuck up in my bedroom. Little did we know that over 500 Palestinian villages were reduced to rubble and eliminated, the ruins to be covered by trees – the former inhabitants camping in neighbouring states as refugees. Over 700 000 Palestinians had been forcibly removed or fled in terror from towns and villages into exile. The names of those villages were erased from the maps of the new Israel. Ignorance was bliss.

The only household in the neighbourhood without the JNF box as far as I could ascertain was the Sachs family home. The Sachs daughters ridiculed the Zionists. They said they were as dangerous as the Afrikaner Nationalists. While they were in favour of Jewish refugees from the concentration camps going to Palestine if there was no other option, they said that was okay as long as they accepted the rights of the Arab people and were prepared to live with them in peace. They argued that countries like America, Britain and South Africa should take in more Jewish emigrants. I was bemused by all this and had nothing to say in reply.

They invited me to join a Jewish youth group called Hashomer Hatzair which, they explained, were building *kibbutzim* (collective farms) in Israel where everyone worked and benefited equally. I said it sounded to me like Orwell's *Animal Farm* and they jeered, saying that was Cold War propaganda.

Jewish youth groups, somewhat like the Boy Scouts movement, were flourishing. Ivor and I were attracted to one of these where, unlike Hashomer, smart military-style uniforms were worn. This group was called Betar,[37] and it happened to be the off-shoot of the most extreme of the Zionist groups, the most brazen in carrying out terrorism in

Palestine; it advocated seizing the land on both sides of the Jordan River. None of this was advocated in our activities other than the latter objective, which appeared in one of the songs we were taught. I learned that the organisation had been founded in my mother's beloved city of Riga in Latvia in 1923.

We had a very active junior leader in his late teens who had us marching in the streets to a drumbeat in search of new recruits. He taught us boxing and wrestling and never intervened, even when we were beating one another's brains out. We needed to toughen up, he told us, as he goaded those of faint heart to take the 'medicine' without complaint and give it back in 'double dosage'. The most interesting activity was war games on the koppies, engaged in battle formation, with pellet guns or sticks to simulate weapons. He ordered one of us to shoot him in the chest at ten yards to demonstrate the need to conquer fear. The pellet bounced harmlessly off but we knew it could sting. He took it without blinking, emitting the cry 'Geronimo!' I was told he died in the Israeli attack on Suez in 1956. Most interesting was that he taught us how to use a compass to find direction and to read maps.

Ivor and I were looking forward to a camping holiday with the organisation. When I informed the Sachs sisters about this, expressions of shock appeared on their faces. They asked if I knew who the leaders of Betar were. I hadn't a clue. They told me that one of the leaders was a man called Jabotinsky,[38] who had visited South Africa to collect funds and enlist support for his party several years earlier. He modelled himself and his group on Mussolini, the former Italian dictator and ally of Hitler. They warned me not to join any group because it seemed 'exciting', as they put it. Every group, they cautioned, served particular interests and one needed to check on that first. That was a bit beyond my comprehension but I was very worried about the Mussolini connection. They told me that no less a person than Albert Einstein had issued a warning about the Betar leaders being 'fascist' or at least fascist connected. They had to explain that 'fascist' meant like being Nazi and that it was Einstein who had made the comparison. I found this hard to accept. How could any Jew be compared to the Nazis, I argued. They said I was being naïve – another word I didn't understand.

I was able to check the story in later years and found an Einstein letter and denunciation of the Irgun leader Menachem Begin who, like Jabotinsky, had been a prominent Betar leader when younger, even more shocking than they had depicted. Not only did it highlight his authoritarian policy but it recorded his organisation's cold-blooded massacre of 240 men, women and children in the Palestinian village of Deir Yassin in April 1948. The letter, co-authored with Hannah Arendt and other prominent Jews, carried the warning that if Begin's party came to power its racist-fascist character would be imprinted on the Israeli state. [39]

Menachem Begin, leader of the ultra-right-wing Likud Party, was Israel's prime minister from 1977–83. Einstein's warning was prescient as Likud broke the hegemony of Ben Gurion's Mapam (labour movement) ruling from Ariel Sharon's election in 2001 to Netanyahu's reign to 2019 and still going strong (except for Olmert's brief period from 2006 to 2009).[40] My eyes were later opened to the fact that the Palestinian *nakba* or 'catastrophe' – the dispossession of land and ethnic cleansing of the native population, including the sowing of terror by deliberate massacres to force the terrified populous to flee – was essentially the planning of Ben Gurion and other Zionist architects.[41]

When I came to this realisation I felt a searing pain and anger at the extent to which I had been abused by Zionist propaganda and it has left me with an abiding understanding of how the minds of the young can be poisoned relative to countless forms of prejudice and racism in so many different circumstances and history.

It seems the Sachs girls, out of concern, informed their father, who in turn spoke to mine. That scuppered my membership of Betar. My father had taken no notice of all the goings-on until Solomon Sachs alerted him to the dangers of Betar. It was clear that my father greatly respected the views of Mr Sachs. My father then persuaded me to choose a different youth group.

Since Hashomer did not appeal to Ivor and myself (it had no uniform, after all), we joined the more acceptable and mainstream group called Habonim (The Builders). Opportunistically, that was just in time for a camp they were preparing on farmlands a couple of hours from Johannesburg. My father paid the fee and I used my savings to purchase

Habonim's blue shirt and scarf. We arrived at the campsite by train together with boys and girls from various parts of Johannesburg. We were highly excited. This was the real thing. We learned to pitch tents, set up the kitchen, organise a campfire and rotate night-time guard duty, which heightened the serious purpose of our activity. For the latter we were issued with torches and whistles and taught how to sound the alarm in case of emergency. Under the night sky and doing the rounds of the sleeping camp it was easy to imagine we were on duty in a danger zone under possible physical attack somewhere in Israel. In charge were two junior leaders in their late teens. We were taught the rudiments of farming and participated in potato harvesting for the established farmhouse, which appeared to be inhabited by senior Habonim members who, as we learned, were preparing for their *Aliya* – migration (ascending) to *Eretz Y'israel* (the land of Israel).

Although we were spared the agony of knocking the daylights out of each other in boxing or endlessly marching about, there were similarities to Betar. We learned how to read maps and use a compass and engage in Boy Scout-type activity. Sing-songs around the campfire were more interesting than the jingoistic Betar themes as we sang amusing ditties such as:

> 'You can't go to heaven in a ten-tonne truck
> 'cause a ten-tonne truck is likely to get stuck ...
> And you can't go to heaven in a Ford V8
> 'cause a Ford V8 won't reach the gate.'
> 'You can't go to heaven with the SAR
> 'cause the SAR don't go that far.

Some of the more fervent would ad lib lines such as:

> 'But you can get to Israel by Habonim mail
> 'cause Habonim mail won't derail.'

This as a prelude to a lecture on how to get to the Promised Land. We sang the more patriotic songs like *Hatikvah* and formed a dance circle, arms linked, as we performed the celebratory *Hora*.

Just as we were establishing a happy routine the situation turned nasty. There was a group of scruffy boys from the tough suburb of Mayfair who differed from most of us coming from better off parts of Johannesburg. They began showing indifference to the camp routine, sleeping late, ignoring the exhortations of the leadership, and flouted the non-smoking rule. Things came to a head when they refused cleaning-up duties. A huge row broke out between them and the two junior leaders. To our shock one of the group picked up an axe and, swinging it aggressively, chased the two around the camp. Whistles were blown and soon reinforcements from the farmhouse took control. The group were ordered to pack up and were marched off the property. They complained that it was a long way from the railway station and that they needed transport but this was refused. Once they were gone normality returned and it was with considerable relief that we got on with camp life.

Several hours later Ivor and I were dispatched with a horse and cart to fetch supplies from a distant store. It was fun being in charge of this form of transport and we set off at a sedate pace. Ivor was given first chance at the reins and I would take my turn on the way back. We chatted away, not a care in the world, as the horse trotted on. Shock is precisely shock because of the unpleasant jolt that stops one dead. Turning a bend in the dirt road we were upon the group of expelled ruffians before we knew it. Quick as a flash they seized the horse's reins and brought us to a rude halt. They turfed us off the cart, which they hijacked before our eyes and off they trotted to the railway station, saying we would find the contraption there. We plodded along the road disconsolately, having gone from a feeling of ecstasy to despair in a moment. So this was Habonim, I thought, wondering whether anything as awful could have happened at the Betar camp with its strict discipline. The hooliganism of the group certainly dented my romantic tendency to idealise my fellow Jews seeking to serve the Zionist cause. If an axe could be wielded so threateningly against a fellow Jew as had been the case in the camp, then pity the poor Arab who got in the way.

Zionism continued to absorb me two years after the birth of Israel had become a *fait accompli*. I was in my 12th year, my final year at Yeoville

Boys. We attended Hebrew school to learn the language but our teacher took every opportunity to use biblical analogies to celebrate the birth of Israel. The Philistines of course were likened to the Palestinians; Samson's powers in slaying a hundred enemies with the jawbone of an ass to Israel's victory; and similarly the annihilation of Goliath by the comely young David. He turned to the story of Moses and the Exodus and how the Canaanites had been defeated. It was when he referred to the 40 years wandering in the desert before the Hebrews reached the Promised Land that a subversive thought struck me. I had a good feel for geography and anyway there was a map of Africa and the Mediterranean basin on the wall. I pointed out the short distance from Egypt to Israel and asked why the Israelites had not simply followed the coastal route to find their way home.

If I had enraged Mrs Sieve over the paintbrush episode, my Hebrew teacher went apoplectic. He hit me across the back of the head with a force greater than that of a leather football soaring off Graham Bales' mighty boot. He screamed louder and in as guttural a tone as Prof Pearls raging at Bubi.

'They were being punished for their sins!' he ranted. 'The weak and the less devout were being weeded out. Of *course* Moses knew the way, you idiot,' he snarled. 'He had to test his flock!'

I was on my feet, battle-ready to counter-attack.

'Is that why six million Jews had to die in the Nazi camps?' I wanted to know. 'Were they weak and not good enough to survive as Israel's new inhabitants?'

'Get out! Get out!' he ordered.

Off I went, spewing out a word I had recently learned: 'Fascist!'

The teacher came to visit my parents to complain. He wanted an apology. My mother explained that I was very serious about Israel and that I read the papers every evening from the time the state was decreed until the war with the Arabs had concluded. But I refused to apologise and an alternative Hebrew teacher was arranged to prepare me for my bar mitzvah. This coincided with my going to high school in 1951, which was also my bar mitzvah year – the occasion of my rite of passage to manhood – a Jewish boy's coming of age.

After much practice and preparation my bar mitzvah duly arrived. My uncle Solly had been my role model for he had a fine singing voice and by my mother's account had greatly impressed the congregation when he was a bar mitzvah boy in 1923 some 28 years preceding me. My father had doubts about my voice and wisely advised me not to strive too hard with the high notes. It would be okay, he said, to recite my passage of the Torah without too much of a sing-song attached. I sat with my father and grandfather while my mother and sister were upstairs as Orthodox synagogues practised gender segregation. There were a lot of relatives and friends and the usual congregation present, as well as one of my schoolteachers who had asked to be present. I found that very touching. He was the opposite of Mrs Sieve and had taken an instant liking to me. My father had been strangely suspicious of him, which I realised when the teacher enquired whether I would like to accompany him and his wife on a motoring holiday to the Kruger National Park and my dad had instantly refused. I nagged and nagged him but he just would not relent. I just couldn't understand the reason why he was so distrustful.

I don't think the regular congregants of the Yeoville synagogue thought much of my bar mitzvah rendition but my family certainly did. There was a celebration afterwards in a nearby hall in which I gave a short speech of thanks. The gifts I received were numerous, although predictable. Along with several fountain pens and writing cases were books about Zionism and its luminaries such as Theodor Herzl and Ben Gurion. One of the books was *The Revolt* by Menachem Begin, prominent leader of the Irgun Zvei Leumi (National Military Organisation) terrorist organisation, responsible for attacks on both the British and the Palestinian Arabs, as well as fellow Jews, especially teachers, who did not support their extreme measures. In later years Nelson Mandela and his guerrilla fighters such as myself studied the book, not because we admired Begin, who became prime minister of Israel and precursor to the likes of Ariel Sharon and Benjamin Netanyahu, but for the operational information disclosed in it. What was interesting were two coffee table books: *The Splendour That Was Egypt* and *The Glory That Was Greece*. Clearly there were some guests for whom civilisations other than the Jews were important. My parents allowed me to have a party at home, with some 40 boys and girls squeezed into our small apartment.

While I had always been attracted to older women like my mother and Bella Sachs, I was now finding 13-year-old girls rather cute. I continued attending synagogue but that lasted only a couple of years. I had prayed regularly at bedtime as a child but gradually became an atheist during my teens. By the age of 16 I came to doubt the existence of a spiritual being. This coincided with my break with Zionism, even though at that time I was not aware of all of its crimes – which included the dispossession of Palestinian lands and rights and the brutality Palestinians suffered under Israeli military rule. As I became older my South African identity became paramount and my doubts about Israel and religion increased. It was not that I came to disrespect the true believers and the religions they followed but I just did not incline towards blind faith in the existence of a deity.

There was awareness that Jewish boys could get into trouble, particularly when it came to sex with Christian girls – a phenomenon which led to many an anti-Semitic accusation. A sensational murder case in 1949 reminded the community of this Achilles heel. A so-called 'good-time girl of easy virtue' called Bubbles Schroeder was found strangled in a plantation in the wealthy northern suburbs of Johannesburg.[42] Three young Jewish men were charged with her murder. She had been in their company at a posh house in the area the evening of her disappearance and they were the prime suspects. Other than circumstantial evidence of their partying with her and one of them having dropped her off in the vicinity where her body was found, the prosecution was unable to prove their guilt and they were discharged. Another theory circulated that she had been murdered by an African, although there were no signs of rape or robbery attached to that bright idea. Some lime was found in her mouth, which came from a nearby building site. As ever, the race card was played for the theory was that certain African groups placed earth in a victim's mouth to prevent them talking in the afterlife about who the culprit was. The police actually pursued that line of investigation as well. The notorious crime has remained one of South Africa's unsolved murders, clearly of fascination because it involved three Jewish males from wealthy families and a vulnerable and beautiful Afrikaans woman.

The Jewish community has always been a small one with multifold connections. The district surgeon who examined the young woman's body, Jack Friedman, was related to my mother. On holiday in Muizenberg at the end of that year we stayed at a hotel where the youngest of the three accused, Hymie Liebman, aged 19, the man who had dropped Bubbles Schroeder off at 2 am in a remote part of town, was taking a holiday break. The hotel was full and I was lodged in an annex along with Hymie Liebman. He was a handsome, cool and relaxed young man who, having been found not guilty, seemingly paid no attention to the gossip being whispered about him. He certainly was not short of company. Several young women were inclined to make a fuss of him. I found that bizarre.

One evening I was larking around on the hotel veranda with a few pals. We had got hold of some kids' bubble-soap and played about blowing bubbles into the air. Hymie Liebman came by with a girlfriend and behind his back we were singing 'I'm forever blowing bubbles, pretty bubbles in the air …' when someone came over and slapped me hard on the shoulder. 'That's not funny,' I was told. 'That's rude and idiotic.' That was the only time my mother ever struck me.

PART THREE

1951–1956

Education doesn't change the world. Education changes people, people change the world..

– PAULO FREIRE

Human beings are too complicated for rule books. Problem is, we are too unruly for freedom.

– STEVE SALAITA

CHAPTER 7

Six of the Best

MY PRIMARY SCHOOLING AT Yeoville Boys was enjoyable. It was my sporting ability that gained me a place at KES – King Edward VII School for Boys – with a dozen other *boykies* in 1951. For otherwise, along with most of the primary school graduates I would have been admitted to somewhere less prestigious like Athlone.

When the Sachs girls heard I was going to KES they chided me for enrolling at such a snobbish school. They *charfed* (Yeoville slang for chaffed or joshed) me not to become a little Englishman. Even Faygie got in on the act, the first time I had heard her open her mouth. 'Papa says Athlone is a better school,' she said, 'and that their debating society discusses whether war is inevitable, and whether money is needed, things like that.' I fleetingly came to see wisdom in her large grey eyes, but retorted that KES had the top sports teams, to which they groaned in fake pain. Bella, commissar in chief, jumped in to inform me that several Athlone boys from Yeoville joined the Communist Party after matriculating. That was true as I learned later in exile when I befriended the likes of Joe Slovo and Harold Wolpe, who had been at Yeoville Boys some 15 years before me.[43]

Although exclusively white, as was the norm throughout South

Africa, KES was a different world from the one in which I'd grown up. Yeoville Boys was a typical low-income, concrete and tarmac school. KES was a government school but aspired to the standards of so-called public schools in England. It was both elitist and authoritarian and established by Johannesburg's founding fathers, the mining magnates and property tycoons under military hegemony, to be part of an educational system designed to produce and shape South Africa's future leaders in line with the requirements of the British Empire – the largest since the Roman Empire.

It was Lord Milner's vision, victor over the Boer Republics in the South African War, that consciously set in train the need for such an educated elite to run society as one of the white dominions under the leadership and control of the English upper class. On the basis of language the defeated Boers led by the likes of generals Botha and Smuts, albeit their compromise with the British, distanced themselves from this hegemony and set up their own elitist schools and universities in Pretoria and elsewhere to keep their version of Afrikaner nationalism alive in opposition to Milner's English-speaking elite.[44]

Whatever its pretensions, KES was second-tier to the upper-class private schools that only the very rich could afford, such as St John's, which was a stone's throw away and part of the pantheon of prestigious Anglican schools throughout the country that would take pride of place in Lord Milner's project.

In the leafy setting of the prosperous suburb of Houghton, an upper-class Jewish area, KES boasted an Edwardian-style main building with an impressive clock tower surveying numerous playing fields. We wore smart green blazers – crown insignia on the breast pocket – grey flannel trousers, school tie and, on special occasions, straw boaters.

On the first day of school the small group of Yeoville *boykies*, sought after for our sporting ability and the first from that side of the tracks to be admitted through the hallowed portals of KES, were sneered at for wearing long trousers. We were standing together in a group feeling self-conscious, anxious about fitting in, and to make matters worse we had to put up with the snub: 'You're obviously the Yeoville lot.' It was a boy with dreadful acne, a year or two ahead of us. 'Can't you wait until second year to wear long pants?' he drawled. Ivor Lazerson was quick to reply: 'Why? Do you want to admire our legs?' That was a neat retort and saw the boy backing off while we Yeoville boys laughed, if a tad nervously.

Ivor was soon recognised as a wise-guy and given the name 'Foxy'. How I wished I had his neat turn of phrase and spontaneous retort. I could come up with something witty but it normally occurred to me long after I needed to shine. I was referred to either as 'Castor Oil', which I tolerated, or 'Casserole', which I liked. Everyone had a nickname of sorts, teachers and pupils alike, and this served, together with easy banter and shared experiences, to diminish ethnic divisions. The atmosphere on sports days when our team took the field and the school belted out the war-cry – *'Itchy ballagoota/skiet a ramma doota/suskanada, son of kanovsky/ boom!'* [45] – was like being part of Montgomery's charge against the Germans at El Alamein.

The uniform we wore and the school culture was designed to make us all part of a ruling elite. There might be differences between us, of religion and class, but without realising it I am sure virtually everyone from First Form to Matric was able to realise, if they thought about it, how similar we were in terms of our received prejudices and the superior attitude in relations with the vast majority of the people of our country. To be sure the education system would strive to keep us strictly on the rails. What we learned in the classrooms and on the playing-fields was ostensibly designed to help us get on in life and have good productive careers so that we would be able to have happy families and play our part as law-abiding God-fearing citizens in building our country as a bastion of the free world. But there was more to it than that. It did not mean that headmaster, teachers and prefects were part of a conspiracy. There was a system in place and an ethos that many could not perceive, which effectively ensured the security and propagation of a particular attitude to life. Mere mortals simply and in most cases willingly fell into place as cogs in a machine to maintain the status quo as far as relations of power were concerned between class, race and gender at both the micro and macro level. In essence as white school pupils we were being shaped to become masters, managers, officers and property owners, instead of critical thinkers. In contrast black or brown children, those lucky enough to gain some kind of education, were being panel-beaten into becoming obedient semi-professionals at the top level but in general low-skilled workers or servants.

A good number of the pupils at KES were boarders from the East and West Rand mining towns where some of their fathers worked as engineers on the mines. They had to fag for masters and prefects and they always appeared to be hungry – or maybe it was yearning for something more appetising than boring boarding house grub. I made several good friends among the boarders, possibly because I was prepared to share some of my mother's scrumptious sandwiches with them. Shrewd owing to her own school experience, she put extra into my lunchbox for that specific purpose. One of them was a witty boarder called David Mackenzie, with whom I shared many mischievous experiences, and another was Grenville Middleton, whose friends called him 'Muntu' (black person) because he joked with black labourers in Xhosa.[46]

My mother gained a reputation for being a kindly woman in Yeoville and years later at Mandela's inauguration as president of South Africa in 1994, one of KES's most notable international sports stars, Gary Player,[47] on the VIP list, even though he had been apartheid's sporting ambassador at large, was keen to shake hands. 'Your mother was one of the kindest women in the neighbourhood,' he wanted me to know. Privately, I felt he was more than anxious to be seen in the company of an ANC activist.

Actually, there was exclusion of a kind. The school had an impressive Scots band of bagpipes and drums, boys dressed in traditional sporran and kilt, which performed at cadet training and important occasions. Membership was limited to those of Scots descent only on the grounds that this had been so decreed by a school governor of means who had contributed the funds for the musical instruments. Such exclusivity did not in those days arouse even the faintest concern.

Every Monday we went to school in our cadet uniforms to play at soldiers, marching and wheeling in platoon formation across the sports fields. The boredom of the square bashing was only alleviated by the skirl of the bagpipes and the accompanying drumbeats which certainly livened things up.[48]

School prefects acted as the officers, including a head cadet, under the supervision of a strict Afrikaans teacher called Jock Muller in his wartime uniform with battle ribbons across his left breast. He became irate and red-faced when anybody was out of step. Those who were sloppy in performance were made to report after school hours for an extra workout under his direct supervision. It was not at all rare for me to be part of some half-dozen recalcitrant boys marching up and down as he barked out commands.

'Attenshun!' Jock commanded and descended on the boy next to me, who had been totally out of step. He raged at the poor lad like an incensed sergeant major one saw in the movies. I found myself struggling to suppress a giggling sensation welling up in my abdomen but the more Jock yelled, and the more purple-faced he became, the more difficult it was for me to control myself and the chuckles forced their way through my clenched teeth into the open. Jock turned on me in an instant, losing self-control, as I had lost control myself but in a different way, and he lambasted me into the ground. I got back onto my feet in a groggy condition but Jock had retreated from the battlefield by then and was busy shoving tablets into his mouth – clearly a case of a man with high blood pressure. The fact that he had served in the war was a reflection that he was at least a Smuts man and not a supporter of Verwoerdism.

What surprised me donkeys years later in a free South Africa was learning more about the man when I met his daughter Joan, who had joined the Communist Party. She told me that her father had admired Bram Fischer and played social tennis with him before his imprisonment. There were a few surprises like that. Ivor was in the A-stream and ever ready to comment about communism. He told me that in a class discussion, where the overwhelming view was that it was an evil system, one of the top scholars threw a cat among the pigeons by suggesting that maybe people in the communist countries regarded us in the same way. I believe that boy became a senior civil servant in Britain.

Although I did well on the sports field, especially in athletics, I clashed with teachers who regarded me as 'unruly'. (In later years the word would be 'ungovernable'.) It was not that mine was a conscious rebellion. I simply could not contain my contempt for the high and mighty attitude of those in authority – and there was plenty of that on display, especially with regard to the prefect system. It was boarders who mainly suffered because the prefects were served by junior boys called fags, who carried out all sorts of menial tasks for them in the boarding houses. They were also given authority to cane any underling they considered to have failed in their house duties. This only applied to the boarders. The system was intrinsically authoritarian and anti-democratic. If you refused to abide by such a 'philosophy' and showed any signs of rebelling or dared break the rules, you were up against attempts to humiliate, degrade and strip you of self-respect. In such a process there are those who become passive and others with a streak of stubbornness who not only don't give in but become more rebellious. For whatever reason, I feel I displayed a resilience. I believe the confidence I fell back on to sustain me emanated in part from my sporting ability – more particularly the 'never say die' spirit of the long-distance runner.

One of my favourite teachers was 'Boetie' van der Riet, who taught us Afrikaans and coached us on the rugby field. He was straight, direct and approachable, so that when he whacked us with the cane we did not mind. It was a question of keeping the stiff upper lip and taking punishment like a man. I had an unfortunate injury early on in the rugby trials which affected me playing in the A team. With my running speed and not being averse to the school of hard knocks, I had been tipped as a possible centre for the First Team. I sprained my wrist badly in a tackle and a visit to the family doctor saw it heavily bandaged and advice that I should not play for several weeks. We reached a vital stage where Boetie honed the possible rugby pool down to just two teams with an important play-off prior to the final selection. I reported for the trial in my rugby gear but when he saw my heavily bandaged arm, he ordered me to stand down. It was a huge setback because I had great ambitions to make it as a rugby player. Once I was out of the initial matches, it was difficult to even get into the B team. Playing C team rugby was not so thrilling, although eventually I made it into the B team before being elevated to a reserve for the A team. That meant acting as linesman for their events. This was a task I messed up, for I tended to mix up soccer with rugby rules, often to the detriment of my own team. In the former the football had to be 100% over the touchline; in rugger if the foot of the player with the ball simply touched the line he was deemed out of play. Unfortunately, a wrong decision by me cost the KES under 14A the match, which led to my relegation back to C team rugby.

There were not many games played at that level and I craved action in winter, no doubt owing to my high testosterone levels. I consequently secretly played soccer on weekends outside the school system, which was treachery.

In summer I laid down my mark on the athletics field and won a number of races over the years, most notably the half mile in my senior year and dominating the same event in a hot competition with Jeppe Boys on their athletics track. That made my father, a Jeppe Old Boy, as pleased as punch and he even attended the event, slipping away for an hour from the nearby Turffontein racecourse.

Running for me was sheer bliss; my closest experience to the spirit of freedom as a youngster. I had loads of energy as well as stamina and could do well in the sprints and longer distances, which was rare. In my first year I came third in the 100-yards under 13 event against stiff opposition and it was regarded as a good achievement. I fancied myself in the longer distances and got through the heats of the 440 yards for under 14s. The boys I was up against appeared to be giants to me but when it came to running I was a cocky little bugger. I put in a gallant run, if I say so myself, starting too slowly but finishing with a strong burst of speed. This saw me being shaded into third place. The winner, a boy called Nash, was twice my size and had an immense stride. He later became a famous athlete. My mother attended sports day as my number one fan; my father, being held up at the four-legged races, was apologetic about not having been present. I didn't mind that at all but I never forgave my mother ... Although she boasted about how well I had done, she kept explaining that because my opponents were much bigger than me, I was given a start over them. I could never get her to understand that being drawn in the outside lane was a disadvantage and that my starting position only *appeared* to be ahead of everyone else but in fact wasn't.

No one ever taught me anything about athletics. The boarders had the advantage of living with house masters who often were all-round sportsmen and were quite zealous in focusing on their own charges.

I invested in a book instead, following the training routines and training exercises that were outlined. I was naturally gregarious, and enjoyed team sports, but found in the loneliness of long-distance running and training a welcome break from company and the chance to dig deep into my developing cognitive processes. I found over the years that distance running not only built up my stamina but gave me a dogged determination never to give up, even when I was tiring and every fibre of my body was crying out for me to stop. I used to run through the most painful stitch but fortunately rarely got that kind of cramp. I loved challenging myself to keep that little extra in my tank so that I could finish off a race with a burst of speed as others were tiring.

Overhearing Boetie remarking that athletes were no good at rugby because they feared being tackled caused me to believe the statement was meant for my ears. I was extremely depressed for some time, thinking that maybe he was right. I took solace in the fact that the injury I had sustained to my wrist was because of a last-ditch tackle I had made on a huge boy bearing down on me. I had brought him down but at the cost of injuring myself. It was when I felt the disapproval of others that I found some remedy from the depression by trying to analyse what had occurred. This was not at all easy at first but I found that I grew better with time. Being able to reason things out at least served to provide some comfort.

One day during lessons a senior boy came to Boetie's door. After conversing outside, Boetie returned to tell us that the *kêrel* (youngster) he had been talking to was making a terrible mistake by leaving school prematurely. 'He thinks he can make a living playing golf,' Boetie said, visibly upset. The *kêrel* was Gary Player, world-famous golfer-to-be, who also found time to praise my mother when I met him 40 years later at Mandela's inauguration.

Mind you, Boetie himself could be totally unreasonable. Something had happened in the class, I can't remember exactly what, and nobody would own up. He was so angry that he threatened to cane the lot of us if the culprits were not forthcoming. One after another of us received a couple of light cuts from his cane, including a boy called Fair, whose legs were in iron braces owing to the polio epidemic of recent years. But he would make no exception and ignored the protestations from Fair who kept complaining, 'It's not fair! It's not fair!' This became a chant in Boetie's classroom every time we had cause to object to anything we disliked. It followed him to the rugby field. If he awarded a penalty to one side or the other, those of us from his class would chant out, 'It's not fair!'

The school principal, whose name was St John B. Nitch, was an austere, intimidating man with a high forehead and bald dome. He was referred to by masters and boys alike in an undertone as 'The Boss'. Perpetually unsmiling and aloof in his black gown, he reminded me of a sadistic medieval monk maintaining his domain by an invisible force. As we intoned the Lord's Prayer at his assemblies and murmured, 'Our Father who art in heaven ...' I wished that The Boss, too, was not of this world and would disappear. I soon found that he had a distinct dislike for me. Like my mother, I smiled easily when happy but also when I was nervous or the centre of unwelcome attention. It appears that those in authority, and particularly those who take themselves too seriously, are not amused when so confronted and are easily moved to anger. The Boss took us for Latin, a subject for which I had zero aptitude. When I messed up the conjugations he was exasperated and, sure enough, I would giggle nervously. With quite a few others I was relegated to studying Geography instead, a subject that people like he seemed to regard as for the duller boys, but one of the subjects I enjoyed and certainly had aptitude for. It gave me a love of maps and of foreign countries. I was relieved to be out of his clutches – or so I thought.

Some teachers used a light cane to instil discipline, some simply cuffed us across the head, and a few preferred to use a ruler to strike a boy on the hand. A few desisted from corporal punishment entirely. If they used the cane, the rule was, as I understood from rumour, that they could not draw it back above the waist. The headmaster, though, had licence to do so, thus having greater effect, but the cane was not to be drawn above the shoulder. The Boss was there as some sort of supreme judge and he acted as the Lord High Executioner. For serious offences, as deemed by a teacher, the unfortunate pupil was sent to report his misdeed to The Boss. That was my fate on more than one occasion.

It started off in my second year when I stupidly whistled at a newly recruited young female secretary who had brought the registry book to our class teacher in the science laboratory. I had become something of an impulsive joker; with no thought of consequence, I would sometimes just give way to a natural mischievousness. I couldn't sit still for a moment and always had to be up to something. For sure some must have thought I craved the limelight. What I regret was that this sometimes meant I lacked sensitivity such as not even imagining what kind of embarrassment the poor young woman would have been experiencing on her first day at work by my crass sexist behaviour in a classroom full of silly boys. Instead of being taken aside and given a lecture as to why my attitude was so wrong, there was no educative effort at all other than to punish me for the offence. The practice at KES in those days was one of caning and not explaining. The result was that one simply went on committing the same offence time and time again.

The teacher ordered me to report to the headmaster. Entering The Boss's office was a daunting experience. This was the first time that I had come face to face with the man in his lair. The grimness of the man, his black gown worn like a shroud, icy gaze looking right through me, was overpowering. He was a man who believed in a retributive deity and in a school where he was God he would perform the Superior Being's will. The portraits of imperious and daunting officers of Empire on the walls, the dark curtains and furniture and a floor that creaked only added to the menacing atmosphere.

The Boss listened to the brief reason for my presence without expression and then, taking hold of me by my shoulders and pants, forced me into a bending posture over a chair, pushing my knees inwards so that my posterior was more vulnerable. He hitched up my blazer so it would not get in the way. I could hear his heavy breathing. I detested his hands all over me and his close presence. I was like a trapped animal in a forest, all my senses geared to his movement, my ears sensitive to the opening of a cupboard and the swishing back and forth of his cane as, like an executioner, he psyched himself up for the assault. The movements spoke of the ritual of a man working himself up into a state of sheer vengeance or excitement. Possibly a little bit of deliberately prolonging the moment and anticipating the enjoyment of the pain he was about to inflict.

I made the error of turning around, wondering where on earth he had got to, just as he sprang at me, cane raised above his shoulder ready to descend like the instrument of an executioner, muttering through his teeth, 'Buck down' – the stinging blow hissing like a serpent, catching me partly on hand and buttocks and shooting blades of agony throughout my body and brain. One spins drunkenly into a black void almost to the point of losing consciousness with a bitter metallic taste in the mouth. I felt his strong hand forcing me down, controlling my reaction as I danced on the spot from the searing pain that seemed to set every nerve of my body jangling like a percussion instrument, and waited for another agonising blow. He halted and came around to me, his face pressed into mine, like a mask of doom, his breath stale and overpowering, and he growled in a threatening voice that if I didn't stand still for the second stroke there would be a third. He bodily grappled with me to get me back into position. I bucked down obediently, bracing myself for the inevitable, teeth clenched, as I received another fierce blow which pitched me into the black void again. My eyes were moist but I was determined to hold back the tears and not utter a sound, having stifled a cry. It was he who was breathing heavily as he finally gasped, 'Get out!' It was as though my pants were alight but I held back from rubbing my bottom until I was out of his space and into the cool emptiness of the school quadrangle, where I strove to control myself.

I went straight to the washroom to gulp down cold water and splash my face. I stopped rubbing my bottom because it seemed simply to exacerbate the pain, the like of which I'd never ever had to endure in my life. My thin trousers offered no protection at all and I might as well have been beaten without any clothes on. Who was more guilty of a beastly crime? St John B. Nitch of assaulting an undersized 13-year-old with tremendous adult force or a silly young show-off for whistling at a young girl who would have been shocked out of her mind had she seen the punishment meted out? I have no doubt the man was a sadist who enjoyed the pain he inflicted, for what I had endured was a vicious and common practice. In later years such punishment would be condemned as criminal abuse with a suspicious paedophilic tendency. What I had experienced emanated from a vile history of whip, lash, *sjambok* from the time of slavery in the Cape and colonial conquest by an authoritarian culture that believed corporal punishment was the natural way to acquire obedience, whether from slave or the misfit within colonial ranks.[49]

Canings always became the prime topic of conversation in the school. When I returned to class everybody was silent, knowing the worst and gauging from the paleness of my face and my body language that I must have received a severe whacking. 'How many?' everyone wanted to know. And, like all who had received such punishment, I indicated with my fingers. That time it was two strokes of the cane since I was a younger boy. Woe betide those who received 'six of the best' for the gravest of reasons, according to the gospel of St John B. Nitch, which was something I would endure in years to come. The teacher who had deemed my offence so grave as to relieve himself of dealing with me directly ignored my return to the class and simply went on as though I did not exist.

The teacher was Mr Benjamin – we called him 'Dumbo' because of his large ears. I discovered years later that he had been a trade unionist who lost his job owing to the National Party repression. He was one of a handful of surviving teachers from my time to attend the school's 90th birthday celebrations at the Carlton Hotel in downtown Johannesburg in 1992. I was there thanks to the kindness of my old school buddy David 'Mac' Mackenzie, who provided me with an invite costing R200 for at that point I did not have that kind of money. I was something of a hero to a few of my former schoolmates and even to Dumbo, as it appeared, when he proudly disclosed to me the fact that he had been a man of the left. I thought that, given that fact, it was surprising he had so unhesitatingly sent me off for corporal punishment from The Boss.

Of all the physical brutality I personally endured as a rebellious teenager or later as a young adult, generally in fist fights – including with the police – the sheer viciousness of such beatings when I was a young boy at KES was the worst I ever experienced. It developed within me an intense hatred for those who wielded power as a result of position or size, displaying a bullying predilection to assault other human beings, especially those smaller, younger and vulnerable. When it came to abuse by men of women or adults of children, I found it difficult to contain my temper. I came to associate such inhumanity with that of entire state systems such as apartheid or the conquest and invasion of countries by colonial powers where the underdog was ground underfoot not only by policy and regulations but by human beings dutifully following orders with sadistic force. The kind of violence which was a feature of KES in my day reflected the practice of a colonial cult and a machoism that imbued patriarchal, class, race and gender relationships of all kinds throughout society and had been brewing in its womb for centuries. Yet KES was considered one of the more liberal of the white schools and we were all ready, rebels like myself included, to put up with physical abuse as part of our rites of passage into manhood. The violence was sporadic, in fact, and nowhere near part of a daily or even weekly routine so it simply hovered menacingly in the background while we enjoyed school until the occasion that it surfaced, as had happened to me. And then a beating was inevitable, following which one was expected to get on cheerily with life.

What was happening in the Afrikaans-language schools with a greater level of patriarchy and patriotism was worse. But worse still were the goings-on in the posh English-language private schools, with their narrow Anglican breeding, insufferable snobbishness, heightened levels of authoritarianism and patriarchy, cold arrogance and almost inherent sadism and even masochism – products of upper-class English in-breeding and Lord Milner-style of Rule Britannia. Such thoughts that I had only arose after I had completed schooling and, through the education I received in the liberation struggle, came to understand that the Boers themselves had been involved in an anti-imperialist struggle against the English. If they had had the capacity to drop their racism and had formed an alliance with the African people, the so-called 'Boer and Bantu' could have defeated the Brits and South Africa might have been a uniquely independent country from 1900. If only?

Back at Albyn Court on that day of first being caned by The Boss, I went at once to the bathroom to examine the damage to my bottom in a mirror. There were raw welts on my buttocks, swollen and red, which had shed some blood and stained my underpants. I panicked. My mother mustn't see this was my immediate thought, but how to conceal the evidence? I tried washing out the blood-stains with soap and water but no matter how hard I rubbed I couldn't get rid of the marks. Nanny Poppy Molefe was in the kitchen and my mother would soon be home. 'Poppy, dear Poppy, what am I to do?' I cried, once I had explained to her what had occurred. She was shocked that such an assault had taken place, not really understanding that such a thing could happen in a white school to a white boy, but she soon got hold of herself and came up with a plan. She worried that even if she washed the tell-tale underpants with the regular wash the blood-stains might still show and my mother would notice. But my mother wouldn't notice if there was one pair of underpants less. It would be best for her to dispose of the tell-tale item of clothing by burning it in Albyn Court's boiler room inferno next to the servants' quarters.

Poppy's immediate concern was how to stop infection, learned from the days when I was a small boy and she the nanny looking after me when my mother was at work. 'You must put *muti* on the wounds,' she advised, taking a tube of cream from the medicine chest and leaving me to it. I could not satisfactorily reach the damaged areas and had to call her back from the kitchen. I gingerly lifted my shirt and dropped my pants. 'Eish! Eish!' she intoned in the African way, horrified at the sight of the damage. 'Sorry! Sorry!' she wept in sympathy as she delicately rubbed the soothing cream over the raw welts. After a minute I became more conscious of Poppy than of the physical damage done to me. I was at that age of sexual awakening when strange things happen to adolescent boys and I actually found myself beginning to experience an unwelcome erection, which of late had become my secret at bed-time. I held my hands over my growing manhood to conceal my embarrassment from Poppy. Oh hell, I thought, what was happening to me? Gritting my teeth, I endured the torment for a few more minutes and then hastily told her everything was now fine. I was very relieved that she was unaware of her effect on me.

I was amazed at how suffering physical pain could be erased by sexual arousal or perhaps mix with it. I could vaguely understand what made The Boss tick. But this sexual arousal phenomenon, with the accompanying comparisons with my pals, had become an overpowering obsession. We all gawked at girlie magazines but also something as innocent as a Folies Bergère programme which a friend's father had bought home from Paris gave us a thrill. Did I know, the pal asked, that 'Negro soldiers had the time of their lives in France and Italy during the war because the women there did not believe in the colour bar?' Some boys familiarised themselves by playing 'touch-touch' with one another. I knew that was not for me

Izzy, René, Hilary, Ronnie, 10 months, Durban Beach, 1939

TOP LEFT: *Ronnie, Durban*
TOP RIGHT: *Hilary and Ronnie, aged 18 months, Durban 1940*
BOTTOM: *Little tadpole – Ronald, 10 months, Durban, 1939*

TOP LEFT: *Hilary and Ronnie, Durban*
TOP RIGHT: *René, Hilary and Ronnie, 1939*
BOTTOM: *Rene and Ronnie, Durban*

Ronnie, aged 7, Durban, 1945

TOP LEFT: *René, Hilary and Ronnie, Durban 1940*
TOP RIGHT: *Hilary, Ronnie and friend, Durban*
BOTTOM LEFT: *Hilary, Johannesburg 1942*
BOTTOM RIGHT: *Gran Clara, René, Hilary and Ronnie, Durban. Hilary had been ill for many months and gained weight.*

René with Gran Clara, Hilary and Ronnie, aged 3, Durban, 1941

TOP: *René, Hilary and Ronnie, Muizenburg.*
BOTTOM: *Cocky Feldman on Danny Boy Turffontein, 1946, Fred May standing on the left*

Kasrils, Durban beach front, aged 15, 1953

because I could only find arousal in private. One learned to keep a box of tissues by one's bedside to avoid tell-tale stains on the sheets. A school friend told me that if he had an 'accident', he would tell his mother that he had spilled custard while eating his dessert in bed. The idea of going through a rigmarole of asking my mother to make custard and somehow fooling her that way was ludicrous to me. My mother had given me a slim volume on sex education to study. It had all manner of diagrams of birds and bees and animals leading up to medical-type drawings of the male and female reproductive organs. There were two nude photos: one of a young girl almost in silhouette with small breasts, which I would gaze at for ages; the male nude was Michelangelo's David.

CHAPTER 8

Poppy

OH POPPY, DEAR POPPY, HOW INSTANTLY you came to my rescue. And how we couldn't come to your rescue when the blood flowed outside your room at Albyn Court that very year.

Poppy Molefe and the other domestic workers of Albyn Court had a godfather who kept them in line and made sure they came to no harm – on the premises at least. Baba Tshabalala was a tough Zulu cleaner, who acted as their *induna*. His key work was to keep the stairs and long passageways of the building clean and polished, sweep the pavement outside and ensure that the boiler providing hot water was effectively maintained. There must have been numerous other tasks but those were the most visible to me. The man had a sour smell about him – which whites referred to as the 'K' odour but which my father told me was simply the smell of sweat and labour. 'Charlie', as he was called by all of us whites, who couldn't pronounce his surname, my father said, washed daily just like we did.

Baba Tshabalala was dark and wiry and very strong. He could lift heavy weights and had powerful wrists that could open the most stubborn of taps. He wore the standard clothes of all 'flat boys' who were employed as cleaners in all apartment blocks. The uniforms were made of canvas, either dark blue or khaki, lined with red trimming. They wore short pants as we KES boys aged 13 had been advised to do. And they were invariably addressed as 'boy' by those who did not know their names. Those people who didn't like to call a grown man 'boy' simply addressed them as 'Charlie' or 'John'. Baba Tshabalala was a proud traditionalist who came from the rural parts of Zululand. He wore decorated plugs (*amashaza*) within his earlobes, which had been pierced and stretched to accommodate them, as was the custom, and he wore sandals made from cast-off tyres. He sniffed snuff and every time we went on holiday to the coast we brought him back a bottle of seawater which he used for medicinal purposes. He brewed a sour milk concoction and every week he wheeled a drum of the stuff around the neighbourhood in a battered old pram, making a little bit of money on the side. He did not suffer fools lightly and if I made a mess along the passages he would admonish me with the words '*Aikona*, Lonni.' The threat was simply to make me realise his displeasure for he never actually lifted a hand against me. Zulus such as he, like some Chinese, could not pronounce the letter 'R', hence 'Lonnie'. Once I was rude to him and he escorted me to my father with his complaint and I was made to apologise and told never to speak to him like that again. That was another of my earliest memories.

Baba Tshabalala had a good relationship with my father, who was for a time caretaker of the building and supervised his work and paid him his wage, which came from a levy. The female domestic workers respected him and were careful not to answer him back. He treated them like his daughters and would not tolerate any misbehaviour. There were three servant's toilets and one was reserved exclusively for him; it would be a sign of disrespect for a woman to sit on his lavatory seat.

By the age of 12, if my parents were out and Baba needed permission to be on the streets, perhaps to go and see a relative for an urgent reason, it was me he approached with a request to write a letter of authority: 'This is to provide assurance that the bearer, Baba Ngomezulu Tshabalala, is employed as general cleaner at Albyn Court, 22 Raymond St, Yeoville. (Signed) Ronald Kasrils. Phone 43 1903.' Together with his passbook, this letter hopefully sufficed to ensure Baba's safe movement in the streets after nightfall – safe from the police, that was. While the passbook gave him permission to be in the white man's city, it did not provide him with the right to be out on the streets after dark. Without such papers he ran the risk of disappearing into a police cell and possibly ending up in prison for three months or on a farm as a virtual slave labourer.

When I signed the letter of authority I felt very grown up but also depressed at the kind of indignities men like Baba had to contend with. There was I, a mere child, with power to authorise permission for a man who could be my father to be out on the streets after dark.

This was not the only way I assisted Baba Tshabalala. Along with the sour milk he also dealt in a little illicit trade in what was referred to as 'k****r beer'. To brew the alcohol, he needed yeast, which was difficult to come by if you were an African. A boy like me, however, could buy a quantity for him and I was willing to do so without any qualms. His sour milk business served as a convenient cover for the sale of the beer. It was with some pride that I would see him pushing his pram around the neighbourhood, knowing that he had a quantity of beer to deliver to select customers. I enjoyed being in on such a subversive secret.

The owner of the building, a Mr Zeger, moved into the apartment vacated by the Lazersons after they moved on to a more upmarket suburb. He proved to be unpopular by giving the elderly Wolov couple – apartment 5 – notice to quit in order to bring in his friends. Within a week we heard the terrible news that they had perished in their new apartment, which was serviced with gas for cooking and heating. Gas was something they were unused to and one morning they were found unconscious in their beds. Since there was no suicide note, it was presumed they had accidentally left the gas-tap on after cooking their supper. This did not endear the Zegers to the Wolov family, who placed the tragedy at their door, nor to the residents and domestic staff at Albyn Court where the old couple had been popular. From Germany, that they had escaped the gas chambers ironically to end up that way was so very sad.

Zeger took the caretaker duties into his own hands but consulted my father for advice within the first few months. He demanded of Baba Tshabalala that the 'girls', as he referred to the domestic workers, should not be allowed visitors. This caused considerable disquiet and led to a tragedy. Baba Tshabalala was certainly a person who did not shirk his duties and one night we were disturbed by a huge commotion from the yard. We were witness to a surrealistic scene as we gazed down into the well of the building from our first-floor apartment. Baba Tshabalala was thrashing a young man with his fighting sticks and blood was flowing. There was a gasp from the onlookers as the man fought back. We saw the flash of a blade in the moonlight and Baba stepped back from a knife wound. The man flew into him again and again, stabbing mercilessly. Baba was very strong, however, and managed to get hold of his adversary and wrestle him to the ground. All the domestic workers, including Poppy, had gathered around and were wailing.

The white onlookers were equally horrified, with someone shouting about calling the police. My father was the only one who was willing to put his life on the line. He dashed down the iron stairs, my mother shouting after him, 'Come back!' Together with a deeply disturbed Poppy in her nightdress he pulled the young man off Baba Tshabalala and threw his dagger into the gutter. I ran down to help my father. I joined him as we rushed Baba Tshabalala to hospital while the man who we thought was an intruder was left under the control of Jock Silver and other residents, waiting for the police to arrive. He was battered and bleeding and in a groggy state but otherwise not in mortal danger. Baba had come off far worse. We knew the doctor on duty in Casualty and Baba was rushed into the operating theatre. We hung around until we heard he would survive. He had to have a blood transfusion, considerable stitching up of the wounds, and would be in intensive care.

When we got back home, we heard from my mother that the intruder was Nanny Poppy's boyfriend and that he was in police custody. My mother had tried to check how Poppy was but she was so embarrassed that she locked herself in her room. Over the next few days she did not report for work and she would not see any of us so my mother sent soup and other food down to her. The next few weeks were very problematic as a traumatised Poppy mooched about our apartment in silence, not wanting to talk about the incident at all. Although we had tried to reassure her that she had done nothing wrong, this failed to console her. The following Thursday she did not even go to Sophiatown but simply went to her room to mope.

She was terrified of Baba Tshabalala's return. There would certainly be a trial of Poppy's boyfriend. Both she and my father would obviously be giving evidence. It appeared that she was afraid of that prospect for one morning we found she had simply disappeared into the night. We could get nothing from her fellow workers, who all clammed up about where she had gone. My parents tried to trace her, and apparently so did the police, but to no avail.

My father did not have to give evidence in any trial. In answer to enquiries at the Yeoville police station, where the man had been detained, it appeared that he, like Poppy, had also disappeared. There was no satisfactory answer as to what had become of him. After a while a police sergeant came to see my father to explain that the man had received treatment in hospital as he was suffering from several fractured limbs, but one day when he was not being watched he had simply walked away.

We lost Baba Tshabalala as well. The stabbing had affected his physical ability so that he could not work and he disappeared to his home somewhere in Zululand. At long last we received a letter from our Poppy. It came from Bechuanaland but with no return address. She begged forgiveness over what had happened, and the way she had left. She thanked my parents for the way they treated her. She asked my mother, to whom the letter was addressed, to tell my sister and me that she loved us like her own children. She also had very good news for she had given birth to a healthy baby boy and she was calling him Ronnie. She ended by saying that we should please not worry about her or come looking for her because she was far away on the farms.

I must have been 14 years old at the time and have never cried so much in my life. My parents would have sent her some money but the trail was closed. We tried again to prise some information from her one-time fellow workers from Albyn Court but if anyone had any clue, they were not talking. My father's deduction was that they and Poppy herself were so wary of the police and possible consequences that they all just shut up. I also overheard him saying that the man who had nearly killed Baba must have been the father of her child and was possibly even in Bechuanaland with her. My mother shuddered at the thought that Poppy was having to rely on him.

It wasn't long after that that Albyn Court was rocked by another tragedy. Our dinner was interrupted one evening by an anxious Mrs Zeger. She was looking for her husband who had been gone for several hours saying that he needed to obtain some advice from my father. She was an old grey-haired woman, uncommunicative with the neighbours, but something of a shrew at home as she was often heard nagging and scolding her husband and bawling out their domestic servant. She was in a highly agitated state. They knocked on a few doors but no one had seen Mr Zeger. There was a new cleaner in the building who had replaced Baba Tshabalala and he reported that he had seen the old man going into the boiler room. My father went down the iron stairs and into the boiler room with the cleaner. He was soon calling up to my mother to call an ambulance. He told Mrs Zeger to stay in her flat, saying there had been an accident, but she rushed down to see and we soon heard her screaming her head off to the point of sending shudders down my spine. My father had found the old man hanging from a rope around his neck tied to an overhead pipe. He was already cold and blue when my dad and the cleaner cut him down. The corpse lay there until the ambulance men arrived.

I was ill in bed with a high temperature and needed no tadpoles to jolt my memory. The screams of Mrs Zeger and her daughter were indescribable, poor things, and did not abate, neither that night nor for several days. Each time relatives arrived and especially a number of married offspring from around the country, the wailing and shrieking was renewed, made louder by the cries of the arrivals who joined in. I heard from my parents that at the funeral Mrs Zeger and her daughter had to be restrained from jumping into the grave.

The domestic workers, still smarting from the incident with Baba Tshabalala and Poppy's boyfriend, claimed that Mrs Zeger had driven the old man into the grave by poisoning him. In this instance the word 'poison' would have denoted casting some sort of spell on him which led to his suicide. My parents and other neighbours were baffled about Mr Zeger's motives but concluded that they might have been financial.

CHAPTER 9

Growing Pains

THE ILLNESS I REFERRED TO SET me back at school. I was indisposed for several months and the doctors could not diagnose what was causing a persistent fever and my body to bruise very easily. Just the slightest knock on my limbs or joints would result in the development of heavy bruising.

I was having my blood regularly tested without any conclusive evidence emerging. There were suspicions that I might have had polio moving fleetingly through my body at some stage, for it did not always lead to paralysis. The thought of that possibility frightened me because there were still outbreaks of poliomyelitis and the invention of the vaccine that put an end to the terror was some years off. There was another theory that I was suffering from rheumatic fever. My father was convinced that whatever was wrong it had been caused by my suddenly gaining several inches in height in just a short time. A 'growth spurt', as he put it. I had a minimal tremor, noticeable in my hands from a young age, which appeared to be in my genes; both my mother and Grandpa Abe had it as well. Doctors described it as a familial tremor, meaning that it ran in the family and was harmless. However, with the malady it became more marked and I had to learn to control it through deep breathing. Some people thought that it denoted nervousness but it was more like the feeling of butterflies in the stomach I experienced before a race which disappeared the moment the tension of waiting was over and the adrenaline kicked in rather than anything denoting fear.

When I got back to school, I found myself behind Ivor and my other pals and it was thought best that I repeat the year. I picked up greatly and did well – but not in History.

We had a teacher from Scotland called Mr Smart, who was with us on an exchange with a very popular KES teacher I had been looking forward to learning under. His name was Teddy Gordon and he was reputed to be a liberal, possibly even a communist. He was in Scotland that year.

Mr Smart was the opposite. He was short, pugnacious, with mean close-set eyes and a bald head. His idea of teaching was by way of droning on about names of kings and generals, dates and events and the superiority of the British Empire. We learned from his remarks that he had served as a police sergeant under the British Mandate in Palestine. Without a doubt he was a real anti-Semite and was soon making biting jibes aimed at the Jewish boys present. It must have come as a surprise to him that in a school named after King Edward VII there were so many of us. He made references to the problem of policing in Palestine. You couldn't tell the difference between the Jew and the Arab. The bombing of the British headquarters in the King David Hotel, Jerusalem, in 1946 by the Zionist terrorist organisation Irgun riled him the most. Mentioning it, he said Jewish terrorism was comparable to that of the Irish - both cowardly and incompetent. Jews and Arabs had died together with the British in that attack. Such remarks were accompanied by him folding his arms, rocking back on his heels, and peering at us while he rolled his tongue within his mouth as though ruminating.

On another occasion he passed a jibe at me thick with sarcasm. Having got the measure of the man I was not going to let it pass. Looking for a book in my school bag, I placed my tracksuit and running shoes on my desk. He had the temerity to suggest that I was revealing the trade of my ancestors and enquired whether I was looking to sell second-hand clothing on school premises. I stalked up to him, pleased about the inches I had gained in height so that I looked down on him, and showed him my fist. I threatened that I would gladly beat him up if he cared to meet me on a weekend in my Yeoville ghetto. I was 16 by then and scared of nobody. He rushed off to consult The Boss. While he was out the whole class pledged that they would stand by me. When he returned, he curtly told me that The Boss was waiting for me. I had no fear of that man, having had several encounters with him and his cane since that first occasion in his office. I had often behaved stupidly but this time I knew I stood on justifiable grounds. More than that, I was aware that about one third of the school's pupils were Jewish and many from prosperous homes in Houghton. If St John B. Nitch laid hands on me over my altercation with Smart he must realise there would be repercussions beyond his door. He was prepared to listen to my side of the story. When I completed my allegation against Mr Smart, he simply told me my complaint would be noted but that he could not tolerate threats against any of his teachers and dismissed me.

When I returned to the classroom Smart affected not to be interested but I could see him slyly scrutinising me through the corners of his beady eyes while rolling his tongue around in his mouth. It was obvious that I was cool and unperturbed – certainly not somebody who had received a caning. Just then a wag at the back of the class shouted out a word guaranteed to sting a Scot's ears.

'Murrayfield!'

The victorious cry was immediately taken up by the rest of the class and 'Murrayfield!' echoed round the classroom walls.

The single-word reminder and underlying message of solidarity – something I came to appreciate from that time on – would have rubbed salt in the wound for the mean-spirited Mr Smart, coming after the resounding South African victory over Scotland on the famous Murrayfield stadium – a record 40-0 drubbing on the part of the touring Springboks.

I can't say we encountered any other teacher who was anti-Semitic in my time at KES. In fact, one of the most lovable characters of all was a true-blue Scotsman, a physical training instructor named Derby Whyte. Derby looked like a portly boxer gone to seed. It was clearly the sagging beer belly that had been his undoing, not that he ever appeared intoxicated. He was a dour Scot who had escaped from a POW camp during the war and survived for a time with the French Resistance, before an arduous crossing of the Alps into neutral Switzerland. He often recounted his wartime experiences. There were two stories about Jews. One was witnessing a German soldier bayonetting a pregnant Jewish woman in the stomach. He described his anger and frustration as his French comrades had to restrain him from attacking the soldier. The other story was about being in a party crossing the Alps which contained a Jewish family who they were helping. He praised the bravery of the daughter but denounced the son who he described as a yellow-bellied coward who had to be goaded to keep moving when the going got tough. When the young man was given a swig of the brandy they were sharing to keep the cold at bay he drank the lot before they could stop him. Derby said he felt like strangling the guy. The sister had wanted to shoot her brother then and there but Derby had stopped her.

Derby Whyte supervised swimming lessons in summer and our indoor gym sessions in winter. He was intent on turning us into men – Real Men. We started the swimming routine on the first day of spring in September when it was still cold in early morning Johannesburg. He would be barking at us in the changing room to hurry up and without any tardiness ensured we had taken the plunge into the pool. The temperature of the water at that time would have been around 14°C. He would be at the back of slackers who were holding proceedings up, bawling that they were a 'dozy lot' and quite prepared to push them into the pool. The height of the nervy experiences was the day we had to perform what he called a 'dead man's dive'. We had to ascend the ladder of the high diving board one at a time. It was some 5 metres high. Each one of us had to walk to the end of the board, stand stiffly to attention, raise our arms high in the air, and allow ourselves to fall into the pool below head first. If you did this correctly, you'd succeed. If you faltered, and many did, usually at the last moment, you would topple awkwardly into the pool and execute a painful belly-flop. Quite a number of boys hesitated on the brink and Derby would bellow angrily at any 'yellow-bellied coward' to 'Get on with it!'

There was one boy who stood frozen on the brink, who just could not relax and let himself go. The more Derby yelled the more frozen to the spot he became, even when Derby in an impatient frenzy ascended the ladder after him. It was only when Derby appeared at the top of the ladder that the boy did the sensible thing and jumped into the pool. That boy was me. I felt I had behaved in a cowardly manner and confessed to my father, but my dad was critical of Derby's teaching method. He felt he should have engaged us in a drill on the ground or at least on the side of the pool rather than sending us cold out onto the diving board. He drew a stool up to the foot of his bed, told me to climb up on it and assume the dead man's position. He then gave me the order to simply fall forward, which I did, landing lengthwise across the bed. I realised if I did that gravity would act to pull me head down into the pool as long as I kept perfectly still and straight.

Next time we had swimming we were expected to execute the dead man's dive. When my turn came, although the butterflies in my stomach were engaged in a lively St Vitus dance and I was very aware that Derby and the rest of the class were closely watching, I performed what was required. Derby said nothing to me. He simply called out, 'Next!' I knew I had earned his respect and was grateful to my father, whose creativity assisted me to teach others in various situations in future years.

Derby greatly admired the brave. There was a boy who contracted polio and returned to school a year later, his leg withered and in a brace. His name was Bobby Fussell, who had made a mark in primary school as a promising cricketer. Not to be deterred, he built up his upper body with weights and became a champion in the swimming pool, specialising in backstroke. Derby hailed him as the bravest boy in the school.

When there were altercations between boys he would have them sort out their differences by putting on the gloves and getting into the boxing ring. Such occasions were not everyday events but when they happened the gym would be full of boys supporting one or the other of the pugilists. It appeared to be a successful way of working off grudges for under Derby's supervision enmity between the two protagonists invariably wore off.

My turn came in my matric year, the week we were off on a month's swot leave before returning to write the final exams. Towards the end of the school year discipline always became lax in anticipation of the holidays. Some fancy water-pistols had come onto the market and rowdy duels were becoming evident during school breaks. The Boss was annoyed and gave a stern warning at assembly that such behaviour would not be tolerated. Anybody continuing with the unacceptable practice would be severely punished. One of the more zealous prefects caught a group of juniors in the midst of transgressing the order. I came across him balling them out. I stood behind the prefect, who was a top school rugby player of considerable physical stature, and while he was giving the culprits a verbal tongue-lashing, I emptied the contents of a borrowed water-pistol into the seat of his pants. As laughter broke out he whirled around in a livid state. He couldn't contain himself when he caught me, metaphorical smoking gun in hand, and immediately rushed off to The Boss to report my infamy.

Alone with The Boss in his office, he told me that if I hadn't been due to write the coming matric examination he would have had no hesitation in expelling me then and there. 'Six of the best,' he announced. 'Buck down.' I heard him psyching himself up with what must have been his most potent cane, swishing it around in preparation. I will spare readers the description of 'six of the best' handed out to me by the biggest sadist I had ever encountered, save to say that every slash of his cane was a blow of rage that shocked my entire physical and nervous system. I did manage to maintain my dignity and more, for I was immune from further punishment, including expulsion. Like a man who has been sentenced to death and has nothing to lose, I muttered to him as I walked out: 'You enjoyed that, didn't you?'

The prefect was standing outside Nitch's office, looking quite contrite and apologising to me; he understood how extremely severe 'six of the best' was. I cursed him in the foulest language I could muster and challenged him to a fist fight after school, telling him exactly where we should meet. I was in such a rage, so intent on revenge, so oblivious of the pain I was enduring, so uncaring of the fact that he was taller, heavier and bigger than me, that I could barely restrain myself from lashing out at him with my fists then and there.

As the school bell rang at the end of the day, I made my way to the bottom of the nearby Munro Drive to meet him, despite a limp from the flogging I had received as a result of one of The Boss's cuts striking me on my thigh. The prefect duly showed up but so did half the school, anticipating a lively spectacle. We took off our ties and jackets, seconds and a referee were allocated, and we squared up.

Before the first blow was struck, my name and that of my opponent was bellowed out from above the ramparts at Munro Drive. It was Derby Whyte, demanding to know what the flaming hell did we think we were up to. He called us up to him at once, forbidding us to fight. That was unusual because Derby liked to see enmity discharged in a fist fight, although he preferred the gym. I was well aware of that and said to him, 'Okay, but let's get into your gym, sir, boxing gloves will do.' Derby shook his head. He didn't like the situation one bit, seeing how deeply angry I was, and he ordered us to get on home. The crowd dispersed.

My fall-back plan was a garden in a nearby house and I sent my second to that of the prefect and the referee to meet within ten minutes at that address. The referee I believe was Richard Goldstone who would one day be an internationally renowned judge. He was a very passive boy and I don't think he blinked once or had a single word to say during the entire fight that followed. We lined up again in the quiet of a Houghton garden. There were no rules – just a fight until one of us gave up. I literally tore into my opponent, keeping low down so that his long reach was neutralised and his big fists whistled behind my head. It was the Kasrils tactics of going in fast and hitting the opponent in the face from my southpaw stance. I was very athletic, no longer the smallest boy in my year, and my anger was pumping the adrenalin in hot fury. I was hurting him badly and he desperately tried to avoid my flaying fists connecting with his mug. I closed in on him as he sagged, changed tactics to grab him in a wrestler's hold and, using his weight, threw him heavily to the ground, which knocked the air out of him. I set upon him like a demon and began throttling him in a half nelson arm-lock.

He was helpless, gasping for breath, but I kept squeezing mercilessly. 'Do you give up? Do you give up?' But he hung on, trying to squirm out of the position. 'Give up! Give up!' That was what I wanted and that was what his dignity could not allow. He continued to squirm and I continued to strangle him. In the end he did give in and my second cheered. I was victorious. I did not so much as look at my defeated adversary as I walked over to a garden tap to drink some water and wash my face. Then I heard his challenge – 'Come on, let's have another round!' Even though the fight was over, his loss of face couldn't allow it to be. Now it was the prefect's turn to be driven by anger. He desperately needed to prove his mettle and save face. I saw the punch coming from a mile away, but my arms were limp from the stranglehold I had put on him, and it was like raising them in slow motion, as his fist drove into my nose, putting it out of joint. As I stepped back to recover, a second blow caught me on my cheekbone. At least I was able to duck down, get back inside him and hang on like a flagging boxer in the ring. We grappled, both exhausted, he like me at least satisfied that he was not down and out.

Tales would be told by both sides and rumours would be circulated but I was satisfied that I had had my revenge and the fact that he would carry more bruises than me. His mother wrote an anonymous letter, which was published in the *Star* newspaper, denouncing the activities of thugs who attack prefects, complaining that her son had come home from school with torn and bloodied clothing, in a battered state, for merely doing his duty. My defiance was a signal to The Boss that he could bugger off. I would not bow down to his edict and in any case I was now beyond his reach.

And didn't he know that. The year before I had defied convention and came to school having dispensed with the regular short back and sides haircut with formal parting. I sported a Tony Curtis hairstyle with the forelock dyed blonde. I and a couple of others rebels had been told by Nitch to stand up at assembly while he denounced us, advising the school not to follow in our footsteps. What else could the man do, since it would take months for the peroxide to fade and there was no rule against having to have your hair parted. It did cost me the school colours though. One of the housemasters, Dan Henning, had found it necessary to explain to the boarders that there was no way I could be awarded full colours because of my hairstyle. Instead I was awarded what was called a 'team blazer' for my athletics achievements which, although second best, was much sought after. No one ever saw me in that expensive blazer. For a start I did not want my father to have to lay out the extra money and by then I'd lost all interest in school awards. The fact that I had done well in athletics was sufficient in itself. I made the school athletics team every year except for the one when I was ill. I won the 880 yards championship in my matric year and came second in the 440 yards. I cherished those achievements all my life but they weren't definitive. All I desired was to attain a matric certificate and get the hell out of the place. There were several teachers that I learned a lot from but Teddy Gordon, my history teacher, who was the one who made the most difference.

The year 1955 was my Tony Curtis year and, on a more serious note, also a major turning point in my life.

CHAPTER 10

Liberty, Equality, Fraternity

TEDDY GORDON HAD BEEN ABROAD teaching in Scotland in 1954 and we'd had to endure the anti-Semitic Mr Smart, but in 1955 he was back.

Teddy was sprightly, keen-eyed and bird-like. He had a receding hairline, high forehead and sharp nose. He spoke with a fine voice, had a witty turn of phrase and wore a university blazer. He had served out the Second World War in the Royal Navy but he barely spoke about that time. He was probably only 15 years older than us.

I will never forget his first words to our class as he stood confidently before us.

'This term we will be studying the French Revolution.'

My seditious ears pricked up. I liked the sound of the word 'revolution'.

Neither will I ever forget his next words.

'Liberty, equality, fraternity.'

He looked around the classroom. 'Who's heard those words before?' he asked. I don't think anyone had. He went on to ask us what each word meant. The response was not satisfactory. We were not articulate about the full meaning of liberty and equality and I cannot recall anyone making sense of the word fraternity. Once we had cleared up those meanings to his satisfaction, he asked us to imagine what the results would be if we stood on a soapbox and called for the adoption of the slogan. First, he asked about the response in the well-to-do suburb in which our school was situated. There was much levity. Then he asked us to imagine the results in the black township of Alexandra some 14 km north along Louis Botha Avenue.

I was probably the only boy who had ever been near the township when I went along with my father on his rounds. But virtually everybody had motored by. I'm sure that most of us were wondering what on earth this had to do with France but we were soon put in the picture. Teddy gave us a riveting exposition on the conditions in 18th-century France: what the meaning of absolute monarchy and feudalism amounted to; the privileged life of the nobility waxing in obscene luxury; the ambitions and frustrations of the emergent bourgeois middle class; the dire conditions of the destitute peasantry. He explained all this with a degree of quiet passion, ridiculing the excesses of the parasitic royal court, oppressing and exploiting masses of people who had no rights and were treated like animals. What was so magical about his use of words and comparisons was that one could not but help see the same conditions between the white rulers of South Africa and the African masses.

Up to that time I had not paid much attention in class. But listening to Teddy speak, and very unusually for me, I found myself sitting back, totally relaxed, soaking up his every word like a sponge without realising it. That there was some change taking place within me was something I did not detect. I was so interested in his narrative that I read Charles Dickens' *A Tale of Two Cities* again, absorbing it in a new light and not simply as some kind of romantic story. I found a book about Robespierre in the library and skimmed through that. At the end of the term the usual tests were set covering all our subjects. For history we were required to write an essay on the causes of the French Revolution. I did not realise that for the first time in my schooling I was accomplishing a task in an effortless way. Normally I would sit looking at the question, fretting about it and experiencing difficulty in my response. Now I completed the essay with ease and that was that. It was a rite of passage for me which occurred without my realisation, far more relevant I would say than my bar mitzvah.

There was an interlude over the Easter holidays and I was invited with a few other boys to stay at the farm of one of our classmates in the Bethal area of the then Eastern Transvaal (now Mpumalanga). His father was a wealthy potato farmer in an area where some of these farmers would later be exposed for subjugating farmworkers, supplied by the police, to conditions akin to slave labour.[50] Not that we noticed anything amiss. Typical hedonists living off the fat of the land. We had a carefree time – swimming, playing tennis and riding horses but we debated politics late into the night for I threw a spanner into the complacency. When I forced my friends to accept that black people were being mistreated, they responded that it was impossible to overthrow white rule. I argued passionately – if romantically – that just as the French peasants had risen up with pitchforks, so, too, would black South Africans.

The holiday coincided with the Jewish Passover festival, which celebrated the exodus of the Jews from Egyptian slavery led by Moses. We sat around the family table with the head of the household and other relatives dining on the traditional food together with *matza* – the obligatory unleavened bread. We all joined in reciting with gusto the vengeful incantations about the ten plagues that God visited upon the Egyptians in order to induce them to release their Jewish slaves, the ultimate plague being the slaughter by an Angel of Death of the first-born son in every Egyptian household.

In retrospect I found this traditional celebration of freedom ironic, given the conditions that were revealed in the newspapers about the brutal abuses under which the farm labourers lived and worked on that very area for next to nothing. Luckless Africans swept up in police raids in city streets, without the required documents, appeared before magistrates in summary trials and were sentenced to a term of hard labour on the farms all over the country. Conditions were appalling. They were kept in makeshift farm prisons, worked from dawn to dusk, and subjected to savage beatings. Those who died were buried in the potato fields. This 'farm labour scandal' was exposed by investigative journalists Ruth First and Joe Gqabi of the left-wing newspaper *New Age*, among others.[51] People I would in time meet and befriend.

It was after the Easter holidays that we were again sitting in Teddy Gordon's class and he was calling out our names in alphabetical order, handing back our test papers and making comments in each case. When he came to my name, he enquired what my History mark had been the year before. That was Mr Smart's year. I told him I had got an E. He replied that I had done much better than that this time. I couldn't believe my eyes when I saw I had received an A+. The top mark! Not only was it the top mark in our class, but in all the four classes for my year. Results were displayed on boards in the school quadrangle outside The Boss's office. There was much interest in my achievement. After all, I was in lowly Form Four D.

The Latin swots in Four A were expected to sweep the board in all subjects. What books have you been reading, I was asked by such luminaries as Richard Goldstone, a future celebrated judge to be, and Tony Bloom a friend of Ivor's and mine who would become one of the country's leading businessmen and in the 1980s would call for the ban on the ANC to be lifted. Teddy had unlocked an interest in me for study and my marks in other subjects consequently greatly improved, particularly in English literature. I developed a taste for poetry and English novels, which launched me into trying my hand at creative writing.

I was captivated by the English Romantic poets and in particular Coleridge, Wordsworth and Shelley. I could recite long tracts from Coleridge's 'The Rime of the Ancient Mariner' by heart and was impressed when our teacher told us that the poet was of mixed race and that his father came from Sierra Leone. Among my favourite poems were Wordsworth's 'I Wandered Lonely as a Cloud', which appeared to sum up my personal angst, and 'My Heart Leaps Up', with what initially for me was the most enigmatic line, 'the child is father of the man', and which caused much debate in class. How could a child be the father of an adult? Most interpreted this as a boy becoming a father, siring a son who in turn becomes a man. The teacher explained that it was thoughts of the poet's childhood and things that moved him, like the joy of seeing a rainbow, described in the poem, which persisted in his adult life and could take on many layers of meaning, particularly as one experienced life and matured. In many respects you are a product of your childhood years. What I found so compelling and beautiful was the simple construct of the problem which awakened the imagination and had one grappling with the message for years to come.

And then there was the decided appeal of Shelley's 'Ozymandias', expressing his contempt for tyranny and power. It was poetry like that which made me feel that my rebellious attitudes which landed me in trouble at KES did not mean I was an aberration. Not that higher authority sought to radicalise us, and by that I refer to the High Priests of the Transvaal Education Department. But in the prescribed anthology books one could find specific gems.

Disappointingly, the textbooks set for English literature were a mixed bag. Shakespeare could certainly enlighten if one had the mind to concentrate with the aid of a good teacher; and the likes of Charles Dickens and Joseph Conrad were entertaining and thought-provoking. But this was mixed with outright colonial monstrosities such as John Buchan's *Prester John*, which was about a daring Scot caught up in a melodramatic 19th-century Zulu uprising.

I enjoyed Geography and gained a great deal from it. Our teacher was Dan Henning, a dry straightforward man without a hint of humour. He was a good teacher and I quickly learned the attributes of physical and economic geography, which proved of use in later life whether as a guerrilla fighter in the African bush or visiting foreign climes. I developed a facility to draw maps, understand contour lines and reproduce them, describe and sketch such features as the Nile and Congo river courses; and memorise the characteristics of the Po Valley, North American Great Lakes, Germany's industrial heartland, and the Lancashire and Yorkshire wool and cotton industries. I had gained an early interest in the subject from my family's immigrant background and childhood discussions with my father on his rounds as a traveller which aroused my fascination with different peoples. Generally looked down upon as a non-intellectual subject, it made one aware of the world and connected logically into history, politics and economic development. Without realising it, my curiosity about the world was establishing a platform for my later development.

My time spent at KES had certainly seen a transition within me.

The turning point in my life had clearly been encountering Teddy Gordon and his lessons on the French Revolution. That and my mother's reflections on the beating of the man in Joburg's streets in 1946 was another key event. If she had not kept my mind open, I doubt I would have been so susceptible to Teddy's lessons. I owed a great deal to Teddy

Gordon and after I had to flee the country for political reasons in 1963, I heard that he had departed for Britain a few years later owing, I thought, to his disapproval of the increasing repression in South Africa. I never met him again but I came across a young cousin of his in Britain and was able to send him warm regards and a message that he had profoundly changed my life. In exile I learned from a fellow comrade, Sadie Foreman, that she had known Teddy and that he had been very close to the Congress of Democrats in Yeoville, and was a sympathiser of the Communist Party. I also learned that another wartime communist, Cecil Williams, had been a teacher at KES shortly before my time. It was as Cecil's chauffeur that Nelson Mandela posed when the vehicle they were in was stopped at the ill-fated Howick roadblock on the road from Durban to Johannesburg in August 1962, resulting in the latter's more than 27 years of imprisonment.

I paid a visit to KES around 2002 in its centenary year. It had greatly changed and had begun to enrol black students. I was asked to be a patron of the celebrations along with people like Gary Player and Tony Bloom. It was a novel experience to enter the principal's office for a convivial discussion instead of 'six of the best'. I looked around, visualising the tortures I had experienced and the brooding presence of St John B. Nitch. Amidst the small-talk I asked about Teddy Gordon and heard that he had died. The principal asked whether I had seen a drinking fountain on my way into his office. Yes, I answered, as it was a hot day and, feeling thirsty, I had taken a drink. He told me the fountain was a commemoration to Teddy Gordon's tenure. There was relevant symbolism in that because at that time I was the country's Minister of Water Affairs.

The visit made me think of the line from my favourite Wordsworth poem, 'the child is father of the man' and how relevant the formative years of my childhood and schooldays had been to what I had become – with all that was positive and indeed the flaws.

The last time I encountered Headmaster St John B. Nitch was when I matriculated.

I did not initially gain a university entrance level but along with a dozen or so other boys could do so if I came back within a month and wrote a supplementary examination. He discussed our marks and gave

Liberty, Equality, Fraternity

advice. It was as though no enmity had existed between the two of us as he congratulated me on getting thus far. Scrutinising my marks, he advised that I repeat the Maths exam. I declined and chose to write Science instead – the man simply could not make me out; his advice appeared logical. Maths and Science had been my two lowest marks but I had done better in Maths than Science. I knew that I had done next to no preparation for Science and, unlike Maths, it was far easier to learn by rote if I applied myself – so my logic was also sound. I borrowed one of the Latin swots Science notes and got a B in my supplementary exam. I achieved my university entrance certificate that way.

As I shook hands with Nitch he appeared to have softened, indicating his satisfaction that I had achieved a crack at a university entrance certificate. Perhaps his relief arose from the fact that the war between us was at last over or more like the prison governor bidding farewell to an old lag. In a sense I felt that way, too, and I was prepared to forgive and forget. After all, I was not going to see that man again so why allow him to continue to bother me. I was so relieved at completing high school that I burned all my notes, except Teddy Gordon's. Those were seized a few years later by the Special Branch.

I had consulted Teddy about the political situation in South Africa and a bit later on he sent me a copy of *Naught for Your Comfort* by Reverend Trevor Huddleston, which had recently been published. He told me to begin with that, which I did; I read what apartheid was about as a political system and of the cruel oppression and suffering of black people. I had instinctively felt and seen just a very little bit of that but never realised how pervasive and far-reaching that was. I had thought Teddy would provide me with communist literature but after reading Huddleston I realised you did not have to be a communist to be brave, confrontational and radical. Although Huddleston painted a pessimistic picture, given the power of white domination and apartheid in particular, his powerful narrative provided a message of hope. He implored all people, white and black, to stand up together, raise their voices and act in united and militant but non-violent action. His passionate plea for justice and morality was particularly aimed at white South Africans, prisoners of their privileges, hence the book's title. It made an enormous impression on me. All thanks to Teddy for opening my eyes. Huddleston's religious order was the Community of the Resurrection. I heard from Joe Slovo later that the communists, great fans of Huddleston, referred to it as the Community of the Insurrection. I like to recall Joe's anecdote: after working closely with Huddleston, the latter remarked to Joe that for a communist he would make a good Christian. Quick-witted Joe's retort was 'Well, Reverend, for a Christian you would make a good communist.'

With tongue in cheek the three best accolades I ever received from my time at KES were:

1. Meeting Ivor Lazerson at a KES reunion in 1992 at the Carlton Hotel, Johannesburg, after I had returned to the country after 27 years in exile. The ANC was on the cusp of coming to power under Mandela's leadership and my former schoolmates were debating what I might become. 'Governor of the Reserve Bank,' Ivor declared with the assurance of his father Six Finger Sam. That was not a post I had any interest in or indeed thought highly of but for Ivor that was top of the totem pole. It was that which impressed me.
2. Tony Bloom meeting me at a Sandton hotel after I became a government minister remembering me as the best pinball player in Yeoville.
3. Bumping into a KES Old Boy in a doctor's consulting room. I was a government minister and what he immediately noted was that I still wore my tie with the top button of my shirt undone. That about summed up my approach to life.

My overall judgement of the value of those school years was developing an appetite for Geography and History, infused with poetry and literature. I can't think of better subjects to lead the young into a better understanding of the world we live in.

When I bade a private farewell to Teddy Gordon just before the matric exams were to begin, he winced at the sight of my black eye and damaged nose, consequent of my rumble with the prefect. He wished me well for the exams, saying he expected me to get a distinction for History. Then he asked me what career path I was choosing. I was unsure at that point and said I would give it more thought the following year. He had come to know that I was doing well in English, particularly poetry, and he advised me to read more deeply into the work of Shelley. 'Ozymandias', he said, was one of the rare radical poems in the school syllabus. He advised me to read more of Shelley's revolutionary poetry and ignore the 'tame' romantic stuff that was generally studied.[52]

I lost no time in reading a good biography on Shelley and discovered in him a kindred spirit.

From his schooldays Shelley had developed a hatred towards tyranny and the established order of church and state. At Eton, England's top public school, he denounced the antiquated system of fagging for prefects. A child of the French Revolution, he championed the ideals of liberty, equality and fraternity and proposed the redistribution of wealth. He was regarded as a dangerous subversive by the ruling class. He was also a powerful advocate for women's rights and equality in the male-dominated society he condemned. He asked the question, 'Can man be free if the woman be a slave?' He did not shirk from suggesting that the established order needed to be overthrown by the use of mass insurrection and armed force.

Shelley's epic poem 'The Mask of Anarchy'[53], exhorting England's downtrodden to rise up in the wake of the Peterloo massacre in Manchester of 1819, intoxicated me, and particularly the celebrated final stanza:

Rise like lions after slumber,
in unvanquishable number
Shake your chains to earth like dew,
which in sleep had fallen on you:
ye are many – they are few

What nobody ever tumbled to, not even my closest KES buddies from our days at Yeoville Boys, was that I was occasionally playing soccer for a semi-league team on weekends. Once I was not playing rugby regularly at KES I partially returned to my football roots. I occasionally played out on the wing for the railway workers' team Ramblers when they were a player short. Not the senior team which played in the Transvaal first division but one of their feeder teams for apprentices. We played in red-and-white striped jerseys and I enjoyed mixing with the white working class. They spoke a mixture of English and Afrikaans embroidered with slang and cursing galore. An opposing player who was committing fouls would be jeered at as playing like a *doos* (cunt).

They were tough young men, already working as apprentice engineers or as artisans of various types; some even drove locomotives. There was a small following of spectators, mainly their girlfriends, who they referred to as their 'cherries'. These young women drank beer from bottles and chain-smoked throughout the matches, shouting encouragement for their lads and jeering at the opposition as a load of 'moffies' (homosexuals); or if they picked some poor fella out they called him a 'nancy boy'. Which also meant they got involved in shrill arguments with the cherries supporting the opposing team and sometimes almost came to blows. We played all over the southern suburb working-class areas, against mine workers' teams like Benoni, Boksburg and Brakpan, and against my old favourite team Rangers in their black-and-white stripes. This was a world as distanced from KES and the northern suburbs as the white areas were from the black townships. I felt safe in the environment because it meant I would not be exposed; if I had been found out, I would probably have been expelled from KES.

This double life helped me to maintain a dual identity. I attended some of their functions, and particularly Saturday night events at tough working-class hotels where I first became acquainted with the wild beat of rock 'n roll, Bill Haley & His Comets, the emergent Elvis Presley and ducktail culture. I enjoyed dancing with their women and soon learned some fancy rock 'n roll routines. I learned to rock with two women at once, one on each arm, which I thought was the height of cool. The guys drank brandy mixed with Coke, smoked fiercely strong Texan cigarettes, rode motorbikes and were extremely jealous of their women. Brawls in the hotels and nightclubs broke out at the drop of a hat. They regarded the glance of a stranger at their women as a challenge to their manhood which required the assertiveness of an alpha male response. This was the time of James Dean, Hollywood legend, in the film *Rebel Without a Cause*. They reminded me very much of the waywardness associated with that movie. I, too, fancied myself as similar to James Dean but I was beginning to feel that I was a rebel *with* a cause.

There was a song I liked which had hit the charts and I knew it off by heart. They all knew it, too, because it was a working man's tune that was sweeping America. It was called 'Sixteen Tons' and the lyrics told about the sweat and tears of a coal miner.[54] As the band in the hotel began to thump it out, their lead singer in jeans and a leather jacket, with an Elvis quiff, got into full stride. Bottle of Castle beer in hand, already quite tipsy, I joined in as the chorus was belted out and my Ramblers buddies linked arms, the whole team in on the sing-song. The feeling of solidarity was palpable as we sang the lines about getting 'deeper in debt', gesticulating to each other, the women forming a circle around us and clapping in support. We were attracting the attention of the whole damn dance floor. Again the chorus in higher decibels yet, again mimicking the action of the miner loading 16 tonnes, his soul owned by the company store. The whole house roaring us on as at a Cup Final as the miner stoically meets his fate. The finale was accompanied by ecstatic applause.

'You know who sings the original?' our goalkeeper asked me through the din.

'Yes, of course,' I replied, and as one man we all shouted out 'Tennessee Ernie Ford!'

There is nothing like a sing-song, but particularly one with meaning, one that resonates with one's workmates or comrades, to break down barriers and build a team. If they had previously respected me, the song had brought about a qualitative change. They realised I was more educated than they were but did not see that as my being a snob or a larney with airs and graces, thinking myself better than them. They referred to me as their *china* (mate). That was owing to the fact that I was prepared to play soccer with them. The song 'Sixteen Tons' showed I could relate to the working man. The next soccer game we played we thrashed our opponents and sang 'Sixteen Tons' with gusto in the showers.

I hid the fact that I was at KES, though, and pretended that I was at Highlands North. This was far from being a prestigious school and as far away from their territory as one could get in Johannesburg. I liked to think I was getting back at the authoritarian snobbishness of KES and the tyranny of St John B. Nitch. What I was quite unaware of at the time was that Nitch had been headmaster at Highlands North before 'ascending' the dizzy heights to the far more prestigious post at KES. The elevation must have added pressure on him to succeed. Not quite the Messerschmitt up his arse, but reason to perhaps deal with arses like me.

While I had been on that Easter holiday in Bethal my mind was clearly percolating. I remember one afternoon watching a gardener on the farm chopping down a tree. He was barefoot, wore dirty blue overalls, a battered hat on his head, was muscular but had an exhausted air about him. He slowly hefted a heavy axe and brought it down with a powerful blow into the tree time and again until it fell. I found myself scrawling words in a notebook and soon completed the first poem I ever composed. It is an amateur effort but projects something of the mood I was experiencing.

Wrecking a Dream
like a thick-skinned oak
solemnly accepting
axes bite
torn by insults
loath to fight
branches cleaved
leaves discharged
stripped bark
sterile
master commanded
chosen to defile
yet beneath the greenery
he has helped create
destructive roots
unseen
interlace to wreck
tyrants dream.

When I wrote that poem I had the song 'Sixteen Tons' on my mind. I realised the genius of working-class songwriters such as Tennessee Ernie Ford.

CHAPTER 11

Girls, Pinball and High Treason

BY 1956 MY POLITICAL AWARENESS, although in a nascent state, was beginning to develop. I had been unaware of the ANC-led liberation movement's adoption of a Freedom Charter in 1955 addressed to all South Africans regardless of colour. The apartheid government, about which the Sachs girls (long disappeared from Yeoville) had warned me, was increasing its repression. Hundred and fifty-six activists of all races, including Chief Albert Luthuli and Nelson Mandela, were rounded up and charged with high treason.[55]

Their trial began in the Drill Hall in downtown Johannesburg. One of the accused was my mother's first cousin, Jacqueline Arenstein, from Durban, Aunt Rala's daughter and Gran Clara's niece. My mother was devastated. The trial preoccupied my family and became the central topic of conversation at Albyn Court. A number of Jews were among the 156 detainees and some nervy neighbours bemoaned the fact of their involvement in politics since Jews had enough to worry about without getting involved in other people's troubles and ought to avoid criticising the government. Most members of the Jewish community, misled by the Jewish Board of Deputies and the Zionist Federation of South Africa, ostracised the handful of Jews who aligned with the ANC and had stood up against the government. There were honourable exceptions but there were no Jewish rabbis who stood shoulder to shoulder with the likes of Reverend Trevor Huddleston.

My mother was anxious to visit Jacqueline. She took the tram down to the makeshift court, where the accused were caged in, having packed a package of food for the trialists. There were dense crowds of Africans demonstrating in the streets and as my mother arrived the police moved in, firing weapons and beating people back with their batons. My mother was shaken but, being white, managed to avoid being targeted by the police. She was lucky to manage to see Jacqueline. The news was abuzz on the radio and in the evening papers and my father was beside himself with worry. They had long arguments about my mother's attendance at the trial. She herself was shaken and intimidated. In the end she compromised by getting foodstuffs delivered to her cousin and the trialists via Jacqueline's sister, Charlotte Lowenstein, one-time Party member, who lived in Johannesburg and was attending the court hearings on a daily basis.

I was very attentive to what was going on but owing to it being my last few months of the matric year I confess I lost sight of the proceedings. The trialists were soon allowed bail and the hearing was cut to some 30 of the original detainees in 1958. They were all found not guilty in 1961. Like others, Jacqueline was freed to go home to Durban sooner than that.[56] She had remained cool and unperturbed throughout, her sole anxiety her two young daughters.

While I continued to attend synagogue on high holidays, regular attendance only lasted a couple of years past my bar mitzvah. On occasion I bumped into Teddy Gordon at the Yeoville synagogue and it was always interesting to exchange pleasantries with him. During my teens I more or less became an atheist; I had outgrown fairy tales and came to doubt the existence of a spiritual being. Even as a bar mitzvah boy I was questioning God for inflicting such barbarism on the world from the Nazi gas chambers to polio victims consigned to the iron lung. I could never buy the idea that human beings needed to be purified by undergoing such suffering. I found believers extremely intolerant of such questions raised. I had experienced this not only at the hands of my Hebrew teacher but in so many other ways. Although as a child I found the biblical stories beguiling, as I got to my 'teens I found them weird and unbelievable – Jonah living in the belly of a whale and Moses parting the Red Sea just didn't do it for me, never mind all the miracles attributed to Jesus. Why had God ceased to perform miracles in modern times, was something I wanted to know. People who claimed they were hearing voices were regarded as crazy so why did we take their word as the gospel in ancient times?

The story of Moses and the Exodus was one that fascinated me. If Moses was able to throw a stick to the ground in front of the Pharaoh and it turned into a serpent, then surely that was a conjurer's trick? I read the detailed account about Pharaonic Egypt in the glossy tome I received as a bar mitzvah gift. That at least was based on scientific fact. It was filled with photographs and artefacts that existed in museums from Cairo to London. The historical record of the reign of all the pharaohs found in the tombs was inscribed in hieroglyphics, which were translatable. I sought reference to Moses, the ten plagues, Exodus and the Pharaoh in pursuit perishing in the Red Sea. To my astonishment there was no such reference to Moses at all. Well, maybe that book was incomplete, I conceded, but the mystery engrossed my mind and in later years, in travels to Egypt, to Luxor and the Valley of the Kings, to the pyramids at Giza, and with all that antiquity on display, I was unable to track down a single reference to Moses.

Later on I read all sorts of books about the case for and against atheism but already in my teens I had come to the view that I could not accept through blind faith the existence of a spiritual being creating the universe and all life, whether described in the Book of Creation or in other ways. My reading led me to accept the theory of evolution as far more acceptable than some imaginary spirit creating the universe and our world even if the Seven Days of Creation and the Garden of Eden should be understood as symbols of God's work.

The germs of my earlier disbelief in God coincided with my re-addressing the Zionist narrative. I had certainly been caught hook, line and sinker when I was ten years old but a blind allegiance to Israel began to wither away, even though at that time I was not aware of the dispossession of Palestinian lands and rights through the systematic campaign of terror and ethnic cleansing of the *nakba*.[57] As I became a young adult I was finding my South African identity paramount. This was to develop with my entry, which was just a few years away, into the national liberation struggle. The reading and enlightenment I was to receive about Israel and the way the Palestinians had been dispossessed of their land, as was the case in other colonial settlements such as South Africa, led me to take up the just cause of the Palestinians in keeping with our struggle to free South Africa. It was ironic that when I began to raise my voice in criticism as a minister in South Africa against Israel's brutal aggression against the Palestinian people, a spokesperson of the Zionist Federation tried to smear me by claiming I was not a proper Jew and had most likely not even had a bar mitzvah. That was just one of the minor barbs fired at me.

Involvement with women was a completely different matter. I was rather shy at first, often tongue-tied and wishing I could think of things to say on the rare occasions that I was alone with a female other than a relative. Thankfully this did not last too long and by 16 I was very much at ease, having had several girlfriends, the majority of whom were Jewish. From the age of 17, when I began playing football with Ramblers, I forayed into new territory. There was an embarrassing episode when I found myself in the back of a car at a drive-in cinema in the clutches of one of the tough cookies who supported us. We started kissing and she began laughing out loud, telling her friend who was smooching in the front seat, 'This *larnie oke* hasn't French kissed in his life!' I owe her some gratitude for from that time on I never looked back.

I took a fancy to a German girl my age who was one of the most gorgeous young females in sight. I confided in my mother and once more she reiterated that not all Germans were bad. I withheld from René the fact that the blue-eyed Gisela happened to be the daughter of General von Mellenthin, who settled in South Africa after the war. He had served under Rommel in Africa as his chief of staff and on many other fronts with the unrepentant opinion, as asserted to the Americans that '... we always felt superior towards the Russians ... we were not afraid of them ...'[58] Gisela had many suitors, mainly young Germans, who clicked their heels in the general's presence at a tea party I was invited to. Witnessing that turned my stomach and I departed the scene in disgust, although not disgust with Gisela. She eventually became betrothed to my old friend Tony Bloom and they have had a very happy marriage. My mother would have held her in good stead, not blaming her for her father's sins. I did learn from Gisela that her mother had divorced the general and married an Englishman and that she had lived with them and not her father.

From our early teens we boys had sex on the brain, and the anxieties of where and how we could end our accursed virginity became paramount. Some of my friends achieved the target by spending ten shillings on prostitutes in Jeppe and Bree streets, which were notorious hangouts for down and out ladies of the night. That avenue did not appeal to me; one look at the wares on display put me off entirely. I continued suffering for a few more years, despising the tales some of my friends recounted ad nauseam.

There were the inevitable braggarts whose tales appeared improbable. One such guy, Nossie, insisted on giving me the name and phone number of a woman ironically called Virginia. He claimed that not only was she beautiful but also of very easy virtue. All I needed to do was give her a ring and say I was his friend. It was the way he described his encounter with her that made me believe he was living in a fantasy world. His story sounded like the lurid tales one read in the illegal pornographic magazines doing the rounds. There was even an epic poem as long as 'The Ancient Mariner' with the title 'Eskimo Nell' which passed from trembling hand to hand and was read in the toilet. I soon got back to Nossie with the appreciative news that I had made it with Virginia, although in fact I was simply testing him out and had never even attempted to meet her. I had indeed phoned the number just to check and indeed a voice answering to the name had responded, but I put the phone down. I gave him a description of my (purely fictitious) sexual encounter with Virginia. Even though I had no experience to speak of, that part was quite easy since I had heard stories about others' sexual exploits until the cows ambled home. All I did was poach from those and embellish my own rendering with the more lurid parts of Eskimo Nell.

It was clear from Nossie's response that he was flummoxed. He positively drooled with excitement, asking me to repeat this and that detail of my story. The way he hung onto my every word made me believe

I might have a career in writing for the pornographic magazines. I could see that like many of us Nossie still needed to summon up the courage to venture into the land of sexual intercourse.

Women were regarded as sexual objects and were divided into two categories: those who stubbornly clung onto their virginity until their wedding day – allegedly the Jewish girls; and those who would jump into bed at the drop of a hat, itching for the male organ – mythical Christian girls (especially Afrikaans girls) or *shiksas*. God help the Jewish boy who broke ranks with the tribe and married a *shiksa*. Even if they converted, they were never really regarded as the genuine article. There were stories about how some fathers totally dissociated themselves from their sons if that happened and sat what is called *shiva* – mourning for the dead. There were myths galore about how to arouse females of all ages into dropping their pants. Get them on the roundabouts at funfairs was one – this apparently excited them sexually. There was one boy who cited his older brother as getting dates 'hot' by taking them to the horse races. How's that, I asked. And then listened to the erudite theory about how girls would automatically rock back and forth as the horses galloped by, simulating sexual movements and not resting until they could be satisfied.

There was a young girl who lived in Berea, a suburb neighbouring Yeoville, and it was rumoured that she would allow her breasts to be fondled for five minutes for a shilling. A friend of mine managed to arrange a date with her. Out of apprehension he asked me to accompany him. I was naturally interested and, just in case, had twelve pence in my pocket. She was a freckle-faced redhead of about 15, not bad looking and with large breasts for her age. It was agreed that my pal would be first. I sat in the lounge reading body building magazines. I noticed some sports trophies on the mantelpiece and a photograph of a body builder who must have been her father. Before long I realised that my friend had managed to wheedle a hand-job from her. This had the effect of him begging her to keep going although his allocated time had expired. This went on for an additional five minutes without him climaxing. Five minutes more and his pleading did not abate. The exhortation went on and on without the conclusion he desired. He kept assuring her that it was just about to happen. I was feeling rather sorry for her; her hand must have been going lame.

Then in horror I heard the front door opening ... I prayed it wasn't her father, the bodybuilder. To my relief it turned out to be a domestic worker arriving with groceries. In any event the visit had come to an abrupt halt, with my friend going home visibly frustrated. He told me that despite the extension of time, he had only given the girl one shilling, which she had promptly put into a piggy-bank. For some reason this made me extremely depressed and I regretted having been party to the sordid event. I was haunted by the memory of what had happened to Bubbles Schroeder in 1949 and the involvement then of young Jewish men, regardless of whether they were innocent of her murder. I feared we could be propelling a 15-year-old towards that sticky end. Had I still been religious I would certainly have prayed for her soul. I went to a café and spent my shilling playing the pinball machines. I encountered her a couple of years later working as a dental receptionist. She looked smart and respectable in her white uniform, and her breasts were certainly alluring. Neither of us expressed any sign of recognition.

When I think back to those days of adolescent sexual predation, I experience an acute sense of shame, notwithstanding that it appeared to be a universal human conditioning to which we so easily succumbed.

My first steady relationship, and most indicative of my passing from being a young boy to becoming a young adult, was with a pretty girl a year younger than me named Suzette, who lived in a fine home in Houghton with a swimming pool. She had a slight gap between her two front teeth which I found very attractive. When she spoke, I found myself fixating on the gap. She spoke rapidly and the light glistened off the ivory whiteness of her teeth in the most tantalising way. She hadn't a clue why at times I appeared to be totally hypnotised; sometimes she would stop in the middle of a conversation to ask me if I was okay and I had to pretend that I was thinking of the importance of what she had just said. That mystified her even more, especially when she had merely been telling me something utterly mundane like that her cat was constipated. Although I was lusting to have sexual intercourse, when I lay in my bed thinking about Suzette it was always about her front teeth. She listened endlessly to the popular music of the day, such as the velvety voice of Johnny Mathis, for whom the girls went wild, and the phenomenon of

Elvis Presley, who unleashed an undreamed new passion in our lives. We would smooch on the dance floor at Saturday night parties to *Love Me Tender* and *Heartbreak Hotel*. By then, at the advanced age of 17, I had mastered the art of French kissing, which I regarded as the pinnacle of pleasure. Our mutual commitment was called 'going steady' for as long as it lasted and was taken very seriously, with the exchange of personal items such as bracelets. I gave Suzette mine, which was silver with my name engraved on it. My sister had given it to me for my 16th birthday. I would visit her in the evenings and her parents would allow me to stay until fairly late on weekends. They would have long gone to bed, leaving us smooching on a couch in the lounge listening to records. We got into divine petting sessions but never to the point of actual sexual intercourse. I was sure Suzette was a virgin, just as I was, both of us looking forward to the full experience of bringing this condition to a conclusion with an attractive partner.

My mind, however, was so full of the gory details of sex with a virgin as recounted by my ignorant friends that I felt I was not up to that kind of penetration. Because I lacked the skill, I felt I might harm her. Just when all the signals between us were ringing green for go I suffered from acute anxiety and the red light would begin flashing – stop! Regardless of this she always welcomed me and when her parents were out of the way, and Johnny Mathis was getting us in the right mood with his dreamy romantic tunes, the petting sessions were back on track. Despite my obsession about sex I found that I could enjoy her company by chatting about books and films, and began seeing her serious side. She was intelligent and I began to appreciate her mind as well as enjoy the physical attraction.

This relationship was about the time that I matriculated. I was soon to depart for the coast for a long summer break and Suzette was going elsewhere. We sensed maybe things would not be the same between us into 1957 when we were both due back in Joburg, so one night we gave it full throttle and I stepped on the accelerator. The end of innocence might have been reached, for the heightened tension resulted in both of us losing our inhibitions and it was not only I with the wandering hands. I forgot about my anxiety even as I began fiddling with the condom

I routinely kept in my pocket in those days – you never knew when an opportunity might arise. Just as the magical destination appeared within reach, beckoning us two innocents like a mirage in the desert that had just materialised, Suzette's father called out from the depths of his bedroom that it was time I went home. I consequently finished high school still a virgin into my 18th year and feeling I had been missing out on an essential experience, without which I could never remotely understand 'the meaning of life' or, as my best pal Vic Katz called it. 'The Royal Hunt of the Cunt'.

As I was saying my final farewells to Teddy Gordon and some of the other teachers, on a visit to KES early in 1957, nearby Louis Botha Avenue – the divide between Yeoville and Houghton – was witness to masses of Africans walking between the city and Alexandra township. They were engaged in a historic ten-week boycott of the buses owing to a penny rise in fares. These were the mean-looking single-deck Putco[59] buses, dubbed 'green mambas', normally overcrowded with down-at-heel African commuters, belching oily black gas into the atmosphere as they recklessly careered back and forth between town and township.

As usual KES boys were crossing the road at the traffic lights. I wondered what impact the desperate downtrodden protesters were making on their young minds. I thought that it would only be Teddy prodding them to think.

PART FOUR

1957–1958

Escape from the Grave

Sleep my little baby – oh
Sleep until you waken
When you wake you'll see the world
If I'm not mistaken...

Kiss a lover
Dance a measure
Find your name
And buried treasure...

Face your life
It's pain,
It's pain
It's pleasure,
Leave no path untaken.

– Neil Gaiman, *The Graveyard Book*

CHAPTER 12

A Short Walk with July

A POST-MATRIC VACATION WITH PALS in Durban, among them Peter Louis and Jasper Brener, had me pining for Suzette, despite the wild parties we engaged in at the coast. The only memorable event of note was a ridiculous pub brawl between us so-called Vaalies and Banana Boys following an impromptu arm-wrestling contest.[60]

After the holiday break I passed my driving test but was generally at a loose end, pondering what to do with my life, and feeling depressed for, as anticipated, Suzette had moved on and was going steady with another beau. I never saw her again but years later in exile one of her former chums gossiped that she had become a librarian and was drab-looking because she did not bother with make-up. The young woman telling me all this had become a bimbo – a typical Johannesburg *kugel* (all teased and lacquered hairdo, war-paint and fancy robes) and didn't realise that I was impressed about Suzette's preference for looking natural. Who needed make-up, I thought, when you had such a sexy gap between your two front teeth? I asked her to pass on my fond regards.

I was more in need of the elusive ending of my frustrating sexual status. Against my better instincts, I was lured by a friend to foray into the less reputable parts of downtown Johannesburg where the ladies of the night plied their wares in the notorious Troye and Bree street area on the rundown east side of town. We met two bedraggled-looking women over drinks in a shabby hotel. They wore cheap clothing with off-the-shoulder blouses designed for young women half their age. Their make-up was plastered on, they reeked of cheap perfume, and the phrase 'mutton dressed as lamb' came readily to mind. I felt terribly sad for them for life had not treated them kindly. A big show was made of ordering preposterous cocktails in loud voices that hopelessly aped upper-class accents. They were tired and worn out and struck me as desperately in need of cash. We purchased a packet of Peter Stuyvesant King Size smokes at the request of the ladies before proceeding to the downbeat rental where they claimed they lived.

In a room full of packing cases and odd items of machinery I found myself on a battered couch with one of the pair, while my friend was already active with the lady of his choice. I could hear the squeaking of an asthmatic old bed in the room next door. My partner asked me whether I had a 'letter' and for a moment I actually thought she was requesting some form of written introduction until she added – 'a French letter'. As I fumbled for the condom all interest drained from me. I made some excuses and beat a hasty retreat, leaving a ten-shilling note in the woman's hand, having to explain myself to my friend afterwards.

Then I struck gold. It is common experience that something you have long sought and felt would never arrive appears when least expected. I was with my friend Vic Katz at the Clarendon Cinema in Hillbrow when I heard a cheerful voice calling: 'Well, if it isn't the Lone Ranger long vanished.' I was pleasantly surprised to find myself in the company of two Ramblers soccer fans, Melanie and Jill. They were staying at an aunt's in the area and readily accepted an invitation to join us for drinks. One thing led to another and we retired to Vic's Houghton home. His parents were conveniently away on a holiday. Being in an upmarket residence was fascinating for the girls and they gazed at the chandelier in the entrance hall with awe. Jill was attractive, with the knowing look of a damsel experienced in the art of lovemaking. As we got into Vic's parents' double bed (Vic was with Melanie in his own room) all inhibitions vanished and we melted into one another's arms – might I add body and soul. At last I was at peace. Afterwards Jill and I shared a fag. She had been everything I desired. There were no pressing questions about whether I was a first-timer, which I had feared might arise, so I felt particularly proud of what I regarded as my command performance. Most of all I felt I could happily die since I was no longer a virgin.

As luck and circumstance would have it, I was able to make full use of the romance. It turned out Jill was staying with her aunt for a few weeks, a convenient drive from Vic's place. My father was generous in letting me borrow his car some nights. I had access to a garden cottage at Vic's and on and off (no pun intended) for almost a month had a royal time with the long-legged, green-eyed and ever willing Jill. She was confident in water and we would swim endlessly in the pool where even there she would take me to new heights of experience.

As I swim, lost in memory, the tadpoles have long been sorted – always more to catch – but most are under control and herded into sequence.

Jill soon disappeared to a job on the Natal coast where her family lived and we lost touch. But after a few years when I, too, had a job in Durban and played in a company cricket team, there she was, babe in arms and married to one of the Ramblers guys in the opposing team.[61] When the teams socialised over lunch I was able to chat with her and even hold her baby.

Meanwhile I was still at a loose end in Johannesburg, still unsure about what to do with myself. I had thought of either journalism or law but had made no moves in either direction. A relative directed me to an attorney's office, M&J Marks and Kaplan, who were looking for a clerk. If I took the clerk's job it meant I would have to sign on at law school. I got the job and was officially employed at the princely salary of £7.10 a month. I attended late afternoon classes at Wits University. The firm was situated on the fourth floor of Eagle Star House in Commissioner Street, an elegant 1930s art deco construction. This was slap in the middle of Johannesburg's CBD, the streets of which were thronged with crowds of bustling pedestrians and heavy traffic. This was a white man's city – even though the majority were Africans, migrant workers living on the periphery – established as such from the earliest gold rush days and laid out in an orderly rectangular block system according to British design, with impressive colonial buildings, upmarket department stores and grand banks. The city had grown dynamically from the very early days of the 20th century with major streets like Joubert, Jeppe, Eloff and Rissik named after its founding fathers and said to be paved with gold. It had all the hallmarks of stability and progress of any white colonial city from Auckland to Belfast, Ottawa to Sydney. Many of the buildings were architectural gems, such as Anstey's department store with its prestigious upper floor penthouses. This had what is referred to as a ziggurat design, the structure rising upwards in step formation like a Mayan temple, much narrower at the apex than at its base. This had the effect of allowing shafts of sunlight to cut across the streets, where other rectangular skyscrapers cut out the light – a photographer's dream. Architectural students visiting from provincial towns would suffer from very stiff necks looking upwards in wonder at Johannesburg's Manhattan-style skyline. It was a very modern city except on the heavily policed periphery where black and brown commuters were disgorged or picked up at grimy bus stations, served by unsavoury eateries, filthy kiosks and muti stores, providing traditional medicines, where no white person dared tread. Such places were Noord and Diagonal – streets that were never free of the stench of diesel, where dog-tired passengers lined up in lengthy queues for the second-class buses to take them home, having to contend with bag snatchers and knife-wielding tsotsis.

Izzy 'Kappie' Kaplan, who hired me for the job, was an affable, nondescript man who proved very easy to work with. His elderly partner, Joe Marks, turned out to be reclusive and I had very little to do with him. He was the initial 'J' of M&J Marks of the practice. He had been in partnership with his father, M. Marks, who was deceased. Joe Marks, the son, was addressed by all and sundry as M&J. He was a kindly old man who apparently only dealt in company law. He had a round baby face framed by a wispy beard, and a large beige hearing-aid plugged into one ear. 'Kappie' Kaplan gave me instructions and he was moderately busy Monday to Friday mornings. On Friday afternoons, however, his inner office turned into a poker club. Several of his legal associates and clients made up the school. A dedicated female secretary, Shirley Gould, ran the office and kept Kaplan on track. She compromised on the Friday poker club and with an assistant provided drinks and snacks all afternoon. I heard from fellow articled clerks that this was not uncommon around town. In later years I learned from Joe Slovo, who was a practising advocate before he became full-time revolutionary, that he likewise played poker in a similar school with his friend and comrade Harold Wolpe, who ran a legal partnership with his brother-in-law, Jimmy Kantor, in the next-door office block.[62]

The person I learned most from was the African messenger, July Marishane. He was a lanky man, well over a decade older than me, with the ebony hew of the Venda people of the country's north, with large expressive eyes which opened wide with wonder when appropriate or cool and impassive when on guard. In time I came to perceive an uncommon nobility about him. July explained all the clerical work to me and I joined him on short walks to the nearby Magistrate's Court where we registered our documents for official delivery such as summonses and writs of attachment and so on amid the clamour of busy clerks and bureaucrats. I had been looking forward to life in the law courts learning the art of cross-examination and defence but was given the inglorious task of debt collector for a faceless firm called Credit Control which sought to extract money owed to a leading retailer. I had hundreds of cases on file in my pokey office of unfortunates who had purchased goods on hire purchase and got behind payment and into debt. Once the firm concerned found that they could not extract payment they handed the case over to Credit Control. That ultimately meant to me.

My starting point was sending out a letter of demand. If no payment was forthcoming on due date a summons was then sent to the debtor. Perhaps 20% of those in receipt of a summons came in to see me; many of the others appeared to simply dissolve in the twilight. These were always poor working-class people, male and female, white, black, Indian and coloured. They were invariably apologetic and promised with the utmost conviction to resume payment without delay. They well knew if they reneged the next step would be the sheriff of the court serving a writ of attachment on them, by which he could remove goods and property to the value of their outstanding debt plus interest and legal fees piled on. They all treated me with excessive respect far beyond my station. At times there would be a policeman who had defaulted on payments and I would be treated as though I was an officer of the court. Yet there were no pretences on my part. Not only was I a youngster half the age of most of the people concerned but you could scarcely swing a cat in my office. I took time to explain the situation clearly and as humanely as I could, and afforded them the dignity they deserved. I tried my best to explain how the system worked and generally implored them to avoid entering into an HP contract which, I explained, was a way of swindling them. But what could they do? They needed to buy furniture or clothing for their children and invariably only had enough for the initial down payment, easily falling into the debt trap. I pitied them and came to regard them as my clients rather than me working for a company called Credit Control. After a meeting with a 'client' I had to diarise the file for a date in the near future. I hoped that when I next saw that file – it was July who placed documents on my desk for attention every morning – my 'client' would have kept to his or her commitment and made the promised payment. I experienced guilt pangs when I found that if this was not the case, it meant trouble for the debtor.

I soon found that going to work in the mornings was a dread. I knew what awaited me: several files of clients who had failed in their commitments. It always made me recall my schooldays fascination with Charles Dickens' characters, the fate in particular of Mr Micawber and the debtor's jail of 19th-century England. I was tempted to relate to my clients Mr Micawber's famous recipe for happiness, which always eluded him:

> *Annual income twenty pounds, annual expenditure nineteen [pounds] nineteen [shillings] and six [pence], result happiness. Annual income twenty pounds, annual expenditure twenty pounds nought and six, result misery.*[63]

As for debtors who changed address to avoid a writ of attachment, the procedure was to turn the matter over to a tracing agency which employed 'detectives' to track the offenders down. The artful ones often changed address to make themselves scarce – and good luck to them. I knew of Jewish families who did just that or adopted other ploys. A distant relative was inclined to order a piano on trial and enjoy some 30 days of free practice and even making a little income by giving private tuition to students. The instrument would be sent back by the 'dissatisfied' customer, who would order a piano from a different supplier and so on. Who was I to be judge in such matters, where even those who could afford to pay were constantly working on ways to beat the system? I had no qualms about mislaying the Credit Control file of the most destitute of my clients.

I was relieved that I had nothing to do with the trackers except when the occasional one came seeking information which might assist them. They were either retired policemen or enthusiastic youngsters who had failed matric. The former smoked non-stop, looked like they possessed only one rumpled suit and wore battered hats. The latter were more irritating, over enthusiastic and asking questions they had learned from the movies or from reading Sherlock Holmes. I made a pretence of being serious in searching my brain for any clues, but never ever gave them as much as the time of day. On one occasion I remember playing the fool with one of the sleuths by pondering on the incessant coughing of the man he was pursuing and suggesting he check out the TB patients at the General Hospital.

It wasn't as though I had any inbuilt respect for authority. My schooldays were evidence of that. The battle between 'them' and 'us' was played out on the streets daily, as police hunted for pass offenders among the throngs of overwhelmingly white pedestrians, shoppers, smatterings of black messengers, street cleaners and job seekers – the latter being their targets. Distorted views were evidence enough among even my fellow articled clerks, who would meet on a nearby corner every afternoon for a lift to law school. One future officer of the court jeered inanely about an African messenger mounting a moped. 'Just look at this squint-eyed boy trying to ride a scooter.' The man turned to him and gave him a piece of his mind. 'The black chickens and the white chickens live peacefully together,' he chided our associate, 'so why can't we human beings? Do you realise how backward you are parading your ignorance?'

White racist attitudes were rife and all around us. My grandfather's driver, a quiet man called Morris Maloi, sometimes drove me into town. It was almost murder when a white driver was held up behind him if he failed to pull away smartly enough at a traffic light. The road rage was palpable as the motorist would swerve dangerously around us, hooting like mad, give Morris the finger and scream, 'You effing k.....!' Morris would simply look ahead but I would notice his knuckles turn white as he gripped the steering wheel. His quiet dignity spoke volumes in comparison to the oafishness of those who insulted him. Such vocal blows rained like vomit on the heads of Africans throughout South Africa every day and one could just imagine the actual physical onslaught often – but not always – out of sight.

On cold winter nights outside the cinemas, small groups of African urchins begged for coins from the well-heeled whites, while always being on alert for the police. It wasn't an uncommon sight to see these kids being chased by policeman lashing out with their truncheons. The white crowds were generally indifferent. Saw no evil – heard no evil. Life simply went on. How many blows would it take, I thought, before the explosion?

One day July Marishane fell victim to the police traps. They patrolled the streets assiduously, with backstops hiding down alleyways waiting to pounce on any luckless victim trying to slip away. Those who were caught were unceremoniously thrown into a pick-up truck if they had no passbook or if it was not in order. It was a hot day and July had left his jacket with his reference book in an inside pocket back at the office as he strolled down to the Magistrate's Court on an errand. The fact that he had a briefcase with court papers inside made no difference to the zealous police. Fortunately, we were alerted to the incident by someone who knew where July worked and an enraged Izzy Kaplan had him released. Otherwise July would have disappeared into the potato fields.

On one memorable occasion we heard singing and chanting welling up from the street. Looking down from our windows we saw a massive crowd of Africans with banners marching along Commissioner Street with the traffic grinding to a halt while anxious motorcycle police tried to head them off. This scene electrified July who ran downstairs to join the crowd without a second's thought. He was away for several hours. When he returned, I was eager to know what the commotion had been about. He explained that the ANC had marched to the Supreme Court to hand in a memorandum protesting current apartheid laws being passed in the whites-only Parliament.

The battle between the races was evident in our own building. There were two lifts, one manned by a surly old white attendant in a tan dust jacket, who would not allow black passengers, and a dilapidated service lift meant for them which was often out of action. Even then he would not allow any black people in his 'white' lift. Even if his lift was empty and they had heavy parcels for the top tenth floor, they had to use the stairs. There did not even appear to be a policy or notice to that effect in place. He was the overlord and assumed he could do what he pleased. Whenever July was with me, I bade him follow me into the lift. The attendant would stall, waiting for the lift to fill up with whites so that he could order July out but even then, we stood our ground. His pugnacious glare reminded me of that anti-Semitic bully Mr Smart at KES. If he stalled too long, I would turn to him and tell him to get a move on as important work was awaiting Mr Marishane and me. I told July not to be intimidated by the man, saying that he could not control his fears. July thought about this but responded by saying that it wasn't so much fear but that the man had a grievance with life. I didn't think much more about it other than pondering on the depth to July's persona who was a simple man from the rural areas.

One day we received a file from Credit Control opening a case against a Mr Wessels for a few hundred-rand worth of furniture. To our amazement in response to a letter of demand the lift attendant, his tail metaphorically between his legs, came to see me. Instead of his dust coat he had put on a cheap sports jacket and tie for the occasion. At first I thought he was coming to make a complaint connected to the use of the lift. No, he said, he was Mr Jacobus Wessels responding to my letter. He was extremely contrite and explained that he was having trouble paying off the debt for a bed he had bought for his children, who had been sleeping on the floor. This was an example of a 'poor white' given sheltered employment, which normally would have gone to a black man, who was battling for survival, and in his ignorance took out his frustration on 'the other'. I asked July to make a cup of tea for Mr Wessels and settled his nerves, for the poor fellow was in an awful state of embarrassment and anxiety. I managed to negotiate a very small monthly repayment on the outstanding debt to

Credit Control on the basis that we could vouch for Mr Wessels' steady employment under our very nose. From then on his lift became a race-free zone – and not only for July.

This incident made me think of July's initial assessment of the lift attendant's hostility and how much closer to the mark his judgement had been than mine. It was not the last time I found this fine insight into human beings of African people. When life is a struggle you develop a facility for assessing the personality of others.

July once told me that I was very different from most whites and I thought he was referring to this incident. No, he told me, it was not just that; it was because I always had a friendly smile for black people, whereas most whites did not even see them and displayed what he referred to as 'a brick face'. In his view Mr M&J was a decent man who had given him opportunities in life. He had first employed him as a gardener when he was an illiterate man from the Limpopo region of the country and had come to Johannesburg seeking work. The family had taught him to read and write and once he could do so satisfactorily Mr M&J had employed him in the office. July hoped to better himself even further and was hoping to achieve a Standard Six school pass. On some Friday afternoons while the office poker game was in session, and there was no law school for me, we spent a few hours going over his studies.

If my work had only been Credit Control, I would have gone crazy and quit the job. I had to prove myself to my parents who had been worried about my restlessness and thought my getting a university entrance matric pass was a fluke. My father could not afford to pay my university fees so I opted to do law as an articled clerk. The pay was pathetic but I didn't have to pay for food or rent at home which helped a great deal. My sister had got married very young and had two children so my mother was very engrossed with her. I needed to persist with my studies at law school, which was something of a mission for I soon became bored and distracted. Like most youngsters, I wanted to reach for the stars. This was at the time the Soviet Union launched the first rocket into space, the Sputnik satellite. I watched it orbiting the earth one night with my father and grandfather. We could see it clearly crossing the star-studded night sky over Johannesburg. Both of them were impressed that Russia, which had been so backward, had achieved this scientific feat. My father marvelled at what he termed man's entry into the space age and what could be achieved by human ingenuity. My grandad, ever the wit, yelled up at Sputnik: 'Ride him, Cocky!'

Such achievements made me even more dissatisfied with my mundane duties at work. A couple of criminal cases I became involved in aroused my interest, though, and kept me on track for the time being at M&J Marks and Kaplan.

CHAPTER 13

Uncertain Justice

My boss Izzy Kaplan instructed me to drive down to the Wynberg police station, next to Alexandra township, and interview our client. 'Ask to see Kollie Moffat Kubeka,' he told me. 'He's being held on a rape charge.' I drove in his car, a very modest Morris Minor, along Louis Botha Avenue, past my old school KES, giving way to boys in their green blazers crossing at the traffic lights, and on to my destination – remembering Teddy Gordon's reference to the French Revolution and Alexandra township.

Once off the main highway I drove a short distance along a rutted dirt road, squalid buildings and shacks on either side and thickening knots of township people. Women hawkers sold fruit, vegetables and the ubiquitous roasted mealies where the green mamba buses disgorged their commuters – the sickening smell of diesel fumes polluting the air. I parked outside a solidly built police complex flying the national flag. There were dozens of police vehicles of varying descriptions parked at the rear, a posse of khaki-clad armed policemen lounging around near the entrance, and a very busy charge office dominated by a portrait of the country's new prime minister, Dr J.G. Strijdom, 'The Lion of the North',[64] sternly gazing at all and sundry. I presented myself at a long counter. I thought I'd have to wait a long time for assistance but after getting the attention of the officer on duty and telling him what my business was, I soon found myself ushered into a small reception office with a table and chairs. Before long a burly man was ushered into the room by a policeman. He was panting and coughing in distress. He was handcuffed and in leg-irons. After ascertaining who he was, I shook hands as best as I could and asked the policeman to release him from his chains. The policeman told me he could remove the handcuffs but the leg-irons had to remain. 'You've no idea how many of these *donners* escape from here the moment our backs are turned,' he told me in the most humourless way possible. He pulled back a chair from the table to sit a short distance from us. Kaplan had alerted me to such a move with an instruction to insist that any escort had to respect legal privilege and wait outside. With tired indifference the policeman agreed, addressing me as 'sir'. 'As you wish,' he said. 'Just call out if there's trouble.'

The moment we were alone I offered our client a cigarette, lit up a couple for both of us, and gave him the pack and the matches. I enquired about his health. He told me he was asthmatic and was waiting for his wife to bring him his medication. I told him that the interview could take a couple of hours so how about something to eat. I relayed out an order to the policeman, who was outside the door, to buy some pies, chips and a couple of Cokes at a nearby store, telling him to get a drink for himself as inducement. As much as the police revelled in their power, the authoritarian nature of the culture was such that they displayed respect even for green 'lawyers' like myself. I don't think they realised how lowly an undergraduate articled clerk was.

Kollie Moffat Kubeka was a taxi driver by occupation, who drove a bright yellow American car and lived in Pimville, on the other side of town. He had dropped off his female passenger in Alexandra township the week before. She had been drinking in Sophiatown, was somewhat inebriated and had invited him to join her for a nightcap in a local shebeen. In a rather hang-dog way he told me he had agreed, at that point looking down at the floor and speaking in a very sombre voice, clearly embarrassed. Our food and drink arrived, which gave me the chance to get him to relax. While he devoured his food, clearly very hungry, I pushed my pie over to him and saw him react with unconcealed surprise. 'You sure you don't need this, boss?' he asked. I told him not to call me boss and we continued where we had left off. As the story went they had a very convivial time in the tavern, both of them getting rather drunk, she more so than he since she had had a head start. She was staggering when they left so he helped her to her room in a shack in the back yard of a house. She disrobed except for her petticoat and lay on the bed while he made some coffee. He said they began embracing and that she had helped him remove his shoes and clothing as a prelude to consensual intercourse. He said he had left her snoring like a merry machine before daylight. Three days later the police arrested him at a taxi rank in Sophiatown on a rape charge and had held him in the Wynberg cells since. He knew of Mr Kaplan through July Marishane, who was a friend.

I had written this all down in a notebook and then asked him to clarify a few things. Had there been any other persons party to the event, I asked him, either her and her friends or his? No, he replied. Were there any witnesses in the shebeen who could comment on their behaviour? Sure, he answered. The place was full and he couldn't say whether any of the patrons had noticed them for any particular reason because everybody was drinking heavily and involved with their own affairs. But the shebeen queen who had been serving them would surely remember. Only he couldn't really direct me to the premises as it was unfamiliar territory to him and he had no idea of the address. There were no street names in the warren of back lanes, sometimes just chalked numbers on doors. If he could get out, he would be able to take me and find the place, he said hopefully.

What about the place where the woman lived, I asked. Was there anyone else in her shack? Were the people in the main house at home? Had anyone seen them enter the shack? He shook his head to all these questions. The main house was in total darkness so the people there must have been fast asleep. If she had cried out for help, I asked, would they have heard her? Of course, he answered, the shack was next to the house and all the windows were open because it was a warm night. But she had kept perfectly quiet because she didn't want to disturb them; in fact when they arrived home she had kept telling him to shush.

In what way had she invited him into her room, was my next question. Well, he explained somewhat tentatively, it just happened. 'Did you push your way in?' I asked. 'Oh no,' he answered quickly, 'we literally squeezed through the door together. She was holding onto me. I had to help her. But she did make me feel welcome, I can assure you of that. I was no intruder, boss – I mean, sir.'

Then I came to the major question because we needed to be absolutely certain.

'Are you sure you didn't force yourself on her?'

'No!'

'There was no struggle?'

'No!'

'Are you absolutely certain that she consented to the lovemaking? The sexual intercourse?'

'Yes! Yes! She was very co-operative,' he repeated, looking me straight in the eyes. 'She desired it as much as I did. You know how it is with the booze.'

'Then why would she be laying a charge of rape against you, Mr Kubeka?'

He was clearly at a loss to provide an answer. His head sagged. His body was weary. He shook his head, muttering, 'I just can't say, sir…'

'Okay, Mr Kubeka, never mind that, I'm satisfied with your story,' I told him.

He must have been thinking the worst, that maybe we would not agree to defend him. So I got that in quickly, not wanting to prolong his agony. His face lit up for the first time with some hope in his eyes. He gratefully clasped my hands and, almost sobbing, his big chest heaving, lowered his head in prayer: 'Nkosi'am! Siyabonga!' (My Lord, thank you!)

I told him that I would be reporting to my boss Mr Kaplan and it was he who would be defending him in court. I said I would also be present to assist my principal and that we would try and press the prosecution for an as early as possible court hearing but warned him that this could take many months. I asked him if he had any funds or property to put up bail as we would be applying for that. He mentioned his car as his only asset and I told him that would be acceptable.

Before leaving I read through my notes to make sure I had everything covered. A few thoughts came to mind. I realised I had left out some crucial details. How old was the woman? Was she perhaps married or did she have a boyfriend who might not have been around at the time? Had she perhaps inadvertently given him a clue? He thought long about this. I could see him thinking hard, trying to recollect maybe something she had said.

'Yes,' he said finally. 'When I picked her up in Sophiatown, and we got talking, she said thank God her man was away otherwise he would beat her for getting intoxicated.'

'And what about her age?' I asked.

'Oh, she must have been about 30 years old.'

'And you?'

'I'm 60,' he said. 'I'm a grandfather. I live with my wife in Pimville and she is furious with me, but at least she forgives, she comes to see me and brings some food. Please ask Mr Kaplan to try and get that bail?' He started coughing again, holding his chest.

'How soon are you getting the medication?' I asked.

'Oh, my wife's coming this afternoon,' he told me, which put my mind somewhat at ease.

When I got back to the office I gave a full report to Izzy Kaplan, both verbal and typewritten. He wasn't so confident about getting bail. The prosecution would say there was too much of a risk of Kubeka absconding, but we would try anyway, he said. In the event the bail application failed and it took the better part of the year before Kollie Moffat Kubeka came to trial in the Wynberg magistrate's court which was linked to Alexandra township.

In the interim we had July Marishane scouting around the township and checking on the various shebeens. Although vastly overcrowded, the settlement occupied a very small space of one square mile, which made his task easier. I had the feeling that he would be able to ferret out some information. It was not difficult in the end to actually trace the woman because her name and address were on the charge sheet but he also managed to identify a couple of shebeens that were close by. In one of those the patronne – the shebeen queen – was easily able to verify the couple's presence because everybody had been talking about the rape accusation. She was able to inform him that the couple were drinking freely and getting on well together. The main information July learned was that the woman lived with a boyfriend or husband – it didn't really matter which – who was with her off and on. Izzy Kaplan's theory was that the man must have discovered that someone else had been invited into his bed and stayed the night. To defend herself the woman most probably had claimed that the taxi driver had forced his way into the shack and raped her. Her man would have compelled her to lay the charge. Her identification of Kubeka, a very large man, and his make of car being an unusual colour, would have assisted them to identify him at the Sophiatown taxi rank.

On the day the case came to trial I took a seat next to Izzy Kaplan. The courtroom was jampacked with members of the public who were there not only for our case. The prosecutor, a man in a cheap grey suit with matching grey shoes and grey eyes peering through round spectacles, over a shabby grey moustache, had come over to greet us and apologised that the court would need an hour to get through some straightforward pass law offences. 'Don't worry,' he told us with cheerful optimism, 'there won't be a hold-up – these people can't afford a lawyer.'

The court orderly barked out in Afrikaans for everyone to stand for the magistrate and glared at the township residents as though warning them to behave. The magistrate looked like the Afrikaner equivalent of St John B. Nitch in his black robe. Except he was not bald but had a head of thick grey hair topping off his angular face, his narrow eyes, his sinister bearing.

The next hour, for someone new to the scene like myself, was unbelievable. A procession of men of all ages in wretched condition, looking wary and broken, were paraded before the magistrate, one at a time, for pass law offences. In quick succession every single one was found guilty and sentenced to several months imprisonment. A few who tried to explain the circumstances of having forgotten their identity book at home, and now had it in hand to show the court, had their explanations brushed aside, the prosecutor interrupting by stating for the record that under the pass laws it was an offence not to have your reference book in your possession when out on the streets. Those who could produce the wretched identity documents had the sentence reduced from three months to one. For two hours we sat as though watching a factory conveyor-belt in operation. This was apartheid law in action – at the sharp end a labour management system ensuring white employers, particularly on farms, of a steady stream of cheap black labour. At that point in time I was unaware of the farm labour scandal but nevertheless I was deeply depressed at the injustice playing out before our very eyes.

The magistrate looked at his watch and announced a short adjournment for tea. Over a cup with the prosecutor he exchanged small-talk with us and for some reason found the need to divulge a dream he'd had the night before which bothered him. He had dreamed he was a black man in the township which was being bombed by aeroplanes. He was shouting to the skies that he was a white man but that made no difference. He was clearly upset and asked Kaplan what he thought of his dream. I was struggling to contain my mirth, realising how delicious it was that people such as he should be plagued by the system which they had put in place. Serves him bloody well right, I thought, while Izzy Kaplan tried to humour him.

When court resumed and the magistrate had taken his seat the orderly called out *Regina v. Kollie Moffat Kubeka*. South Africa was still a member of the Commonwealth and court cases were being prosecuted on behalf of the English monarch – hence Regina.[65] The accused took his place in the dock. Kubeka had on a well-pressed suit and tie which his wife must have delivered to him. After a couple of police witnesses gave evidence concerning the laying of the charge the first witness of note was called, who happened to be the plaintiff herself.

As the woman took the stand, I realised I'd left out a crucial detail in my discussion with Mr Kubeka. She was a massive lady, easily his size but extremely portly. The thought must have struck Izzy Kaplan at the same time it struck me. If it had been rape, even if she had been in a drunken state, it would have taken a tremendous physical effort to subdue her. Yet we knew from Kubeka's condition as an asthmatic that he was in a bad shape. This was not a period of gender sensitivity and even though I had a tender attitude to women I must confess that uppermost in our minds was finding a way to get a verdict in our client's favour, not for unprincipled reasons but because we felt he was genuinely innocent.

We sat through the prosecutor attempting to be sensitive about body parts and sexual intercourse but he and the court clearly had a well-trod formula. 'Private parts' was the term used to refer to the intimate parts of the male and female anatomies. The plaintiff's story was of a simple taxi ride home, no mention of drinking bouts beforehand, but alleging the driver had forced his way into her room and raped her on the spot. She had attempted to resist but he was too powerful for her and had managed to subdue her, hold her down on her bed, fiddle with her 'private parts' and penetrate her with his 'private part'. The only physical evidence shown in court were her dress and underclothes, including her panties, which were a huge spotless white pair of bloomers.

We had almost reached the lunch break. The magistrate asked the lawyer for the defence whether he wished to start his cross-examination. Izzy Kaplan, in a very confident manner, said he would like an early call after lunch because he felt he could come to an agreement with the prosecutor in the interim, which could possibly assist the court in terms of time. This caused quite a stir in the courtroom and an anxious look from our client. I wondered what my boss was up to. Over lunch with the prosecutor Kaplan told him that there was absolutely no case for his client to answer and that valuable time could be saved if the prosecutor withdrew the charge. The man looked quizzically through his round spectacles, all ears, gesturing to Kaplan to proceed with his explanation.

'It's very simple,' my principal explained. 'You have presented evidential proof in court that no rape could possibly have taken place.'

The prosecutor's expression begged for explanation.

'Are you sure the underwear were the actual items of clothing on the night?' Kaplan asked.

'Yes indeed,' was the reply.

'Then how come if there had been such a struggle, as she claimed, such a flimsy garment as those panties had not even the smallest of tears? Surely they would have been ripped?'

The prosecutor was nonplussed. He could not stop blinking. He had no real interest in upholding the claim of a black woman, after all. One could read that in his features. If he could prove that one African was in the wrong over another, he would prosecute but now, in the light of what Kaplan was saying, you could see the wind emptying from his sails. He didn't want to give in that easily, that was clear, and Kaplan knew that.

'Well, Mr Prosecutor, you think about it,' he said. 'I've got a very strong defence. Look at the size of that woman. Kubeka is 30 years older and he is not a well man. To have subdued her without so much as a scratch on her body and her flimsy underwear intact is quite frankly unbelievable. I have evidence and witnesses to show the lady had been on a drinking spree from before she took the taxi ride home, and continued with Kubeka in a shebeen before inviting him into her home. This is going to be a long case, Mr Prosecutor, and you don't have a leg to stand on. She laid that charge because her husband was away that night, found out about her infidelity on his return and she had to lie to him that she had been raped to save her skin. '

I saw the lump in the man's throat – his Adam's apple – moving awkwardly as he swallowed hard. 'Let me think about this before court resumes,' he responded at last. 'I might have a word with the magistrate.' He left us and Kaplan gave me a broad wink. We didn't have all those witnesses lined up but one could see the need to pile on the pressure to get an acquittal.

The case was ready for resumption that afternoon when the magistrate entered and we all rose. The prosecutor stood up, looking a trifle pale, I thought. He announced that he wished to make an announcement and the magistrate, as though on cue, nodded his assent.

The prosecutor addressed the magistrate first. 'Your Worship,' he said, 'I wish to announce that I am withdrawing the charge of rape against the accused in the dock. It is clear to me after the plaintiff's evidence in chief, that no rape could have in fact taken place as she claimed.'

There was a clamour in court and the magistrate barked for order.

The prosecutor then asked the orderly to hold up the outsize bloomers. So huge they could scarcely be referred to as panties. All eyes in court were on the bloomers. One felt the fate of Kollie Moffat Kubeka lay within its ample expanse. The eyes of the plaintiff and of the accused met fleetingly over the nylon sheen displayed before them and the onlookers. I wondered what must be going on in both their minds.

The prosecutor took up the thread of his narrative again. 'This humble article of clothing, which the plaintiff claims was forcefully removed from her body to allow the accused to rape her, is the silent witness of his innocence and of her false testimony. Your Worship, it is not possible that this article of clothing could have survived such an assault without the garment being ripped apart.' He paused to choose his next two words to maximum effect: 'Rent apart!' as though taken from the Bible. 'Your Worship,' he continued, 'it is my legal responsibility to withdraw the prosecution's case against the accused.'

There was a long pause and an excited buzz in the court. Itching to assert himself, the magistrate banged his gavel several times, calling for order. The prosecutor, drawing himself up to his full height and addressing the magistrate, said he had a few words to say to the public and could he be permitted to proceed? Again on cue the magistrate nodded his assent. First in a low, controlled voice, which required the people in the public gallery to lean forward to follow him, he said that the accused had been lucky because the court was always prepared to see both sides of a story. He wished to warn Kubeka and all those males present against 'the township Jezebels' who were devils of temptation that came in different guises. The prosecutor gazed at the citizens of Alexandra township for a long minute as he looked from side to side of the courthouse. In a strident school-masterly tone he warned them not to waste the state's time and money by presenting false testimony. He said he would be looking into a case of perjury against the plaintiff. Law and order was sacred, and the duty of the police was to defend that. The duty of the public was to play their part, otherwise the whole land would face a catastrophe in which every single man, woman and child, irrespective of colour or background, would be destroyed as in the biblical story of Sodom and Gomorrah. 'Remember,' he said sternly, looking directly at the woman who had brought the charge against Kubeka, 'what had happened to Lot's wife.' The courtroom sat, hushed. 'Turned into a pillar of salt!' the prosecutor intoned menacingly.

The man must have imagined himself in the pulpit as the glazed look in his eyes, probably influenced by the nightmare he had experienced the day before, drove him on to the vision of Armageddon. Either way, he was clearly losing the plot. 'The dangers assailing our country from many quarters are right here in this community,' he barked out, 'where there are people aligned with sinister forces planning to bring us to our knees. The courts, the police and the army, the prisons, are God's ordained defenders of our civilisation from communism and anarchy. Tell the people out there of what we have learned here today.' And he pointed over the heads of the public to the imagined demons out in the township. With that peroration he sat down, wiping the sweat from his brow.

The magistrate banged his gavel for attention and in a quiet and subdued voice said what we had been waiting to hear.

'Kollie Moffat Kubeka, the case against you has been withdrawn and you are free to go.'

Years later, when one has learned to be far more sensitive to the plight of women in relation to the inequal power relations between the sexes, I feel pangs of sympathy for the woman in this case, and the offensive way she was belittled by the prosecutor. I have no doubt that there was consensual agreement between her and the man we defended. His accuser, however, was certainly caught in the grip of a domineering husband or partner, and she must have been desperate to save herself from his wrath. In trying to protect herself, however, she clearly was unashamedly prepared to see an innocent man sentenced to a long term of imprisonment. While there might be instances of this kind of malice, I fully support a woman's right to stand up against all manner of abuse. Because this was one of those cases where the accuser was at fault, it in no way casts doubt on the enormous number of instances where women are the victims. It is well known that very few rape cases reported to the police result in suspects being summonsed or charged. South African statistics show that less than 5% of rapists who are tried are convicted. Of 66,000 reported rapes: 250 convictions. By comparison, the figure for Britain is one suspect charged for every 65 reported to the police.[66] The scales of justice are outrageously weighted against women.

CHAPTER 14

Assault and Robbery

THE OTHER CRIMINAL CASE I WAS party to in my time at Marks and Kaplan was that of *Regina v. James and Five Others*. There are some aspects of the trial that are indistinct in my mind – for some reason the tadpoles failed to materialise, or perhaps something bigger happened that overwhelmed some of the earlier details. Could that have been with one of the ladies I met at the end of the trial, I wonder.

The principal young man on trial had a name like James Hilton or Hilton James. When there are two names, both of which can both serve as a Christian or family name, one can tend to get them mixed up. I used this trick several times when I was in the underground and on the run and made up names for my cover stories. One such example was Trevor William so that people, if asked who I was, would be unsure as to whether it had been William Trevor or the other way around. It helped cover one's tracks from any prying enquiry.

James, as I recall him, was a young man who worked as a motor mechanic in Germiston. Like many 'grease monkeys', he liked to be scrupulously scrubbed-up after knocking off, with an emphasis on being smartly attired. Maybe like a surgeon. He was one of those people who immediately strike you as a born leader. It was not a flamboyant style but rather a very calm self-assurance, a direct way of speaking, the facility to listen closely when being addressed, and a light sense of humour. He gripped your attention. I was soon to see him in the company of his circle and he was the man everybody looked to. The charge he and five of his friends faced was that of assault and robbery. It was a serious charge and all but one of them were lucky to have received bail. The sixth man was still in detention and that's where the tadpoles fail again. I can't recall whether it was because he could not raise the necessary amount or whether, as I seem to recollect, he had a police record, which would have been why the court had refused to grant him bail.

There were two lawyers appearing for the accused. Izzy Kaplan was only appearing for James. When the trial started the lawyers and clerks filled a bench. The main witness was the plaintiff.

He was a small man of very slight build a good ten years older than the accused, so he was in his early 30s. His evidence in chief was a story of having arrived in Germiston by train from some rural town with £500 he had drawn from his savings account. That was a very large sum of money in those days. He was looking to purchase a vehicle and had put up at the Germiston Hotel. That night he had a few social drinks in the hotel bar and got into conversation with James and company. When they heard he was looking to buy a second-hand car James told him that he worked in the business and could assist him. The plaintiff was very relieved and trusted them on the spot. He recounted that after the hotel encounter James drove him around as they wanted to show him their town. He claimed they were out to get him totally intoxicated as a prelude to robbing him. They had stopped somewhere for more drinks and at some point he had blacked out entirely. He told the court that he woke up in the early hours of the morning lying on a grass verge to find that he was suffering from head injuries, bruises and cuts. And all his money had been stolen. He managed to make his way back to the hotel and the next morning had sought out James with the assistance of the hotel staff. He confronted him about the previous night's events and demanded his money back. James flatly denied that he or his mates had anything to do with this accusation. The plaintiff had consequently gone to the police station and laid a charge. There were other witnesses, such as the police

Plymouth, Special DeLuxe, Sedan. 1948

TOP: *Izzy's car*
BOTTOM: *Yeoville Boys School Under 11A, 1949. Kasrils seated extreme left, Ivor Lazerson seated extreme right. Brian Henning, seated centre, with ball.*

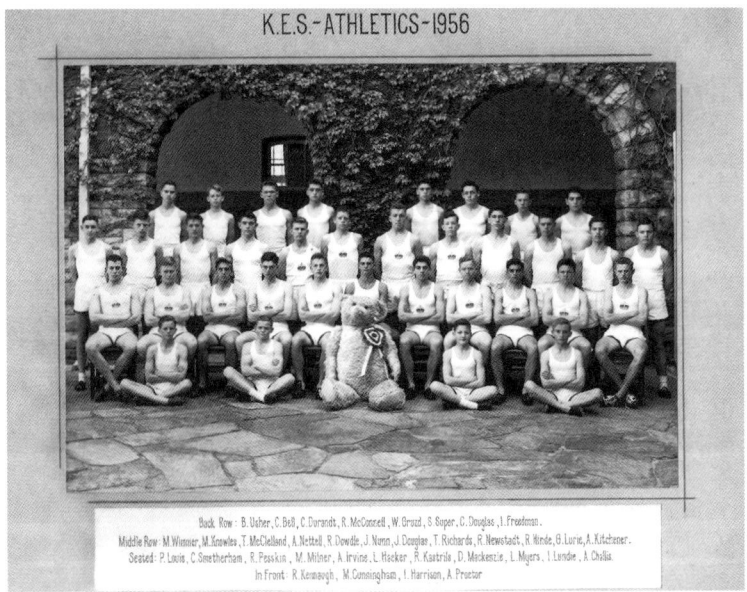

TOP: *KES athletics team, 1953 – Kasrils, front row, second from the left*

BOTTOM: *KES athletics team, 1956, Kasrils's matric year. Kasrils second row, fifth from right, David Mackenzie, fourth from right*

TOP: *King Edward VII School*

BOTTOM: *Ronnie Kasrils, aged 16, his hair peroxided, with friend Peter Louis, Muizenberg, 1954–55*

TOP LEFT: *René and Izzy at Commercial Traveller's Ball, Johannesburg, 1957*
TOP RIGHT: *Kasrils at cousin Judy's wedding 1957 (photo courtesy Judy Feinberg)*
BOTTOM: *René, back row, second from left, Johannesburg department store, staff gathering, circa 1960*

TOP: *A family wedding, Izzy Sonik and his wife Hilary, Grandpa Abe Cohen extreme right, Henk von Gent next to him, 1955*

BOTTOM: *Hilary with firstborn Roslyn and Grandpa Abe Cohen, standing next to the MG sportscar Ronnie adored, 1957*

TOP LEFT: *René on a shopping trip, Johannesburg, 1950*

TOP RIGHT: *Ronnie Kasrils and Peter Louis, downtown Johannesburg, 1957, working as lawyers' clerks*

BOTTOM: *Kasrils, aged 21, Durban, film and TV director, Lintas agency, Lever Brothers*

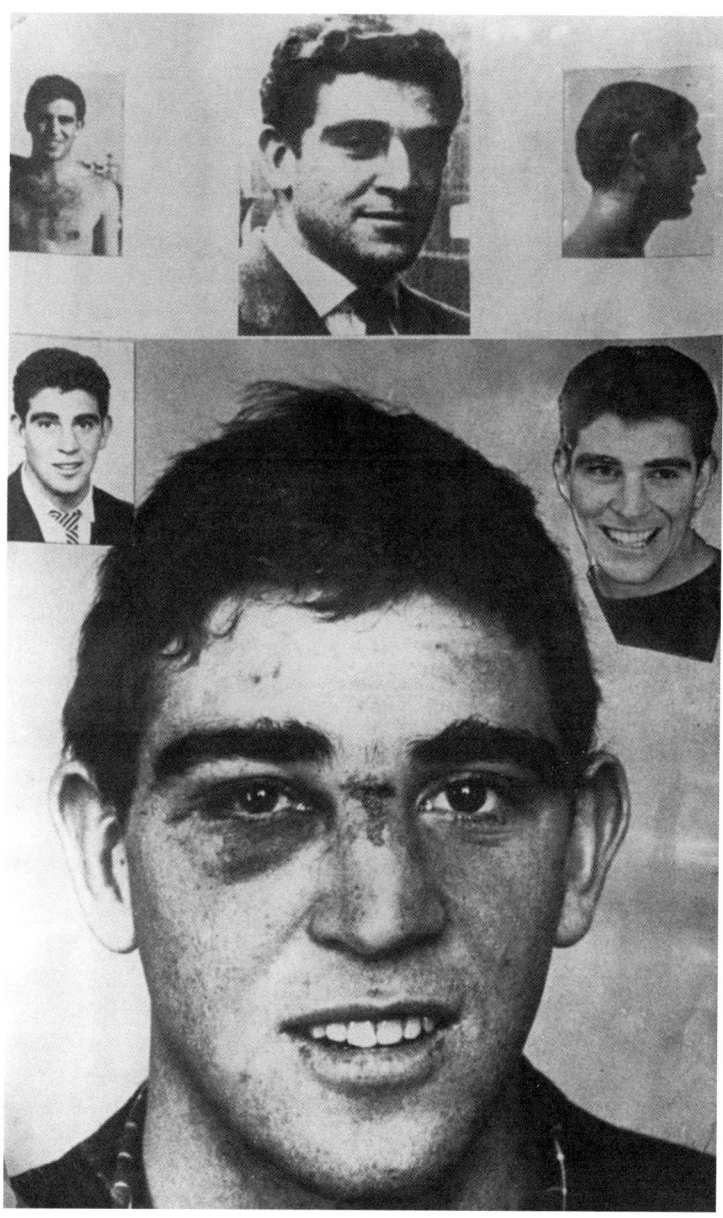

A collection of photographs of Ronnie Kasrils taken between 1956 and 1960, discovered in the files of the Durban security police by Professor Ian Edwards during his research.

TOP CENTRE: *Lintas*

SECOND ROW LEFT: *KES matriculant*

MAIN PHOTO: *Result of Hillbrow brawl, 1960 (photo courtesy John Goldblat)*

OTHER PHOTOS: *Kasrils, 1957-1959*

Author home from exile pays a pilgrimage to the war memorial on the Yeoville Koppie where he played as a child (Photo 1990)

and hotel staff, testifying to aspects of the story; and there was a medical report. The report showed that he had suffered some blows to the face, and had a chipped tooth and a cut on the head. Photographs of these injuries were handed in as exhibits.

James' evidence, corroborated by the others, was that the first part of the plaintiff's evidence was partially correct but much was covered up and the rest was false. The man had been drinking like a fish from the start and was keen to go on a drinking binge. He had disclosed to them about living in the rural areas where there was little opportunity for socialising and little freedom to do as he pleased owing to an overbearing wife and in-laws. His wife controlled him tightly and didn't like him drinking or going out.

James explained that they had humoured the man for a while before taking him for a spin around town. They had then dropped in at a dance hall where their girlfriends were waiting for them. Their accuser did not fit in with their plans, was not interested in dancing, and asked for a lift back to the hotel. James had no problem about driving him back, feeling that the man was already too drunk to wander about town that time of night on his own. On the way back, however, the out of towner demanded to be dropped off at a bar. James tried to dissuade him but he had insisted – and that was the last James saw of him that evening.

I recall the evidence of the one accused who was not out on bail. I remember him as a very interesting character, tough and extremely eloquent. His assured turn of phrase indicated that he was familiar with court etiquette. He was clearly a man who had knocked around a lot but had retained his dignity. His story echoed that of James and the others but he was quite graphic in describing the kind of character the plaintiff was. He asked the judge if he could be permitted to use language that he would not normally want to use in the court but felt it could describe the attitude of the man owing to his form of speech. The judge told him to go ahead.

'Your Worship,' he said, 'when this gentleman approached us at the hotel, he was already inebriated. His language was filthy and when he explained why he was out on the binge he said, "Well, my fucking wife is always on my fucking tail and never lets me have a fuck of a time." Your

Worship, during the course of the evening, when he was almost falling over and throwing his money around, wanting to buy us drink upon drink, I asked him whether as a married man he was being responsible to his wife and his children. Your Lordship, I again ask for your indulgence, for even I was shocked when his reply was: "My wife can go and get fucked and my children can get fucked. I couldn't care a fuck about them at all."'

The attorneys had a simple task. Kaplan was the first to address the court. The gist of what he had to say was that there had been no proof whatsoever that his client or the group had anything to do with the beating the man had sustained or the robbery of his funds. He said it was quite likely that after James had dropped the plaintiff off that his drinking bout had continued. Who could say who else he might have met on the way, whether in a bar or out on the streets late at night on his own? At some unknown and unsubstantiated time that night anyone could have attacked him, beaten him up, taken his money and left him unconscious on the grass verge. For good measure Kaplan added: 'Who knows, he might even have simply collapsed and sustained his injuries through a fall.' As for the loss of his money, Kaplan continued, 'Your Worship, in his state he might have simply lost it on his wanderings that night.'

The next day we assembled in the courtroom to hear the judge's verdict. One could sense from the short summary he was providing the way the verdict was going for he had found the plaintiff an extremely unreliable witness, a man who was 'the author of his own misfortune', he said. He found that the accused were reliable in their evidence and that all six had been able to collaborate their joint explanation in an acceptable and believable way. His verdict was Not Guilty and they were discharged to palpable sighs of relief.

I was back at work the following day trying to catch up with the depressing Credit Control backlog. I was attired for a celebratory party that evening. At the end of the trial and in all the congratulations and backslapping, James had invited me to the event, saying that he and his pals were really keen for me to come along. I agreed and he said he would send somebody that Friday afternoon to collect me from work.

He told me that if I wished he would arrange a hotel room for me to have a good night's rest after the revelry. The office girls greeted me with wolf whistles when I arrived at work. Dressed to kill for a date, they laughed as they heard I was planning to attend the celebrations as the firm's representative. I was looking forward to the evening and wanted to impress so I wore a suit purchased for special occasions from my friend Victor Katz, who was working in his father's outfitters in Hillbrow. It was the trendy new look: charcoal grey suit, pink shirt and socks, pink and grey striped tie and blue suede shoes.

About closing time Kaplan's secretary Shirley Gould popped her head around my door, poker-faced, announcing that somebody was waiting for me. 'A Credit Control client at this time of day?' I asked quizzically. 'It's for your party this evening, I'm sure,' she answered. And then, dropping the poker-face, she gave me a wink and said, 'Quite a knock-out!' I hastened to put my files away, and took a comb from my pocket to set my Tony Curtis hairstyle in place.

I couldn't believe my eyes. I had expected one of James' boys to fetch me but sitting cross-legged and demurely smoking a cigarette was a woman in black leather zip-up jacket and tight blue jeans tucked into black leather boots. She had an oval face with high cheekbones, almond-shaped eyes defined even more starkly by her arched eyebrows and dark hair tied back in a ponytail. Her dramatic appearance was accentuated by the ruby-red lipstick she wore. Jumping up, she held out her hand to shake mine with a very firm grip which spoke of physical strength. 'I'm Jess,' she announced. 'James sent me as I was conveniently in town today. Are you ready to go?' I responded in a breezy voice, 'Ready, willing and able,' and immediately regretted exposing such uncool enthusiasm.

Next she asked if I was okay riding pillion and I realised that she was dressed for a motorbike. It was a fine machine – a 480cc Triumph. She gave it a kickstart and it instantly roared into life, reduced to a purring sound as she throttled back. She's master of more than this beast, I thought. I didn't mind having her in charge. I climbed onto the pillion and put my hands firmly around her waist. The evening had taken on different dimensions from what I had anticipated.

'Just hold on tight,' Jess instructed and off we sped. In those days crash helmets were not obligatory but she had put on a balaclava to keep her hair in place and a pair of goggles to prevent her eyes becoming watery, which made her look even more exotic. She rode her bike with easy confidence, nipping in and out of the heavy traffic going east along Commissioner towards Germiston. It was a good hour's trip and we accelerated in the countryside with a throaty roar of the engine, the wind whistling by and my pulse racing more through the thrill of hanging onto this feline, hugging her tightly, than fear of speed. She suddenly de-accelerated and we went sedately through a series of S-bends where she waved at a couple of traffic cops seated on their motorbikes watching for speedsters. They waved back so she must have known them.

We got to the Germiston Hotel, of rambling Victorian design, established at the time of the gold rush, where party preparation was getting under way. As I went off to be greeted by James, Jess told me she would attend to getting the key for my bedroom and, boosting my ego, booked me for the first dance. I was feeling heady and horny but tried to look as nonchalant as possible.

James escorted me through to the hotel's public bar where his co-trialists were chatting away, all the centre of attention to their many supporters and friends. Everyone gave me a resounding cheer as I arrived as though I had been the sole reason for their victory. After several rounds of drinks, we enjoyed a buffet feast followed by victory speeches. I was asked to say a few words. I encouraged them not to think that the outcome was simply the result of lawyers.' The fact is,' I said, 'you were clearly not guilty; you all gave your evidence in an exemplary way, which impressed the court. And showed what a fine bunch of upstanding, law-abiding, 100% morally tee-totalling upright citizens you are!' That got a rousing round of applause mixed with laughter. I ended by reminding them, somewhat patronisingly, what the judge had said about keeping good company and avoiding unseemly characters and that I believed they would be more cautious in the future.

There was a great band providing the music at the hotel that night and after a slow warm-up on the dance floor, and a few more drinks, everybody was in the mood to let their hair down as the musicians began belting out red-hot rock numbers, with everybody itching like bugs and shaking Elvis Presley-style in his rendition of 'I'm All Shook Up'. I was dancing with Jessie and itching too. She had changed out of her motorbike outfit into a slinky black dress with high-heel shoes, which she had kicked off as we got as wild as veritable bugs ourselves. She had freed her dark hair from the ponytail and let it fall below her shoulders. As I twirled her around her hair whipped provocatively across my face and I pulled her close and then flung her back again as she ducked under my arm and out again.

With every stanza the crowd joined in, shouting out the chorus of being in love – all shook up.

The screaming sax, the throbbing bass, the ecstatic sound matched the pulse beat of a new-born energy frantic for release, as though urging us to break with the stifling conformity of a world that was not ours, even if we could not understand. There I was, Jewish, middle class, liberal-minded and with a professional career in the offing. They were Christian, working class, and no doubt politically intolerant, affected no doubt by racial brainwashing – but the new musical genre of rock 'n roll exploding around cut across ethnicity, gender and class lines. No matter how amorphous the awareness, and no doubt some didn't even have an interest in understanding, the new rhythmic idiom and pulsating lyrics unlocked a dream of unspoken freedom our generation was yearning for.

It being Friday night, and some having to work the next morning, including James, a great evening celebration came to an end before midnight. James bade me a fond goodnight, explaining that he had to get to the garage where he worked very early next day in order to make up for lost time on several cars that were being serviced. 'I leave you in Jessie's good hands,' he said. 'She'll get you wherever you need to go tomorrow morning. Sleep late and have a good breakfast here – it's the feature of the house. Thanks for coming and hope to see you again.'

Jess had taken my arm and guided me to my hotel room. She had the key and let me in. I saw her leather jacket and other belongings on a chair and thought she might just be picking those up before saying goodnight too. I was wrong about that.

'Pretty boy,' she said, 'let's share a shower before we rock and roll.'[67] When I woke the next morning Jess had disappeared. I hoped I would find her at breakfast. Instead one of James' lads greeted me to say he would join me for breakfast if I didn't mind and then drive me to wherever I needed to go. It was pouring with rain and he said that Jess had asked him to do the favour as the weather was unfavourable for a long bike trip. If only she knew how disappointed I was. He handed me an envelope with a note inside. It read: 'Thanks for a memorable time. I never thought lawyers could be so hip.' There was a PS: 'Sorry I didn't stay for breakfast and see you off. There was a message from my mommy to say that my child was unwell. I had to drop everything.'

The phrase 'ships passing in the night' came to mind – only I'd transpose motorbike for ship. I can see Jess clearly to this day. The faces of James and his pals by comparison are blurred but Jess – she was one hell-of-a tadpole.

CHAPTER 15

Rigging the Market

M&J Marks and Kaplan Attorneys at Law was changing. Two characters appeared on the scene and took residence in an outer office in the corridor before our entrance. An outsider would not necessarily notice the connection but their business was clearly linked to ours and they spent much time with the reclusive Mr M&J, as everyone referred to Joe Marks. They were Berman and Chimes, a classy act and the closest of confidants. Berman was tall and slender, debonair, greying hair, inquisitive eyed. Chimes was heavier set, with sandy hair, watchful rheumy eyes, and equally impeccable in his dress sense. They were quiet in their ways and soft-spoken too. Both were smokers. Berman used a cigarette holder and Chimes a pipe. They moved along the passageway as though their feet were in slippers and entered M&J's office with a quiet knock, which Joe Marks would have been incapable of hearing. If by chance you noticed them entering you probably didn't see them exiting. What you sat up and noticed was their secretary, a sophisticated woman with flaming red hair who liked to wear green or black dresses with matching high heels to show off her figure. Unlike them, she did socialise with our secretaries and I enjoyed chatting to her over tea. Not that you learned anything about her bosses or their work other than that they were stockbrokers. It was pleasant chit-chat about films, restaurants, where to buy good clothes.

They had a fourth face in tow, who appeared to have been a long-standing associate of M&J, or so July told me. He was straight out of a Dickens novel. A diminutive man called Dickie, with slicked back hair – a prominent parting down the middle – over a sunburned triangular face, a broad deeply wrinkled forehead tapering to a pointy chin, toothbrush moustache, and teeth so regular and white they must have been false. I figured he was a pensioner with time on his hands and not well off for his shirt collars and cuffs were frayed. He always wore the same brown trousers and plaid jacket and tie to match with a red kerchief in the breast pocket and a stub of military ribbon pinned in place. What was most eye-catching were his brown brogues, which were so highly polished you would probably see your face reflected in them if you knelt down in front of him. He was a bit like the British comedian Terry Thomas, only much smaller but with that same toothy grin.

Dickie would come in mid-morning, seat himself in reception, meticulously wipe the dust off his shoes with his red handkerchief, study the share prices in the office newspaper and gulp down cups of tea and Marie biscuits brought to him by July, who he never so much as glanced at or thanked. I once complimented him on his military ribbon. 'Great War,' he said, referring to the First World War. He told me he had been a *sapper* and asked whether I knew what that was. Before I could respond he clapped his large hands together with a loud bang. 'Blew things up,' he said with relish. 'Worked on the mines after that,' he added proudly, again smacking his hands together. 'Blew things up! and he chuckled.

'Have you ever heard of salting a mine?' Dickie once asked me in a conspiratorial way.

I shook my head and waited for him to carry on.

'You fire gold filings from a muzzle-loader or a shot-gun into the rock-face of a disused mine to give the impression of gold-bearing ore. That was done in the old days.' He chuckled, his eyes darting from side to side. 'Ahh, the stories I could tell you of the good old days. The golden days of mining,' he said, cackling. 'Get it?' And then he roared with laughter at his own joke. Looking from side to side to make sure he wasn't being overheard, he added: 'Can't do that kind of thing these days. They'll catch you out.' He sighed and looked down, deciding to give the brogues a rub with his red handkerchief. I detected the faint smell of alcohol on his breath and as if on cue he offered me a polo mint. 'Good for the throat,' he said.

Only now and again would Dickie be called into M&J's office and he would slide in as nervous as a mouse expecting to find a cat inside. July confided in me that Dickie was petrified of Mr Marks, who would scold him over past misdeeds. Then July told me something even more intriguing. Joe Marks apparently had a brother called Theodore Isaac Marks, who used to be a partner in the business. He was now working in what July called the 'stocking market' and Dickie, or Mr Dickie as July called him, delivered messages between the two brothers. July didn't like brother Theodore. He said he was a sly and cruel man and he had once seen him caning Mr Dickie in his office in the old days when he was in partnership and operated from the office Mr Kaplan now occupied. That was before Mr Kaplan had joined the firm. July often said how kind both Mr Joe Marks and Mr Kaplan were. Once or twice I tried to get some sense of it from Izzy Kaplan, but he would simply say that at last Joseph Marks had some work.

Shirley Gould was more forthcoming with a remark about Berman and Chimes having worked on the Stock Exchange and being some kind of stockbrokers. They had been business partners of Mr Marks's deceased father Morris (the M of M&J). When I asked her about Theodore Marks working in the 'stocking market' she laughed and explained July had meant the Stock Exchange.

It was Mr Chimes who first approached me. He said he needed someone reliable to do deliveries around town now and again. I would be able to use his car, he said. Delivering what, I asked? Share certificates, he said. A morning here a morning there. He acted that out with his hands. He would ask for Kaplan's permission. Sure, I said – if it's okay with the boss. Dickie was the usual driver but I had picked up from office gossip that he had pranged Chimes' car and it was rumoured he had been under the influence of liquor at the time.

Some weeks passed. Then Chimes called me into his office. Tables were piled high with boxes. Dickie was busy packing one with impressive looking A4-size certificates with the title 'Western Main Reefs' embossed on them in gold characters. He asked me to get the 'boy' to help, meaning July, and we filled the car's boot with boxed certificates. He gave me a list of addresses for delivery purposes with the number of boxes consigned to each and an invoice to be signed by recipients on delivery. I drove off. I had no knowledge of how the Stock Exchange functioned and assumed that those who purchased shares would do so through their brokers. Surely that meant the broker would hand the certificate to the client at his office? But I shrugged that off. Maybe if I had been paying closer attention at law school I would have been wiser.

It took me the better part of the day to deliver to a score of addresses. I was surprised that these were in the seedier parts of the city, places like Doornfontein, Bertrams, Booysens and Mayfair. Some were hole-in-the wall businesses, corner tea rooms, backstreet motor mechanics. One ramshackle house in Doornfontein was in Buxton Street, notorious for having housed an infamous brothel. Strange addresses, I mused, for people investing in a mining company, but then again a gold rush attracts all sorts. Indeed if the recipients had anything in common it was only that they were shabby in appearance, had seen better days, signed quickly and seemed to want to get rid of me as soon as possible.

When I got back to report to Mr Chimes and handed him the signed invoices he was pleased and handed me a £10 note – more than my monthly wage. I was delighted. He said there would be more such runs and I assured him of my availability whenever required. He was a reserved individual but I could not resist enquiring whether he had two sons a few years my senior who had attended Yeoville Boys school. I mentioned their names and recalled that they were excellent athletes. He was momentarily taken aback and sucked at his pipe. Chimes was an uncommon name, I added. He gave a nod and replied that they were distant relatives. He abruptly changed the subject by scrutinising the invoices again and questioning me about one or two of the signatures. But I knew he was lying. I have a good memory for faces and I was certain I had seen him with the two boys on sports day. The image of him, pipe in mouth, came back to me. That was not even ten years previously. But why would he dissociate himself from his sons? Maybe he was divorced, I thought, and had bitter memories.

Rigging the Market

Despite his unease at my initial questions, Chimes used me several times more and on one occasion the task took an entire weekend delivering to smallholders in the farming areas around Johannesburg and Pretoria. For this he gave me 50 bucks, virtually six months' pay at Marks and Kaplan, which I set aside for a rainy day.

I had a gut instinct that there was something fishy about Messrs Berman and Chimes but only came to learn about their tricks several years later while I was in exile. I picked up the gossip from home in snippets and it was all rather mysterious and murky. It turned out that Western Main Reefs was nothing more than a glorified scam. Millions of shares in the name of the company had been issued between 1957 and 1958 and never sold to the public but only interchanged between a narrow circle dealing out the entire share capital of Western Main Reefs at ridiculously low prices. The aim was to create the impression of brisk trade in the shares so as to stimulate the market and eventually when the time was considered opportune sell them off to an unsuspecting public at inflated prices. This was a criminal offence known as 'rigging the market'. While Berman and Chimes were at the centre of the operation with Joe Marks – Dickie was implicated of course in a small way – the central figure to emerge as the mastermind was Joe Marks' shady brother Theodore Isaac Marks. This man, who had qualified as a barrister in England, saw uniformed service in the Second World War, had once been in partnership with his father and brother, was charged with seven counts of fraud and one of theft. These crimes were alleged to have taken place while he was a member of the Johannesburg Stock Exchange between 1958 and 1959 until he was expelled. Together with his brother, J. Marks and Berman and Chimes had authored and acquired the entire share capital of Western Main Reefs – buying and selling millions of shares among themselves. Theodore had bought over 28 million shares for himself at a nominal price.[68] This was all preparatory to offloading the shares onto the market where they expected to make hefty profits. My immediate boss Izzy Kaplan was not involved in the criminal enterprise but ran afoul of regulations relating to the transfer of trust funds owing to his responsibilities in the legal practice with M&J Marks and he was penalised in some manner by the Law Society. It might have been a period of suspension.

Police investigations were under way before I left South Africa in 1963. I had become aware of this and wondered whether, if the case came to trial, the prosecution would want me as a witness. By then, however, I had moved to Durban and was on the run from the police and soon escaped into a long exile so I lost touch with the outcome and all the details. To this day, I have no idea of the fate of those concerned or the exact details, and most of the court records are unavailable. What I do know is that the judge delivered a guilty verdict in the trial and rejected an appeal by Theodore Isaac Marks. That appeal is the only document that has come to light.[69] There must have been jail sentences handed down, however. I did hear that some of the culprits saved their skins by giving evidence for the state. From vague stories I picked up while in exile, and therefore I cannot verify its authenticity, a minor figure, who sounded much like Mr Dickie, was said to be one of the state's chief witnesses. I often wondered what had happened to my friend July Marishane, much of whose fortune appeared to lie with Mr J. Marks, and the fate of that rather reclusive man is unclear to me.

Long before this was coming to a head I had been preparing to prematurely end my articles and abandon law school. I was feeling deceitful because the idea had been a long time brewing in my mind. While giving Mr Kaplan the impression that I was studiously attending afternoon classes in fact I was whiling away my time in other pursuits. I accepted study leave before the exams knowing very well that I was not going to even bother to show up to sit them. As almost two years with the law firm came to an end at the close of 1958 I handed in my notice. I felt extremely guilty about my dishonesty but Kaplan accepted my explanation without any problem and thanked me for the work I had done. Shirley Gould put it all down to my 'idealism' for they figured out that I wanted to do something more constructive for the country. That made me feel even more insincere because actually I was planning to cut loose and go in search of a woman I was pursuing who had left Johannesburg for Cape Town. The money I'd received from Mr Chimes made this possible. Had I known at that time of the greater double-dealing of the Western Main Reefs saga centred on my workplace I doubt I would have felt so guilt-ridden about my minor deception.

CHAPTER 16

Rock 'n Roll

AT THIS POINT I NEED TO BACKTRACK in order to make my odyssey clearer. It was more the intoxicating distractions of a racy life that had been affecting me and what was becoming multiple role-playing than a lack of aptitude for law that brought me to this point. Since my mind was preoccupied with much else I was finding law studies boring and too much like a continuation of school, which affected my level of interest. Lectures that rambled on about subjects such as company law and legal procedures which had to be memorised by rote to pass exams had scant appeal, given my low motivation. I fully realised that if I was to qualify as a lawyer I needed to apply myself to my studies. The trouble was I had become unsure of my choice of profession. Maybe I should have taken a gap year instead, in order to better deal with my residue of teenage adolescence, which can of course cling to one well into later years.

Standing in the way was a complexity of immaturity and a restlessness not only for the excitement and gratification offered by Johannesburg's vibrancy but by a deep yearning for a different commitment which I didn't quite comprehend. It was captured by that urge to be free of prescribed conventions and breaking the rules as gyrated within my bones. When I was on a dance floor passion and testosterone surged with the rock 'n roll rhythm. I started cutting classes and began living a double life. The routine had been leaving the office early afternoon to catch a lift or take a bus to law school. I kept that farce up once or twice in the week for appearances sake. Otherwise I would make a beeline for the seedy snooker halls downtown, where many a misspent hour was idled away. Come early evening I would head for cosmopolitan Hillbrow.

On Friday afternoons in particular I was eager to get out of the office as the place virtually closed down for Kaplan's poker school. A typical Friday went like this: I strolled breezily through town to a billiard parlour in a sleazy side street, the additional tenner in my pocket from Chimes a cause for extra delight. On the way I popped into my Cypriot tailor on the upstairs floor of a two-storey building with a bar and a huge balcony. I had ordered three of his fashionable narrow ties at five shillings each and was keen to pick them up now that I had extra cash in the pocket. I played pool with the Greek, Lebanese and Yugoslav lads who hung around there and we traded news as to where Saturday parties and dances would be taking place. Which were the best places to pick up young nurses, was one preoccupation of ours. Among the lads were George and Angelo Maphilas, whose father had fought against Tito on the side of the Chetnik royalists. They were among the toughest and most charismatic guys around and I was glad to be in their good graces. I had introduced George to my old Albyn Court neighbour Valerie who had confided in me that he had been keen to meet her ever since he had seen her as a schoolgirl drinking a milkshake at the Apollo Café across the way from the Yeoville swimming pool. I also impressed them on account of being about the only South African they knew who had ever heard of the Chetniks. I was careful not to let on that I favoured Marshall Tito and was pleased he had come to power.

One picked up a lot of gossip. I heard from them that a Yeoville boy, Sammy Karlin, had been arrested for the attempted robbery of a diamond store, Katz and Lurie, on the corner of Eloff and Commissioner. He knew the owner's son so there were rumours about inside information. I remembered Sammy as having become something of a juvenile delinquent at school. 'Are you gonna defend him?' they asked. 'Only if on request,' I replied – we couldn't run after business. We heard later that the police had shot Sammy dead after a dramatic prison break.

After a game of pool I was off to the real magnetic attraction, which was a short tram ride up Twist Street to Hillbrow. On the way I popped into a gents outfitters managed by my friend Victor Katz. He showed me some of his latest fashions and we agreed to meet over the weekend. I dropped into the Golden Ray Café and played the pinball machines. My objective was a rundown building called Rydal Mount at the top of Nugget Hill and a studio flat in the gloomy basement which I rented for next to nothing with an artist friend, Norman Seeff.[70] I had known Norman at KES where he had been in the athletics team but was better known there as a promising art student. He was attending art school and we had picked up on our previous friendship when I'd bumped into him at an art exhibition. I had taken to composing poems and writing short stories and he was a good critic.

Norman was certainly in touch with the new creative energy that was bursting on the scene. One day he introduced me to a very serious-looking man in a dishevelled suit who I had seen working as a clerk in the law courts. His name was Athol Fugard and he lived close by Rydal Mount in a cheap apartment where, according to Norman, he was beavering away at writing plays. Another memorable introduction was to Lionel Abrahams, who was about the same age as Fugard (a decade older than Norman and myself). Norman had already told me about an exciting literary journal Abrahams edited called *The Purple Renoster* which was pushing the limits and, if I remember correctly, had published a very funny poem called *Ode to a Fly on the Lavatory Wall*. I was surprised to find that Abrahams was severely physically disadvantaged as a result of cerebral palsy contracted in childhood. He had immense talent and extraordinary willpower and drive and was able to live an active life. Norman told him that I was writing poems and Lionel invited me to send them in to his journal, which I did but got no reply, possibly because they were rubbish. Abrahams was 28 when he started his experimental journal in 1956 and it made a great contribution to South African poetry and literature in the 16 years of its existence. He has written that at that age he 'had a great deal of leftover adolescence still to grow through',[71] which I could well relate to. He lived to the age of 75 and was well loved and admired across the colour line. His death left a huge gap in South Africa's cultural life.

Norman was eclectic in his interests and had a deep knowledge of classical music as well as jazz. There were times when we chilled out for long periods in a candlelit room listening to Beethoven and Shostakovitch, Duke Ellington, Dave Brubeck and Count Basie. He covered the walls of the studio with etchings in charcoal of imaginary faces, including a mangled visage of Christ. He had a book of photographs of an alluring Parisian model in backstreet bars and cafés in the Latin Quarter, juxtaposed alongside bloody carcasses in a butcher shop or waiting in the rain at factory gates or in the embrace of another woman. It was all black and white and stark. Pensive, non-smiling faces. 'This is realism,' Norman would explain, like Van Gogh's breakthrough in producing pictures of workers' boots or starving peasants eating onions. We thought smiling faces were superficial and concealed character. The book got into my soul and I yearned for that form of expression.

We experimented with paint, poetry and theatre. We took photographs of friends posing as James Dean or Sophia Loren look-alikes, lighting up cigarettes, inhaling, exhaling, blowing smoke rings, generally looking bored out of their minds. One of our friends was Kendrew Lascelles, a dancer and comedian, who had the most beautiful girlfriend who paired with him in ballet. Her name was Zelide Jeppe – he called her Bobo. They appeared in a cabaret called *Wait A Minim*. She eventually left him for Jeremy Taylor whose satirical songs such as 'Ag Pleez Deddy (won't you take us to the drive-in)', with the alternative title 'Ballad of the Southern Suburbs', became a social anthem of white youth and outsold any Elvis Presley record.

Kendrew's wit was extremely spontaneous. One day we were lounging around as usual at Rydal Mount when somebody announced that they were going to watch South Africa's boxing champion Mike Holt in a forthcoming bout. Mike was known as being rather challenged when it came to cognitive matters and had a most irascible side when it came to the media. Kendrew immediately jumped up and, quite impromptu, acted out an interview between a radio commentator and Mike Holt in contrasting upper-class English and thick South African accents:

Radio announcer: Good day to you, Mr Holt, and thank you for being with us.

Mike: It's a shit day, man.

Announcer: Uhum, well, I'm not talking about the weather, sir!

Mike: Look, meneer, I'm no bloody English sir. I am just a country boy from the platteland.

Announcer: Well, to get to the point, Mr Holt, you smartly halted your opponent in your last fight. I say 'Halted' what! Ha Ha!

Mike: Man, my name's Holt, not Holted.

Announcer: A pun, sir, a pun.

Mike: And I give you a bloody pun on the jaw, if you don't watch your bek!

Announcer: What would you consider your best pun – er … I mean punch, Mr Holt?

Mike: [has problems trying to figure out his right from his left hand] Well, umm, my … er … right – ag, man, asseblief – my … er … left – no, man, dis sommer my reg … umm … right hook! Ja. Korrek. My right hook.

Announcer: On a different subject, Mr Holt, what do you think of William Shakespeare?

Mike: Let me at him. I'll kill the bugger!

Announcer: And who is your favourite sparring partner?

Mike: My boetie. And I have been kicking the shit out of him since we were kids.

Announcer: When you're in training, Mike, what do you eat for breakfast?

Mike: Jungle Oats … And my brother too.

Kendrew left South Africa to reside in California where his many talents flourished as writer, poet, painter and much-loved human being. The west coast of America also lured our friend Norman Seeff, who became a famous salon photographer to the stars in Los Angeles. As I was to discover, Hillbrow in those days must have had an extremely high per-capita artistic talent per street block and must have been for white South Africa what Sophiatown was for black in terms of creative vibe at a particular time in history.

For those of us with double identities from Hillbrow or the northern suburbs, struggling to break out of the South African conventionality cocoon, there was the attraction of post-war neo-realism with films such as *Bicycle Thieves*, *La Strada* and the Indian classic *Pather Panchali*. The movie that really inspired me was *The Grapes of Wrath*, based on Steinbeck's novel about Oklahoman sharecroppers driven off the land during the Great Depression and driving overloaded trucks in convoy to California to pick grapes. It reminded me of Africans in our country and I walked out of the cinema that day in a trance.

Through Norman I got acquainted with a number of his fellow art students, mainly young lesbians living together. I was mesmerised by them for their bohemian lifestyle as much as their artistic talent but above all for the way they dared to subvert conventional rules. They had their hair cropped short, wore corduroy trousers and thick jerseys in the Joburg winter, rolled their own smokes and joints, drank wine from jars and could recite poetry with, in one case, a special proclivity for Dylan Thomas. I realised I had much to learn, especially when I was asked what I thought of *Under Milk Wood* and muttered something trite, which elicited the comment that it was better to be silent than mundane. Special friends were a couple, Rosemary Taylor and her partner Gloria. The latter had a wonderful singing voice and her rendition of 'Summertime' from *Porgy and Bess* brought me out in goose-pimples. She was what was referred to as the 'butch number', being masculine and overweight from a thyroid problem. Some of my former KES friends, who were out on the town, encountered Gloria and myself in a tête-à-tête at the Montparnasse Café on Kotze Street. The expressions on their faces said it all for Gloria's gender – in turtleneck Shetland jersey, trousers and veldskoens, man's cap on her head – was a challenge to the uninitiated.

Most of our gay friends presumed Norman and I were queer – the term in those days for homosexual – and, somewhat opportunistically, we might have thought we needed to use this misperception as a passport into their company. This, of course, was not the case, as I was later to find out. They all remained friends with both Norman and myself when both he and I had found female lovers.

I continued to lead something of a weird double life even in Hillbrow.

On the one hand I was becoming involved with the artistic and bohemian set and getting into debates about philosophy and art; on the other there was the attraction of rock 'n roll.

My friends in this regard were Victor Katz and Ronnie Leader, a rich misfit from Saxonwold who was studying for a BA in English literature at Wits and, like me, was attracted to life on the edge. He was known around the ropey hotels and bars in Johannesburg as Tony Lira and with his thick dark hair he looked like an Italian gigolo.

For weeks we had been looking forward to the première at the Plaza Cinema of Bill Haley & His Comets in the sensational movie *Rock Around The Clock*, which appeared to be part of a cultural revolution abroad. The vast cinema was filled to capacity that evening with restless youngsters from both the northern and southern suburb divides of white Johannesburg, all abuzz with anticipation. Large contingents of police had been deployed along Rissik Street in anticipation of trouble since cities such as New York, London and Paris had seen rioting in the aftermath of the film. Johannesburg was a city buzzing with energy anyway.

Bill Hayley's bestselling record had already conquered us and his signature song was being sung with gusto in the streets with ranks of mainly working-class white youth in their ducktail hairdos linking arms, charging down Rissik Street and jeering at the police about their intent to rock around the clock. It was as though they were laying down a challenge. Black people might normally be the main target for the police but this by no means meant that the anarcho-nihilism of white working-class youth was tolerated. The lyrics about rocking from one o'clock through midnight were mundane, to say the least, but charged with the 12-bar blues beat they were explosive.

We couldn't wait to get into the movie house and there was a lot of good-natured pushing and shoving. The restlessness inside the cinema was electric. Even the slow start of the movie had everybody hanging onto their seats in anticipation of seeing Bill Haley in action, by no means put off by his smooth egg-like appearance and silly curl dangling down his forehead. There was pandemonium the moment the music broke out. As if lured by a Pied Piper we danced on the seats, in the aisles and even up on the stage. All inhibition vanished. And nobody was aping what we had heard about the crowds of youth abroad going ape-shit. South Africa's authoritarian and patriarchal society and conventions were far more of a straight-jacket needing to be torn open than class and ageist control in Europe and America. I was at one with every brother and sister in the house as we belted out the intention of rocking 'til broad daylight.

Afterwards we burst out of the cinema into the cold night air in a jubilant and united mood. I jumped onto a passing bus, which had slowed down to a crawl amidst the happy throng, grabbed the white conductor's hat and put it on, then swung around the pole to put it back on his head – an early exhibition of pole-dancing – and jumped back into the street. The surprise on his face turned into a grin and he cheerfully waved us on.

Then the police, batons drawn, charged into our midst. Young men and women mostly in their teens were sent flying, some trampled underfoot, while the crowd ran in all directions. The breaking of glass windows flung back the crowd's rage with the police. I found myself on a street corner where a massive plainclothes policeman was hammering a young man into the ground. Pedestrians on all the four corners were mesmerised as other policemen joined in.

Then a solitary voice rang out loud and challenging: 'You police should be ashamed of yourselves! You're nothing but big bullies!'

People around me stiffened and moved away in fear. The plainclothes policeman came over and grabbed me by my shirt collar and began beating the hell out of me. I sank to my haunches and received a massive kick in the chest which knocked me back a yard. I staggered to my feet, raising my fists in retaliation, but who was I kidding? My head was spinning and I could barely see as another blow slammed into my face and I half grabbed him around the neck to hang on. He dragged me over to a police van and threw me in among a dozen other lads equally roughed up. We were driven through the crowds with people beating their fists on the side of the van in solidarity and were soon at Marshall Square, the central police station, where we were booked in and thrown into a large communal cell which was filling up all the time until there were some 60 of us in there. There was some excited discussion but my jaw was extremely sore – I thought it might be broken – so I wasn't in a mood to talk. At a glance I could see that my cellmates were overwhelmingly the southern suburbs boys. I had a dreadful night trying to sleep because of the pain and because of the screaming from down the corridor of what must have been prostitutes dragged off the streets as part of the normal haul of a Saturday night. In my half-asleep state, partly dreaming and partly awake, I imagined the screams were from my mother in the charge office demanding that I be released.

The weekend was drab and boring with some awful porridge and dry bread and at noon watery stew. The talk was that we would be appearing before the magistrate on the Tuesday. I was spared the extra day in *chookie* when Izzy Kaplan came to bail me out. He accompanied me to court. I had washed and changed into a suit and tie. He went in to have a discussion with the magistrate before cases were called and when he reappeared gave me a wink. While we had two witnesses in Vic Katz and Ronnie Leader, who would state that I'd done nothing more than call on the police to stop beating people, they weren't needed at all. Class status clearly came into play for the magistrate must have been impressed that I was an articled clerk. Kaplan told me that a charge of disorderly conduct and attacking a policeman had been dropped. What was more, the hulk who had assaulted me wanted to apologise. It turned out he was a Captain Van Schalkwyk of the Flying Squad. He was a sinister-looking man with thick black hair and a powerful build, someone you wouldn't want to meet down a dark alley. He smirked in a cowardly manner, apologised for having made a mistake in my case, and shook my hand, clearly relieved that he wasn't going to be sued.

All the other working-class lads who were paraded before the magistrates that day were either given strokes if they were under 18 or fined for disorderly conduct. Those caught damaging property or, in a few cases, trading blows with the police were given short prison sentences of possibly three to four months.

Within the hour of the handshake I was back at work pushing a pen and dealing with Credit Control files. My parents had been worried about my weekend residence at Marshall Square police cells. I felt remorseful about my neglect of the family – in fact doubly so with respect of my philandering behaviour. They had collectively moved into a rented home in Houghton – my folks, grandpa Abe Cohen and my sister with her husband Izzy Sonik and two young daughters, Roz and Michelle. There was a room for Gramps and me to share. Maybe it was his snoring that drove me to Rydal Mount in Hillbrow more nights than not. He was a lovable old man in his mid-70s, still on the road as a salesman, who would wake with a start whenever I raised my voice to plead with him to stop snoring. He would rustle over to the wardrobe to take a stiff shot of brandy in the hope that this might miraculously curb the nasal impediment, or so he claimed. It only made it worse. As his late wife my granny Clara had once observed, he was grossly overweight owing to his love of fatty foods and that he sat around playing cards and never even went for a walk. The big joke was that after a colossal meal Grandpa would take out his sugar substitute pills to stir into his tea.

Izzy Sonik's father became extremely ill and was admitted to the nursing home where one of my girlfriends, Francina, a charming Afrikaans country girl, worked as a student nurse. I was barely around to share in the family's concerns or even visit Mr Sonik. One bright Sunday afternoon I was walking hand in hand with Francina, with whom I had shared Saturday night's company instead of Grandpa's, when she encountered another nurse coming off duty. Francina asked her in a deeply concerned way how the old man was. 'Afraid he passed away early this morning,' was the answer. I had a terrible foreboding. 'Was that a Mr Sonik?' I asked her. She nodded. 'Did you know him?' she asked. 'Such a nice old man, and his family too. They must be shattered.'

My blood ran cold. I felt like such a creep. Here was this simple Afrikaans *meisie* exhibiting such humane feelings about a man she scarcely knew and there was I gallivanting about without so much as a care in the world about a family illness I had barely shown any interest in. I excused myself and rushed home to be with my brother-in-law as he sat *shiva*, to be present at the funeral and the obligatory prayers at the deceased's home until the next sabbath. But soon I was back to the old ways or, rather, my newfound lifestyle.

Izzy Sonik had a small garage in the undeveloped area of Bryanston where he sold petrol and dealt in second-hand cars. He must have been touched at my reappearance and concern for the family because he allowed me the use of an old red MG TD sports car he couldn't find a buyer for and, alternatively, a clapped-out Royal Enfield motorbike – the Bullet model – which had seen better days. With Francina either on the back of the bike or in the passenger seat of the MG, I took to motoring flat out on Sundays to show this out-of-town *meisie* the joys of the many resorts outside the city. Sometimes we drove as far as Hartbeespoort Dam or else I treated her to hamburgers and milkshakes at roadside eateries like the popular Doll House, an iconic red building with steep roof on Louis Botha Avenue; or we'd spend an evening at a drive-in cinema where we could get really cozy in my father's Plymouth. I was a speed freak and would gun the MG's motor up to its maximum speed, the accelerator flat under my foot – 73 mph (150 kph). It's a wonder I didn't kill the two of us. The thought of death couldn't have been further from my mind. I felt invincible. Poor Francina, she needed protection from a madcap like me.

Francina and I had the sweetest little relationship. She was a decent person with very good values. It was my good fortune to bump into her over three decades later when I was back home from exile and visiting a friend in hospital. I was told that the matron in charge wanted to greet me. She was still tall and slender with a marvellous figure and the sweetest of smiles belying her formal uniform and air of authority. 'Well, Mr Kasrils,' she said, 'you have led quite a life, haven't you?' And then she added in Afrikaans: 'Do you remember me?' When I said, 'Of course I do, Francina. How could I ever forget nearly killing you in my MG?' she doubled up with mirth. 'You always knew how to flatter a *meisie*,' she retorted.

CHAPTER 17

Back of the Moon

THE RED MG OR THE MOTORBIKE, depending on my mood, made my life easier, not only for the thrills but for the convenience they provided. From home to Hillbrow in the quiet hours of the night took ten minutes. Driving to work in the mornings through heavy traffic and then law school and Hillbrow meant my choice of vehicle was generally the motorbike, which enabled me to cut easily through the city traffic. Over weekends my choice of destinations widened and the MG was the choice.

Other music and other people began to come into my life – almost in secret.

Jazz at the Montparnasse Café in Hillbrow was the in-thing. Genuine devotees and superficial posers alike were drawn to the establishment but owing to the apartheid laws the musicians were exclusively white. Gloria sometimes sang and I was her great fan. When she sang her signature 'Summertime' and in her husky diva voice she would bring the house down.

Then there was the heady attraction of subversive jazz across the colour line for those in the know and with the courage to risk breaking the law. The constrictions of apartheid created subversives galore and not only in the political underground, although I was still something of a rebel without a cause in the James Dean sense. Chris McGregor, a white pianist and composer from Cape Town, formed a band called the Blue Notes with black musicians. Gloria got the tip-off and we sped off in my MG to a secluded mansion on the outskirts of town. I had imagined the venue would be surrounded by lookouts but apart from a couple of young white guys at the gate, who simply glanced at our faces before gesturing us to park at the back of the establishment, we walked into the house through an open rear door. There was a large crowd, made up mainly of university students, sitting on an assortment of chairs and on the floor, nodding quietly in time to the strumming of the band with a tall, blond, bespectacled Chris McGregor at the piano effortlessly working the keyboard. I had imagined the typical American jazz sounds but somehow there were the strains of Africa within his compositions. The racial mix of his group fascinated me. During a drinks break for the band I heard McGregor speaking in Xhosa to his mates and I wished that, like him, I had been brought up in the rural areas.[72]

We continued to follow Gloria's tip-offs for she would be invited to some of these gigs where older and younger black musicians would appear – musicians such as the venerable Kippie Moeketsi on the alto sax, Dollar Brand (later Abdullah Ibrahim) on the piano and the young schoolboy Hugh Masekela on the trumpet. Who would have believed that they would become internationally famous and South African jazz legends?[73] Of all the remarkable young talent emerging at that time, so many of whom I came across years later when they were international celebrities, Hugh Masekela was most notable in the way he demonstrated a ready memory for some of the faces like mine who would have been only scarcely noticed. Back in South Africa after a long exile, which we both faced, he would greet me warmly as *Buti* Ronnie 'from the old days'. And I had hardly bumped into him in exile.

It was novel and exciting crossing the colour-bar line and breaking its prohibitive laws. Alcohol was drunk with instructions that if there was a police raid all the Africans present would hand in their glasses so that the house could not be charged with infringing the laws prohibiting them from imbibing 'European' liquor.

Gloria would sometimes be asked to sing and she became famous for her 'Summertime' rendition. There were breathtaking divas like Dorothy Masuka, Dolly Rathebe and a shy young woman named Miriam Makeba.[74] Another of them was the dancer Dottie Tiyo, a favourite in the popular African Follies extravaganza who caught my eye. They used to joke with me about how a real man liked his coffee: strong and black or weak and white? I used to retort: 'Whether milky or black, it must be sweet.' Sexual proclivity apart, I learned through close-up involvement how all people are essentially the same. In the South Africa of my early adulthood this was a revolutionary experience.

Those vibrant divas were products of that mysterious place called Sophiatown which Nanny Poppy frequented – a hotbed of jazz and swing where black America and Africa synthesised, epitomised by *Drum* magazine with its sexy covers and racy street jargon, shebeen culture, crime, dames and politics. Those gals, often adorning *Drum*'s glossy covers, exulted about everything going as captured in the sensational musical *King Kong*, in which Miriam was the female lead singing:

Back of the Moon, boys
Back of the Moon, boys
best shebeen in Jo'burg
is Back of the Moon ...

The experience of being present to listen to those minstrels was intoxicating and I would have gladly gone to jail just to have been present. It was a life-changing experience in a sense akin to the thrill of having seen the Russian Sputnik streaking across the skies that year. Those women were so alluring that I couldn't but help wonder what it would be like getting a black woman into bed. Plenty of opportunities certainly arose at the swinging mix-race parties, called *jols*, that I soon found myself being invited to.

Grenville Middleton, whom I knew from KES, remembers the swinging scene: 'I chose a different direction from my old school chums ... partly due to the heady and exciting atmosphere in Johannesburg at that time. Ronnie Kasrils was one of the new influences that came into my life ... Ronnie was there chatting up Miriam Makeba ... We all danced to the pennywhistle street music... I found myself in the arms of Dorothy Masuka ... As I stroked her smooth dark skin the excitement in my innocent youthful soul began to reach fever pitch ... I knew that, despite the ethereal view, the wine and the smoke, I was playing a dangerous game. What if there was a police raid?... I became aware of Ronnie beside me. He put his head next to mine and whispered: "The joint is bugged, get out of here!"[75]

Gloria and Miriam hit it off and became great friends so within a few months I jumped at the opportunity of a clandestine rendezvous with Miriam at Gloria and Rosemary's Hillbrow apartment when they were out and we could be alone.

Early Friday afternoon was most convenient for I could skive off early from Marks and Kaplan. *Poets Day – Piss off Early Tomorrow's Saturday* – was my version of Kaplan's *POOF – Poker Offered On Friday*. Miriam would have arrived in the morning pretending to be the maid and see Rosemary and Gloria off to art school. I wasn't sure whether Miriam had experience of a 'European' male but we were mutually attracted to one another and both experienced the joy of lovemaking, which came naturally to us. Although I hadn't imagined anything different, the actual experience of having a black woman in my arms had a liberating effect, reminding me, if I needed reminding, that there was absolutely no difference whatsoever between black and white except the colour of one's skin and confirming for me how unnatural and stupid racism was. It was a further step I felt along my path to self-liberation and ridding myself of the chains of white conformity. We were curious about one another's backgrounds and I learned that Miriam had spent the first six months of her life in jail with her mother, a Swazi *sangoma*, who was serving a sentence for illicitly brewing and selling beer at that time. She grew up in the peri-urban areas around Pretoria. The poverty induced by landlessness meant that eating meat was a rarity. Sheep were occasionally rustled from white farms and roasted pretty quickly. Her mother would sprinkle water on her and her siblings not just to wake them up but to give them the impression it was raining. When the police came around to the villages and questioned children about when they last ate meat they were able to respond without parental prompting – 'The last time it rained.'

Miriam had made a name for herself singing with a popular male group called The Manhattans, who specialised in a mix of blues and traditional African music. She was most proud of her role in an all-female troop called The Skylarks and despite her shy exterior was determined to achieve success as a woman in what she called a 'male-dominated patriarchal world'. What could I choose to tell her about myself? I thought she would be able to relate to my affection for my mother and what I had learned from her about life and indeed that was exactly what interested her. She spoke about her own mother's hardships and how it was from her mother, who played traditional Swazi instruments, that she got her love for music.

I was becoming something of an existentialist in my philosophy, reading and discussing the works of Jean-Paul Sartre, Simone de Beauvoir and Albert Camus. Life and freedom was all about exercising your own will and choices. 'Man is condemned to be free because once thrown into the world, he is responsible for everything he does,' wrote Sartre. The ability to choose is what gave human beings real freedom. By refusing to abide by the conventional laws and restraints of society, imposed by authoritarian systems such as apartheid, one could live a life of free choice and independence, so I thought. Such was the case with the student artists I'd come to admire like my friends Norman, Rosemary and Gloria. There were homosexuals in our circle, many of whom propositioned me. For a while I wondered whether I was that way inclined but I could not respond to their caresses since it was women who so powerfully turned me on – women like Miriam. She and I were both prepared to risk the apartheid Immorality Act which had a maximum sentence of seven years.

One of my Yeoville friends, Pamela Beira, was caught by the police in bed with her lover, Joe Lowe. Both were well known to me from the jazz scene and both went on trial. When they were out on bail, they managed to skip the country.[76] Miriam Makeba avoided recognising that we had had an intimate relationship, albeit that it was a brief one. I bumped into her at a number of government functions after 1994 when South Africa became free, and although she was perfectly friendly, she avoided past reflections. She brought joy to millions of people in our country and around the world and I was fortunate to have known her back in the old days.

There was another form of music that was hitting the South African scene in a big way.

Straight out of the heart of the townships, and played by creative street-kids on a simple pennywhistle, it was known as kwela.[77] The sound was high-pitched and haunting, and it had one swaying in sexual rapture. Just like rock 'n roll it seized one in the gut but differed in that, like jazz, it was more about the soul. Unlike rock, the movement induced was not like water crashing over rocks but rather the smooth flow of translucent liquid. The master of the genre was a lanky township kid named Lemmy Special. It was the genius of Dorothy Masuka, Miriam's pal, who composed, sang and invented a new dance form which was uninhibited Africa and the natural accompaniment to the kwela craze. This dance form was called *pata pata* (touch touch) named after Dorothy's eponymous hit in which she would sway evocatively to the ground, her hands and fingers caressing an imaginary body before her, bowing low and then up to full height. When you danced with a partner you fondled each other's bodies, doing the *pata pata* as though preparing for lovemaking. That's what 'touch touch' signified just as rock 'n roll in its African-American roots was all about rocking and rolling one's lover.

In 1922, African-American blues singer Trixie Smith recorded 'My Man Rocks Me (With One Steady Roll)'.[78] It was the forerunner of history in the making. When I heard this over discussions with the *aficionados* I remember experiencing a trembling feeling that art and music carried a prophetic message of earth-shaking social change ahead. In those adolescent and romantic years, I had an almost mystical religious regard for the power of art. I consequently used to stalk around the Hillbrow and downtown art exhibitions in vague search of the elusive meaning of life. One of the young artists of the time, Barry Feinberg, describing his first exhibition, reminisced: 'One of [the] visitors whom I met for the first time was Ronnie Kasrils, who later described me as "an acquaintance from my bohemian days in Hillbrow". At that time he was an aspiring writer with a reverence for all things artistic.'[79]

The saying 'All's fair in love and war' certainly applied in those quasi-bohemian circles, irrespective of how close friendships were. Barry had a girlfriend, Helen 'McX', a volatile peroxide blonde with dead straight hair and a severe fringe that cut across her line of sight. She was tall and slender, heavily into alcohol and weed, modelled clothing and was reputedly bisexual. I lusted after her. I lured her away from Barry and we had a short-lived but lively affair. For some reason my friend Gloria detested her; if I was in search of a suicide pact, she warned me, then I should stick to her. A 'suicide blonde' and 'manic' were words Gloria used to describe Helen, but both men and women went crazy for her. One of Ronnie Leader's friends from his Parktown school days, and one of the most intelligent and politically astute guys around, soon managed to attract her away from me. Helen was much in need of drug rehabilitation and Jasper Brener, who was studying psychology at university, rescued her from the toxic Hillbrow environment and secreted her in his grandmother's cottage in the northern suburbs. Coincidently, he was the one who had also wooed Suzette from my grasp. Of all the friends of that time both Barry and Jasper remain close to me almost 60 years later. I deeply miss Vic Katz and Ronnie Leader. Both these friends of mine died violently; ironically, it was always my safety they feared for.

One Saturday morning just before midday I was walking along Kotze Street across the road from the Montparnasse when I came upon a lively crowd clapping their hands and clicking their fingers to the liquid sound of a kwela band. Drawn in by the music and the festivity, I joined the group. A petite woman, with fair hair cropped short and misty blue eyes, in tight-fitting three-quarter-length jeans, flimsy off-shoulder blouse and Spanish espadrilles, was within the joyful multi-racial circle gyrating erotically and performing *pata pata* with an imaginary partner. She was completely stoned and on another planet with no regard whatsoever to the people around. It was only the music that mattered. This was Patsy Rushton.

Patsy modelled at art school and was on friendly terms with Norman Seeff, who introduced us. She lived in a penthouse above the Golden Ray Café and we had visited her on a couple of occasions. Almost ten years older than us, she was of Irish extraction and was possessed of the fiery spirit of that nation. She had been born in Rhodesia, where her father was apparently a stern magistrate, and by the age of 16 had run away from home. She was literally picked up off the streets by a South African artist called Aaron Witkin. According to Norman, she had lived with Aaron for a dozen years, but earlier that year he had dumped her for the dubious attraction of a visiting art dealer from London who had lured him there with the promise of a glittering career.

Patsy and her story were well known to the bohemian Hillbrow set. Like Helen McX, she, too, had her off-days, when she displayed that 'manic suicide blonde' fretfulness. She could not get over being jilted and had made a couple of half-hearted attempts at suicide – overdosed on alcohol and pills, slashed her wrists. The bohemian circle saw much of that.

On this Saturday in Kotze Street, standing watching Patsy dancing, oblivious, I felt she needed assistance. As much as the crowd, and especially the men, found her gyrations alluring, I was embarrassed for her. I also thought she looked like she might pass out. It was the sound of police whistles that broke my inhibitions and as the kwela band slipped smartly down a convenient alley and the crowd dispersed, I took her by the arm and led her away. At first she resisted, not aware of the change in circumstances, but I jostled her gently along. I asked her if she would like to have a cup of coffee and to my relief she suddenly appeared to recognise me.

'Oh, you're Norman's cute pal,' she giggled.

I thought the Golden Ray was probably the best place for the coffee but as we got there she pulled me to the stairway leading to her penthouse. Still giggling, she said: 'C'mon up. I want to play with your pennywhistle.'

CHAPTER 18

Patsy

T͟H͟A͟T͟ ͟W͟A͟S͟ ͟I͟T͟. I ͟W͟A͟S͟ ͟S͟M͟I͟T͟T͟E͟N͟, captured and captivated.

An Elvis song spoke my mind: 'Just let me be your teddy bear.' But life is not about happy teddy bears. When we awoke the following morning, Patsy did a good job of pretending nothing had happened between us. She had raised her drawbridge. She was friendly, even engaging, but had retreated behind invisible parapets and bulwarks, preventing any entry into her inner space. I was left out in the cold on the other side of a moat. I thought maybe she had become off limits because she was suffering from a hangover. As though in answer to that thought, she said, 'Hang on …' and proceeded to mix a drink of flat Coke with a spoon of sugar in it and some salt. 'Got to deal with my dehydration. That's what a hangover's all about. And just a wee bit of the hair of the dog,' she chuckled mischievously, adding a tot of vodka. She didn't mention the assortment of tablets she swallowed with the drink and soon appeared as right as rain. '*Regmakers*,' she explained, rattling a bottle of multi-coloured tablets as though in an advert. 'What every gal in distress needs.'

I jumped to my defence. 'You don't mean it was me who distressed you?' I pleaded. 'No, honey,' she replied, 'just a bugger who one day upped and left me for another, damn his eyes.'

She became rather tearful but composed herself in front of the mirror. 'Just need to put on my face, give me a minute, will you, and I'll take you for brunch at The Florian.'

Well, at least she had not thrown up thorny thickets between the two of us. Ever the optimist, I was grateful for small mercies. In fact it was far more than a minute. Patsy took time to choose a particularly fancy summer dress, all puffed shoulders and flared skirt, in yellow and white polka dots, which she wore with a large white hat. She put on a pair of large dark glasses to hide her red eyes and counter the sun's rays for it was very bright outside. She looked as though she had stepped out of the pages of a fashion magazine. Was this all for me, I wondered? Was I still in with a shout?

We strolled along Kotze Street to The Florian, which was popular with ladies, who enjoyed the tea and scones they served, as well as being a bohemian hangout. That morning she looked distinctly lady-like. She had held my hand but that had been her natural warmth so I did not allow my inner hopes to run away with my deepest desires. The Florian was situated on the second floor of an artful 1930s building with a large balcony where customers could take the sun if they liked and watch the passing traffic. Patsy preferred to sit inside, where the atmosphere was most congenial and the ceiling fans twirled. We ordered regulation English breakfast with lots of coffee and just as I was readying myself for a discreet verbal advance to see whether I could breach her outer ramparts we were interrupted by a gentleman friend of hers. As they exchanged hearty greetings, darling this and darling that, I realised that she had a prior date with the fellow. He was posh, private school, probably a St John's Old Boy, well into his 30s. He was wearing a sports jacket and cravat, despite the heat, and he gave her a copy of Evelyn Waugh's *Brideshead Revisited*. It seemed this was for her birthday. I was aware she was going on 30, a good decade older than me, which was one of the reasons I thought I'd been acceptable for a one-night tumble. The upstart barely noticed me. He charmed her with anecdotes about Waugh's satirical novels, effortlessly mentioning vignettes from *Decline and Fall*, *A Handful of Dust* and *The Loved Ones*. I knew none of those works; an imagined upper-class toff like Evelyn Waugh had never appealed to me, although after that morning I read them all within a week to see what I was missing and better be able to enter the conversation if there was a next time. The posh twit had Patsy in stitches and I was so jealous I could have gladly slit his throat with my bread knife only my hands were trembling. Depressingly for me, they had a formal date and after brunch she bade me a merry farewell, kissed me on the cheek, and sauntered off with him – apparently to watch the polo at Inanda in the mink and manure belt. No wonder she had dressed up in that posh way, I realised bitterly.

I stayed at Rydal Mount for the next fortnight, determined to once again gain her favour. I even spied on her, checking whether she was at home in the evenings (I could see her lights from across the street). There was one frightful moment when I was playing pinball in the Golden Ray, from where I had a good view of the entrance to her building, and I observed her returning home late with the posh twit in tow, chattering away ten to the dozen. I had been hammering home the points and the pin table was rocking with orgasmic throbs, clanking up the number of free games I was winning. I hastily abandoned my activity and the free games to the grateful spectators who had gathered around. I wanted to rush over the road to get a view of the penthouse. Would the lights give me any indication of any promiscuous goings-on? As I took up my position her apartment was suddenly ablaze. Now I had the unenviable experience of watching from a café across the road, drinking a succession of Cokes, my eyes peeled for a change of status. I was literally praying for the posh twit to exit but the lights stayed on and on and then suddenly they were switched off and my heart sank. I literally held my head in my hands, wishing him to exit the damn place within the next few minutes. But he did not materialise on the street, even after an hour. It felt like an eternity, as though my ship had sunk to the depths of the ocean.

I stalked back to Rydal Mount and had a fretful night thinking of the two of them in bed together, visualising their antics in detail, to the point of driving me insane. I did not want to confide my agony to Norman, but I did manage to get him to accompany me on what I hoped would look like a natural visit to Patsy the following Saturday morning. We were going shopping and I suggested we check with her to see whether she needed anything. She answered the bell in a flimsy Chinese nightgown, was happy to see us and begged us to stay and have some coffee. I was dead afraid that we would find the posh twit or another man skulking about the premises but thank god she was clearly alone. Sure, she said, when we had finished the coffee, me in a deep sulking silence, she would be most grateful if we could do some shopping for her. Her list included two bottles of Vodka and a dozen lemons.

The agony returned when we reappeared with her shopping. Patsy was not alone this time. Her visitor was a huge man with a dark mane of hair, and a revolver tucked into his thick leather belt. He was better known to Norman than to me but I recognised him as Jacob Witkin, or Jacko, the younger brother of Aaron, the artist who had jilted Patsy. I detested Jacko. He was an arrogant man who loved throwing his weight around. Jacko was the behemoth responsible for ruining my rugby career when he had slammed me into the ground during the trial school game at KES resulting in my injury. Now he worked for a security company, hence the show-off firearm on display. Norman knew him well because his two brothers were both artists. The middle one, Isaac, was a sculptor and all three had attended school at KES. There was a joke about their biblical names and what their parents would have called a fourth child had there been one.

Jacko was in a huddle with Patsy, who was very tearful. Norman hinted that he was bringing her news of brother Aaron in London. Possibly it was my paranoia but I began to feel that his intentions were not so honourable but related more to his own designs as a possible replacement where his brother had left off. It was clear to me that Patsy was naïve and gullible in this respect and I planned to find some private time to interrogate her. In an unreal adolescent way I convinced myself that all she needed was a strict talking to.

On reflection I knew I was being arrogant and detested myself for the hangdog expression I wore every time I approached the Golden Ray Café. If I could see her, I resolved not to chastise her in any way. It was purgatory, however, for she was much sought after and there were any number of male friends one could count as possible rivals. One of the most irritating was an old Austrian intellectual who called on her most evenings for dinner at The Florian. It appeared she had known him for many years and was seemingly quite devoted to him as though to a father figure. I harboured paranoid suspicions of his intentions as well and could barely conceal my restlessness; he seemed to stand guard over her virtue.

Then suddenly Patsy disappeared from the scene entirely. The penthouse above the Golden Ray was deserted for a week before it gained new tenants. I had knocked on her door only to be greeted by an eccentric man with blond locks in a hair net, wearing a pink nightgown and preposterous fluffy slippers. He had a ginger cat in his arms. My heart in my mouth, I asked if Patsy was in. A rush of relief coursed through me when I was told she no longer lived in the place but at the same time I was devastated to realise she had left without notification. She was no longer a *habituée* of The Florian either. Glancing in on a couple of occasions, I saw the Austrian sitting on his own having dinner but did not want to approach him in case he knew nothing and might badger me for information. Friends like Gloria and Rosemary and many others in our community knew next to nothing. I thought of tracking down Jacko Witkin but decided that avenue would be too humiliating.

I bumped into the posh twit at the Montparnasse at one Sunday afternoon's jazz session and, swallowing my pride, passed by his table and stopped to exchange superficial pleasantries. The band was taking a break, which gave me the chance to greet him and enquire about where I could find copies of Evelyn Waugh's novels. He was incredibly responsive and directed me to a number of second-hand bookstores around the city. As nonchalantly as possible I then asked him whether he had seen our mutual friend Patsy.

'Oh,' he said casually, 'gone off to the coast for a break, or so I understand from our family.'

'From *your* family,' I asked?

'We're relatives, both from Rhodesia, you know. My grandfather and her father were cousins. The old man gave her a shocking time, you know. And her mother wasn't much better. They urged her to be a nun, wanted to send her back to Ireland, that's why she ran away at the age of 16. And that's how she came to fall into the hands of that … that artist fellow.

Patsy

He played her along when it was fashionable to have a young kid in bed with you. All she could do for a living was pose as a model at art school. Lived together for nearly ten years. He was never going to marry her. A cad of a chap, you know. Dumped her when it suited him. Dumped her like a bag of old clothes. Dumped her for that hoity-toity dame with a fake double-barrelled name from London. She made a play for him with the promise that she would get him into the big-time art galleries. Didn't have half the talent of that brother of his. The middle one with a biblical name – Isaac Witkin.[80] Now that's a sculptor for you who is really going places. Dumps her, gives her the cold shoulder, leaves her penniless, poor thing. Fortunately, she had good friends around to help her. Especially … well, especially, you know I suppose, that there was a period when she … er … hit the bottle hard and was quite suicidal.'

All this was vital background information, which I would dwell on later, but I was growing really impatient with him, even though I was relieved to hear he was a relative and not a would-be lover like me. The question was: where on earth was she? South Africa had a long coastline with many resorts and ports. Could he really put me on track, I wondered. He must have sensed my growing impatience because he suddenly added, 'Gone off to Cape Town, you know. Don't even know whether she has any friends there.

'Why Cape Town then?' I asked.

'Scene of the crime,' he replied enigmatically.

'The crime? What crime?'

'Turn of phrase, old chap. It's where she first met him and where the relationship began, although they lived for years in Joburg. And it's where it all came apart in the end. They were in Cape Town on holiday when the Wicked Witch of the North got between them.'

The jazz band got going again and all possibility of further talk was drowned by the music. Evelyn Waugh, as I now preferred to call Patsy's cousin, had stayed the night in her penthouse as a relative and not a lover. What a relief. He was no longer Enemy Number One – in fact I had become quite fond of him – and he had given me a most useful lead that I could work on. I dragged him out onto the pavement in order to conclude the discussion and we shared a smoke. As we parted I embraced him with immense relief and he whispered into my ear: 'Oh my dear boy, we should arrange to meet one evening over a cup or two of wine,' and he stroked my hair invitingly. So that was telling ... Evelyn Waugh was not sexually interested in the likes of Patsy.

The innocent reference to 'the scene of the crime' had pricked my conscience. I was still working at Marks and Kaplan, still taking a monthly wage while ostensibly on study leave, but without intention of returning to work after my law exams (which I was pretending to write) were over. There and then, on the pavement outside the Montparnasse, I decided to resign from the job and go to Cape Town to seek the woman of my dreams. I pictured myself as a knight in shining armour, galloping south on my trusty steed to save the damsel in distress.

It was going to be something of a leap in the dark, however. The question of whether I could actually find her was one thing; whether Patsy and I might have a future together was entirely another.

Other than an urge to find a job that involved writing – I knew I had a bent for something creative – I had no idea how, where and when employment might materialise. That question did not bother me at all. I was young, only 20, with a lot to learn, including what was right for me. One thing I was very clear about, though, was that I did not want to do something I disliked, like having to work as a debt collector for Credit Control; I did not want a career that didn't suit me. I knew I was in a privileged position of not having to do anything like that to make a living. Of course if you have no choice, you could end up doing the most hated job and would do so to survive as long as it was not evil.[81]

I didn't feel I was harming anybody at Marks and Kaplan, although I would have preferred to have been open with them. I found a rationale in a philosophy of sorts based on my rather naïve understanding of Sartre's writings on existentialism. I did not even believe I understood existentialism other than what I actually felt about my place as a privileged white in South Africa. Without any doubt I realised that I had very deep feelings, very genuine feelings about the injustice of the system and the need to do something about it. What I was being confronted with at that time was coming to grips with my own identity, and my determination not to allow conventionality to dictate the course of my life nor the racist laws to prevent me from acting naturally in every way possible. That meant thinking independently, speaking my mind and above all rejecting hateful laws preventing me from choosing my friends and my lovers and my associates. Sartre's message of asserting one's will and one's choices made sense to me and gave me the strength of my convictions. I was not sure whether existentialism made political sense though. Sartre was not the only existentialist. Kierkegard, Dostoyevsky, Nietzsche, Camus – all projected a dismal view of the world and dark suspicion of the masses, which was contrary to my impulses. With the reckless confidence and enthusiasm of youth ignoring all fear of the unknown, feeling invincible, I was prepared to take the plunge into the dark.

PART FIVE

1959–1960

The mystery of life isn't a problem to solve, but the reality to experience.
– FRANK HERBERT

CHAPTER 19

Cousin Joel's Library
Cape Town, December 1958

I ARRIVED IN CAPE TOWN at the beginning of December 1958 with a suitcase, a few books and Mr Chimes' £50 in my pocket. I was made very welcome to stay with my cousin Joel Tobias, a medical doctor, and his family in Oranjezicht, a fashionable suburb nestling under Table Mountain. When my mother and father were on honeymoon they had collected as a souvenir a silver sugar spoon with the motif of Table Mountain and its iconic cable car embossed on the handle. From an early age I dreamed of holidaying by that mountain to watch the cable car in its ascent and descent. My mother would wax lyrical about the laying of the tablecloth, the breathtaking sight of the stealthy build-up of white cloud unfurling as if by an invisible hand along the mountain's length.

Joel was the son of my father's youngest sister Betty. He had a very pleasant wife, Sylvia, and two young children. He had a splendid collection of books and encouraged me to read whatever I liked. He pointed out a few books, having gathered my political interests the first evening I joined them in a meal. He asked whether I'd ever heard of the British communist Harry Pollitt and handed me his autobiography titled *Serving My Time*.[82] I began reading it that very night and was struck by the author's description of going to work with his mother who was a Lancashire weaver: 'It was starting work ... [at the age of 12] with mother that really opened my eyes to the kind of world we live in. Every time she put her shawl round me before going to the mill on wet very cold mornings I swore that when I grew up I would pay the bosses out for the hardship she suffered.'

I had asked Joel whether he wasn't afraid of keeping communist literature? Wasn't the book banned? No, he explained, it hadn't caught the censor's attention, probably because of the benign title. He laughed and said it wasn't like the English classic *Black Beauty*, which had been banned because of its supposedly provocative title. There were Steinbeck novels, which I was familiar with, and Hemingway's *For Whom the Bell Tolls* about the Spanish Civil War, which I read that first week. It has remained my favourite novel. Another lifetime favourite that I pulled out of his bookshelf and read for the first time in Cape Town was *Man's Worldly Goods*[83] by the American Leo Huberman, which was my first introduction to Marxism and the creation of true wealth by labour, the irresolvable contradictions and inequality of capitalism and how the socialist system operated in the Soviet Union. He had a copy of the once-banned Russian novel *Dr Zhivago* by Boris Pasternak which won the Nobel Prize for Literature in 1958. It wouldn't have seen the light of day, Joel told me, but for Khruschev's denunciation of Stalin in 1956. I could see he was much struck by this book as he expressed the view that the problem with communism as exemplified in *Dr Zhivago* was that it didn't take into account the human spirit and the importance of the individual. The Russians, he said, didn't like it because it was a rejection of socialist realism and extolled the cult of individualism. I had been wrestling precisely with this in my reading on existentialism and debates with Norman in Hillbrow. There was an appeal to me in this argument owing to my own existential dilemmas and indeed suffering over Patsy and what to do about my career. Did my own experience not show that for every single individual, as Sartre would put it, there is his or her own specific challenge? While I was caught up with my own subjectivism, my own sense, however, told me that one could not do anything of universal relevance on one's own even if you were involved in an individual pursuit, whether as, for example, an artist, scientist, golfer or boxer. Even then, did not the intellectual labour, the ideas, motivation and stimuli derive from interaction with others? This was contrary to the attitude drummed into our heads at school – notwithstanding the team effort ideal on the sports fields – that anything could be achieved through individual effort if you really tried. But surely that was impossible in isolation from everyone else? There might be some fortunate individuals in their aspirations for success and happiness who might achieve their goals all seemingly through their own personal endeavours, which was the American dream, but I felt that in the majority of such cases there were the advantages of wealth and social forces working to make that possible.

From my reading of Hemingway's great novel on Spain or Pollitt's life story organising British workers and *Man's Worldly Goods* I thought of the interplay between the individual and the collective. I began adopting a view that changing an unjust society was not up to an individual but depended on the uprising of the masses. This had been the case in the French Revolution that I'd been so passionate arguing about with my KES friends on the holiday in Bethal or for that matter the overthrow of the Czarist autocracy in Russia which I was then beginning to read about. Huberman's book was most educative, as was another in Joel's extensive library, *The Socialist Sixth of the World*, about the Soviet Union's achievements compared not only to the backwardness of Czarist Russia but in how it was catching up with regard to the Western industrial powers. The author of that book was Hewlett Johnson, the Dean of Canterbury Cathedral in England; he was known as 'the Red Dean'. Such discoveries generated great interest within me.

Joel and Sylvia could not have been kinder and were keen to show me around Cape Town. They particularly wanted to introduce me to the city's culture. We saw a play called *Kimberley Train* about the dilemma facing people of mixed race where families became divided because some offspring could pass as whites – 'play whites' – while others were very dark in hue and an embarrassment to those accepted by the whites. It was written and directed by Cecil Williams, the former KES teacher and leading member of both the Springbok Legion and Communist Party.[84]

They took me to an event that was attended mainly by so-called coloured people through an invitation extended to Joel, who had patients in the area of the performance. This was a presentation by a Malay cult, practising ratiep,[85] in which the performers in a trance-like state passed needle-like swords and knives through their bodies to the beat of drums and other musical instruments. It had its origins in Indonesian slaves brought to the Cape 300 years before. Joel explained to me afterwards that the trick was having such an acute awareness of one's anatomy that passageways within the body were followed avoiding arteries and vital organs. The more such routes were utilised the easier the skill became. The same performers displayed the power of mind over matter by walking barefoot across hot coals.

Joel had a dry humour. One day asked me, 'What comes first – mind or matter?' and I began to give him a bumbling explanation from what I was beginning to pick up from Marxism about mind being primary and consciousness secondary, all the while looking to him for affirmation. When I ran out of steam, eyes twinkling, he quipped: 'Never mind it doesn't matter.' There was more to his quip than a jest for I had perceived that in all our talk about philosophy and the literature in his treasure trove he had a great fondness for the works of the anarchist Prince Kropotkin.

I had by no means been idle in my pursuit of Patsy. From virtually day one I had begun hanging out at the various beaches, not just getting a tan but in the hope of bumping into her. I had taken note of a few big dances that were advertised, concentrating on hotels in the inner-city area, and had visited those, observing that the Cape Town scene was nowhere near the energetic vibe that was Joburg. There were a couple of clubs in the harbour area, Darryl's and Smugglers Den, which were more promising but looked as though they only got going very late at night, as were an assortment of very sleazy nightspots closer to where the shipping docked and where prostitutes plied their trade. I didn't want to be away from Joel's too often at the time I was settling in. For a couple of weeks I tried keeping my mind off Patsy by the books I was devouring. Then on one of my evening rounds, having told Joel I would probably be quite late, I bumped into Angelo Maphilas who was in Cape Town on holiday. We had a few beers in a hotel pub and I asked him about his brother George, who had been keen on my neighbour Valerie.

'Wouldn't you know it,' he told me, 'the lucky bugger's been waltzing around with that doll of yours from Hillbrow – that sexy chick Patsy.'

I was swallowing the beer from the bottle and nearly choked. He had to slap my back to calm me down. Almost breathlessly, I asked him where they hung out. To my relief he informed me that George had gone back to Jozi but that if I checked out Darryl's or the Smugglers Den late at night, but particularly weekends, I'd probably find her there. 'If she's been with the baseball crowd, she'll be at the former,' he said. 'If she's been with the gin swiggers, she'll be at the latter.

Like me that Saturday night he seemed to be at a loose end so we walked over to Darryl's together. I felt a strange prescience as we walked along the deserted dockland with the dark shapes of ships in the background and occasional couples necking or discussing terms of business. The bouncer at the club door had become accustomed to my evening forays in search of Patsy and didn't ask any question as we passed through the door. It was very dark inside with low lighting and, despite the heavy cigarette smoke hanging in the air, the place was not very full. Soft music wafted across from a quartet playing slow jazz numbers. I saw Patsy dancing in a tight-fitting, off-the-shoulder, white dress with high heels to match, bronzed and fair-haired from days on the beach, with a far-gone, vacant look on her face. Her partner was a palooka of a guy, baseball cap on back to front, impassive expression, light on his feet, skilfully twirling her and another fancy woman around at the same time. That always impressed me – a guy dancing with two women simultaneously. I wanted to stand in the background and first assess the goings-on, but as the music stopped Angelo waltzed over to her to say hello and the big palooka drifted off with his other partner to a table with a rough-looking crowd well into their boozing. Patsy immediately sparkled on Angelo's arrival and then he turned to point my way. Her eyes lit up, mouth opened in an 'oh my god' expression and she came rushing over to embrace me running into my arms. 'I can't believe it! I can't believe it!' She was jumping up and down like a kid. 'My darling, my milk and honey, my peaches and cream, what on earth are you doing here? What a surprise!' And she began kissing me all over my face.

I was having to catch my breath. I stepped back, holding her at arm's length and for an instant a panicky expression crossed her face as though she thought I was rejecting her. 'My honey, I just want to have a good look at you,' I assured her. While I did want to admire her close up, I was really looking to see whether it was the alcohol talking – and I couldn't say that was not the case. But the relief of being with Patsy again and of the raptures with which she greeted me was like a goblet of nectar from the gods. The music had struck up again, nice and slow for couples in search of an intimate mood, which suited me down to the ground. I said, 'Come on, let's dance' and she said, 'Come on and hold me tight.' She did just that, with her head on my shoulder, and I felt that things were going to be just right. No drawbridge, no ramparts to surmount. And that's how it turned out – although we first had to run the gauntlet of a terrifying trio of her baseball-nut admirers, who took offence at her running off with me, she waving them off with a 'Don't be so absurd, dear hearts' as they threatened to beat the living daylights out of me. Thank god they didn't have their bats with them.

We jumped into a taxi, the trio of snarling madmen banging on the doors, and Patsy took me to the boarding house where she was staying called Water's Edge and it was exactly that – perched above a rocky cove with the Atlantic Ocean shimmering under a full moon beyond in a rundown area called Bantry Bay which ages later would become a billionaire's row. As we alighted from the taxi, and she took me by my hand to lead me to her cottage she giggled and said she hoped I'd brought my pennywhistle along. She pulled me down onto her bed, telling me to smother her. I was like the knight who had finally made it into the inner sanctum of the castle, back from the crusades with all my pent-up yearning for my princess and her treasures. One who hadn't been wearing a chastity belt but I was long past that kind of male conventionality. Patsy was in the mood all right.

'Ah ha,' she sighed, 'it's not me you want, it's my body.'

'Ditto,' I said.

'From top to tail,' she giggled.

It was almost with trepidation that I awoke the next morning in fear that, as had happened on that first occasion in her penthouse, her drawbridge would be raised and the barricades rolled out. Instead, as she sensed that I was awake, she rolled over on top of me, pressing her lips to mine.

When a woman or a man keeps desiring it, the reason can be pure passionate romantic love. Wonderful when that happens. All the better when you had to struggle for it. I had become a little bit more experienced and as much as I wanted to feel that Patsy felt like I did, I couldn't help sense how lonely she must have been in the months she was in Cape Town, where I would have guessed she had no shortage of lovers. Angelo had hinted as much when he referred to his brother George having been with her and George was a particularly handsome man. As much as she could put in a sparkling appearance, have fun and be delighted by jokes, there was a sadness in her soul which made me feel very protective of her. I never allowed pensive thoughts and feelings to dominate me because I hated to be depressed and resolved to be ready to respond to her needs, whether physical or spiritual.

CHAPTER 20

Water's Edge

WE ROSE FROM OUR RUMPLED BED at noon and I began to realise what a dilapidated place Water's Edge was. It was a sprawling, rundown property with numerous rooms and decrepit out-houses such as the one Patsy rented – certainly no cottage, as I had thought – filled with broken furniture and a sagging bed that had seen better days. The place was overrun by cats and stank of their pee. No problem for me at all. This was Rydal Mount by the sea. How appropriate my romanticism to Lionel Abrahams's phrase about adolescent years. The proprietors were an elderly couple with ruddy noses and bleary eyes that spoke of addiction to alcohol. The manner of both the man and the woman was grumpy and suspicious, as most landlords are, but they were prepared to tolerate interlopers like myself as long as the rent was paid on time and I didn't fight or make trouble. The female of the pair, by far the more meddlesome, took to calling me Victor Mature, not so much as a compliment but as it turned out because she regarded that film star as having a menacing side and for some reason she had become suspicious of me. 'See that you look after that bonnie lass,' she hissed at me on many an occasion.

Patsy and I walked down a hundred steps to the actual water's edge and bathed in a shallow rock pool, she in a skimpy bikini and I in a swimsuit she borrowed from an American friend for me. The friend's name was Larry Salomon from New York City and he was in South Africa on a Ford Foundation scholarship studying politics.[86] He was a laid-back, lanky chap exactly five years to the day older than me – as we soon found out we had the same birthday. He had minimum clothes, for he didn't seem to care about material things. He generally wore a pair of jeans with a sweatshirt – short sleeves or long sleeves depending on the weather – and a pair of scruffy sports shoes. He looked like he'd stepped straight out of Jack Kerouac's beatnik novel, then the rage, *On the Road* (although he himself had absolutely no interest in Kerouac or his novel, which disappointed me). He had been born in Germany in 1933 and was one of the last of the Jewish children sent out of the country, in his case to Britain, on the *Kindertransport* just before the outbreak of war. I got to know him in due course and found that he remembered *Kristallnacht* vividly, which had taken place just before his fifth birthday – at the time I was born. His home was stormed, the windows broken and the Jewish Star of David crudely painted on the exterior walls. Although his father had been decorated by the German army in the First World War, he was detained at one point but released after a few months as a result of public pressure. The parents had decided to send Larry and his twin sister Silvie to Britain. Just a few days before they were due to depart, they received a message saying that the family that had agreed to receive his sister had changed their minds so Larry departed alone. The poor child was so distraught that he refused to go but of course the parents insisted and on the day of departure he remembered the harrowing parting as they and his twin sister saw him off at the railway station. Once he was out of view he had cried inconsolably. He showed me a photograph of his family: his father appears nonchalant, perhaps by way of reassuring his wife, who has a rather nervous-looking expression in her eyes reflecting her fear of the future. Larry's twin sister is seated at his side – he with a playful grin. I had no words to say at that time but the faces have lived in my mind ever since. I see the four of them, Larry the only survivor – his mother, father and sister ending up in a death camp. You look at a picture of a single family with their hopes of a happy and secure life and a bright future for their children and multiply that over a million times to reach a figure of six million wiped out like flies and you want to rage against inhumanity and barbarism. Your mind tries to encompass the suffering of millions more instances of terror and brutality all over the world.

I had no knowledge of immediate family having perished in those darkest days of the 20th century but over 200 Jews with the name Kasrils or approximating to it are listed as having perished in the Holocaust.[87] Names get altered through immigration, even marginally so, and many of these could have been from a wider family. When I read of Nazi atrocities against Jews in the areas where my grandparents had originated – such as Vilnius, Riga and Libau – I realised how close our immediate family came to being wiped out entirely had they not emigrated to South Africa. Even at the stage in my political adolescence the lesson of the Holocaust for me was not the Zionist position of an inherent anti-Semitism in the world that could never be changed and that Jews were and would always be the eternal victims of such hatred. I could see that racial prejudice existed against many different peoples and groups but I believed the way of dealing with this was by the unity of social forces standing together against inhumanity. The Jews were not the sole victims of Nazi barbarity. The essential lesson was the sanctity of all human life and the need to fight for freedom, equality and justice for all as the basis for peace and decency, security and happiness. This was the summation of earnest discussion between Larry and myself. The Marxism I was beginning to imbibe gave me the view that anti-Semitism and all forms of racial discrimination are the product of class divisions in society, and ultimately serve the interests of powerful corporate interests. Racial antagonisms and contradictions can be reduced and eliminated in the struggle for a common democratic social system.

Larry and Patsy had been invited for dinner at a friend of Larry's, Joseph Kibel, and they took me along. Joseph turned out to be the son of a famous and controversial painter, Wolf Kibel, originally from Poland, who came to South Africa via Palestine and died in 1939. Joseph who was born in Poland, did not work, read philosophy at home, and had an artistic wife named Carmen who looked after him. Larry had already told me that Joseph lived off the sale of his father's paintings and whenever he needed funds would let one go under the auctioneer's gavel. After a meal of chicken soup with rye bread, followed by cheese and grapes with some cheap red wine, Joseph regaled us with the idealistic theory of solipsism, taking off from where he must have been discussing the philosophy with Larry on a previous occasion. Larry was an attentive listener and I discovered that he was prepared to give everybody a hearing on even the most esoteric of things. Wishing to bring Patsy and myself into the conversation, Joseph explained for our benefit that solipsism is a philosophical theory which asserts that nothing exists but the individual's consciousness. He began to demonstrate the theory by taking an apple out of a fruit bowl and holding it up as an example, explaining that it existed for each of us because we could see it and it was lodged in our consciousness. 'What happens,' he went on, placing the fruit in a tin and closing the lid, 'when it is out of sight?'

Larry said, 'Well, we all know the phrase "out of sight out of mind" but we do know that what we cannot always see does in fact exist.'

'That of course is the case,' Joseph responded, 'but how can you verify it? Someone might well tell you that your uncle in New York is still alive but the only way you can verify that is through your own consciousness by actually seeing him or talking to him on the phone.' What that amounted to, he concluded, was that it was impossible to verify anything except through one's own consciousness.

I could see that Patsy was finding all this very dense and incomprehensible and to my mind I thought it was just verbal gymnastics. But Joseph showed that he also had a witty side to his nature. He opened the tin and, removing the apple, said: 'Let's bring this back into existence.'

When we were returning to Water's Edge Larry was still preoccupied with what he called Joseph's semantics. He conceded that one's understanding of reality depended solely on one's subjective feelings. But then where do our subjective feelings come from, was his question. I had been struggling to follow the argument from the time Joseph had begun spouting, but didn't Sartre, I said, even with his focus on individual choices, link that to the social environment as a whole? Larry liked that. Yes, he said, if it wasn't for other people, if we were all Robinson Crusoe, how would we survive and understand the meaning of life? Patsy pointed out that Robinson Crusoe needed his Man Friday.

Very often such dense discussions are baffling and depressing but

I found that somehow over time, in discussion, reading the subject matter, one's ideas fell into place. I wondered whether I should study philosophy at university but there were no funds for that and anyway I felt one could do a great deal of reading on one's own. But then, arising out of what we three had observed, no matter how much reading one did it was necessary to discuss with others if you wished to deepen your understanding. I had expressed this in the car and Patsy, who loved novels – as I had well noticed when she discussed Evelyn Waugh – disagreed. She said that reading was such a healing factor for loneliness so did it really matter if you never ever discussed what you liked at all? We had consumed a fair bit of wine during the evening and I sensed she was dropping into depression so I squeezed her hand and told her that was how I sometimes felt about poetry.

Patsy had a part-time job in an art gallery. While Larry was busy in the university library he had a fair amount of free time. He was beguiled by the Cape and what he termed South Africa's three P's: Politics, Pot and Pussy – proclivity for which he and I shared in common. We spent much time getting tanned on the sandy white beaches at nearby Clifton and climbing Table Mountain. We often stopped to smoke weed and engage in long discussions. He was a good teacher and I a willing listener. He was soon lending me his books about South Africa such as Eddie Roux's history of the Communist Party, *Time Longer Than Rope*,[88] which he considered brilliant. He gave me insights into beatnik culture and black American music. He didn't care much for rock 'n roll, although he pointed out that Chuck Berry was its originator and that white singers such as Elvis had latched onto the genre and presented it to white youth. He forecast that the commercial companies would gentrify it and reduce its potency.

Larry was no Marxist but he was scathing about America's anti-communist phobia and the harm this had inflicted on rational thought. He loathed Joe McCarthy and Richard Nixon with a subtle vehemence. He gave me a graphic account of McCarthy's witch-hunting, communist-baiting congressional hearings which he had watched on television. He described the slimy insincerity of Nixon and how he had appeared on television holding his pet dog in an effort to prove how wholesome he was after some harmful revelations in the media. I was interested in his view on Israel, which he termed a tool of American imperialism. I didn't quite follow the meaning of that and he explained that without the funds the Zionist state received annually from America it would never have survived. Israel, Larry said, had become an outpost of America's foreign policy in the Middle East for domination over the Arabs. Why, then, I asked, had the United States pressurised Britain, France and Israel to withdraw their troops after the Suez intervention in 1956? Owing to imperialist rivalry, he explained. America was looking to replace the former colonial powers all over the world in favour of its own ambitions.

Racist attitudes in South Africa never ceased to amaze him. A student at the university once told him that he had just run down and killed a 'coon' with his motorcar. The guy was so nonchalant about it that at first Larry thought he meant a *racoon*. When he realised the student was referring to a black man, he was mortified. As a result of his studies his opinion was that the black labour movement in South Africa, if it could organise its full strength, was the key to change. He was cautious in his opinions, however, and admitted that he knew very little about the African National Congress. Because Cape Town was predominantly a white and coloured city, he was looking forward to travelling up to Johannesburg to complete his research there and interview ANC leaders if he had the chance.

Larry and Patsy had friends in District Six, the pulsating coloured ghetto on the slopes of Devil's Peak alongside Table Mountain. We spent many weekends there in the company of Zoot and Miriam Mohammed who were of Malay descent, their forebears having been brought to the Cape by the Dutch as slaves from the 17th century. The racial mix of the Cape generated the so-called coloured people of mixed race, who became teachers, intellectuals, artists, revolutionary leaders and, especially the proletariat of Cape Town, workers in the docks and also in clothing factories, which were close by District Six. There one found an irrepressible spirit and humour of a people who refused to bow down to white domination but also many who had succumbed to drink and criminality to survive. Alcoholism had been a curse from the time of slavery and was sustained by the 'tot system' whereby coloured men, women and children laboured for a pittance in the white-owned vineyards and received cheap alcohol in part payment.

While Miriam cooked exotic Malay dishes, Zoot would roll his guests *zols* (joints). Dagga – a word derived from the indigenous Khoi-San people who had cultivated it for centuries for its medicinal and trance-inducing qualities – could be easily bought from peddlers hanging about the Seven Steps, a fabled haunt in the area. Local people referred to dagga as the 'tree of knowledge' for the spiritual insights and meditative qualities produced by smoking the herb. Larry in particular found the effects edifying. There was no shortage of the herb in Zoot's company. Zoot had been in the infamous Roeland Street prison for receiving stolen goods and I'm sure a great many other misdemeanours. He amazed us with his tales about prison life and said he smoked more of the weed inside jail than out. Among his close confidants were Alf and Isaiah – pronounced Eyezay – who appeared to be going through a course of left-wing political studies. Alf would amuse us by analysing any problem under the sun in a mixture of an Afrikaans patois called *tsotsi-taal* and high-sounding English. '*Nou sê vir my, mense* (now tell me, folks) – What's the cause? What's the effect? Understand the dialectics that links with the materialistics.' And then he would lean forward in mock sagacity, revealing his missing front teeth, and explain: 'An' in whose befokked interests anyway?' There was a great deal of merriment and a playful knocking of the Marxist terminology they were becoming acquainted with. They referred, for instance, to the scientific term 'dialectical and historical materialism' as 'diabolical and hysterical masturbation'. Miriam's playful reaction would be to lift her arm as though to strike them. She would nevertheless rebuke them in a thick Cape accent: 'Ag man, moenie so irreverent wees.' Like Miriam, Isaiah neither drank nor smoked, and was a pillar of support for his family. But he and Alf – Alf von Loggenberg – did drive consignments of the best dagga in the country, from the Transkei, where it was secretly cultivated and purchased from the peasants, and smuggled into Cape Town. To be caught in possession of the herb or even just smoking it meant a heavy prison sentence. I met up with Isaiah Stein years later when he, too, was a political exile in England. His sons, Brian and Mark, played first division football for Luton Town, and Brian played for England on an occasion. Isaiah always longed for his District Six home, which had been bulldozed into oblivion by apartheid's forced removal policy which dispersed its inhabitants a score of miles away to the bleak Cape Flats where the suburb of Mitchells Plain arose.

I have mentioned Alf's missing front teeth and thought that maybe he had lost them in a fight. But I also noticed that many working-class people of mixed race in the Cape, male and female, had missing front teeth. I didn't want to be rude and ask Alf about this but referred my question to Miriam. She laughed and told me that it was a custom among working-class people of town and the countryside to have two front teeth extracted. She told me with a bit of a smirk that it was referred to as a 'passion gap' and in answer to my raised eyebrows said it was considered sexy. I immediately thought of the fetish I had developed over my schoolboy crush on Suzette with the mere fraction of space between her two front molars. I switched off from Miriam's explanation trying to visualise Suzette with the passion gap. I snapped out of my stupor with Miriam explaining that the dentists in the Cape made loads of money from very poor people by extracting teeth that were perfectly good. She became quite serious as she explained the background to all this. It started among farm labourers, especially those working on fruit farms, and more especially apple farms. Apart from the vineyards there were huge apple farms in the Cape and the labourers were permitted to indulge. You must know that apples are extremely acidic, she said, and liable to rot the teeth. This led to extractions and after a while the custom set in whereby even healthy teeth were extracted for appearance. For some reason – 'And I wouldn't know,' she laughed – this was regarded as enhancing a sexual encounter – hence the term.

Miriam, dark and sultry looking, was a member of the Coloured People's Congress, an ally of the ANC. They had copies of the alliance's weekly newspaper, called *New Age*, in their house which I began to read avidly. The paper was an eye-opener about militant protest and activity seemingly throughout South Africa which one did not encounter in the mainstream white press. There were photographs of masses of marching people, of clashes with the police, in urban and rural areas. There were exposés of the brutal conditions under which people were living and outspoken demands for change. There was a great deal of coverage of international developments all over Africa, the liberation struggle in Algeria, Vietnam, Cyprus, Cuba, developments in the Soviet Union and China, a world revolution on the march. The editorial comments gave the impression of a coming revolution in South Africa and exhorted the masses to join the Congress movement and struggle for change. There were photographs of prominent white and black leaders at public meetings, some of whose names were already familiar to me, such as the president of the ANC, Chief Albert Luthuli and Father Trevor Huddleston, whose book *Naught for Your Comfort* Teddy Gordon had referred to. There were also photographs of young people of all races marching together with placards, some white youth like Patsy and me.

Miriam was very responsive to my interest and said she would have a copy of the newspaper every Friday as that was the day it came out. She also tentatively encouraged me to think of attending some informal house meetings if I wished where politics was discussed. It was in her home that I came face to face with one of South Africa's prominent communists. This was almost an embarrassment for Miriam particularly because out of the blue the comrade Sonia Bunting unexpectedly arrived. The house was full of pungent dagga fumes. Miriam went out to delay her while Zoot opened the back door and rear windows and we helped to fan out the smoke while he hastily burned incense sticks. Miriam came back into the house with Sonia and a few of her colleagues in tow. They were just passing by and dropped in to say hello so did not stay long after taking a cup of tea. By then I was feeling a little dreamy from the smoke and did not open my mouth except to sit and try to pay attention to the discussion. But I missed an opportunity of speaking to a very influential communist at that time. Within a few short years I would become not only acquainted with Sonia Bunting but actually quite friendly and then extremely close with her in exile. She had impressed me that day at Zoot and Miriam's home for the ease with which she had interacted with them, the warmth she showed for their children and the positive way she had discussed organisational work with Miriam. She had arrived with a gent, Jack Tarshish, who was a member of the Communist Party's clandestine slogan-painting unit. They privately discussed a slogan-painting campaign with Zoot which soon mesmerised Cape Town. Over successive weeks the initials '**VJM**' appeared on strategic walls around the city, even opposite the racist Parliament. At dinner parties, bus stops, in the taxis and trains, everyone was discussing what the initials stood for. Then suddenly in an overnight blitz the slogan painters revealed all. Right where the '**VJM**' initials were painted, the slogan '**Verwoerd Jou Moer**' was painted in bold letters. There were those who were incensed – racists. There were those – the disenfranchised – who had a good laugh. The phrase was particularly popular among the coloured community, where the term 'Jou moer' was an utterance meaning 'Fuck you!'

I sounded Patsy out about whether she would be interested in attending political meetings in future but she showed no interest at all, saying it was one thing to socialise with people like Miriam but some of her political friends frightened her. Why was that, I asked. Well, one needed to be careful about such people, she said, they were out to use you. She suddenly became irritated and said, 'Can't you see that?' which rather startled me. I backed off. I felt it was not a good time for Patsy to have an involvement like that anyway; at least not at present when she had not got her life onto a secure footing. I had tried enquiring why she had abruptly left Johannesburg for Cape Town, thinking of her cousin's words that she was returning to the scene of the crime. Apart from referring to an anniversary event, she avoided talking seriously about her break-up with Aaron Witkin, which clearly preoccupied her mind and hurt her deeply. There were times when she let slip that she had been to one or two of the places we visited, such as a vineyard we went to to sample wine and she commented how the product had improved since she and Aaron had visited. I had picked up from Joseph's wife, who had apparently been a colleague of Aaron's at art school, that it was in Cape Town where Aaron had initially met Patsy and ultimately jilted her in favour of the London lady. 'Look after Patsy,' she had told me. 'She is a very vulnerable woman.'

I did get some further insight from a hedonistic journalist, Denis Kylie, who worked for the *Golden City Post* as their Cape Town correspondent. He was part of the flamboyant crowd that gathered around Miriam and Zoot and was close to Larry and Patsy. While he clearly liked Patsy, and behind my back was constantly trying to get her into bed, he did say she had always been 'full of shit' from her days with Aaron Witkin who, as it turned out, had been a close friend of his. He didn't use that term impolitely nor to hurt my feelings but in a breezy way as though there was nothing really wrong about it but rather a different way of saying that she could be pretty volatile at times. In his opinion this stemmed from her feelings of insecurity as a runaway from home at an early age and the fact that Aaron had failed miserably to provide her with the stability she yearned for. He mentioned that it had been exactly ten years since Patsy's arrival in Cape Town from Rhodesia and initial encounter with Aaron so that would explain her cousin's reference to her 'returning to the scene of the crime'.

Denis was amused and cynical about my interest in communism and on one occasion at a house party when Miriam and some of her comrades were singing 'The Red Flag' and there was a lull, he turned to me with a smirk and sang, 'The working class can kiss my arse, I've got the foreman's job at last.' This caused some consternation and a few harmless blows were struck but everyone ended on good terms. My anger had been raised not so much by his parody of the song but by my irritation at the manner in which he sought favours from Patsy. It also betrayed the adolescence I was striving to get behind me.

We learned that Miriam and Zoot's wedding anniversary was coming up. We *honkies* – Kylie's term for us whites – decided to throw a beach party in honour of the couple at a remote spot on the peninsular near Cape Point where two oceans met. The most accessible and beautiful beaches were reserved under apartheid laws for the exclusive use of whites, which was the case throughout South Africa. Just as with the sports grounds the most inaccessible spots were set aside for the non-white people: in descending order – for Indians; for people of mixed race; and the indigenous Africans. We were quite a mixed bunch and, following Zoot, made our way to one of his secret haunts far from the road where we were less likely to be disturbed. We camped for the weekend with ample quantities of the necessities for such an event and enjoyed ourselves as free beings as we felt South Africa could be. For me this was what existentialism was all about. Free choice. Let the apartheid laws go to hell.

We had an impromptu concert with singing, telling jokes and

comic acts. Having been inspired by my friend Kendrew Lascelles's performances, I presented his parody of Mike Holt the boxer. It was Alf, though, who had us rolling in the sand with his sketch of the architect of apartheid, Dr Verwoerd, delivering a speech about racial classification in his high-pitched voice:

Goeie dag, mense. As is well known, in this racial scrambled egg of a land, we have introduced The Population Registration Act to classify all South Africans into their God-given racial groups based on their physical and socio-economic characteristics – and no bloody communist is going to change that!

Under our apartheid system the white man, the Indian, the Bantu races and the mixed-up so-called coloureds – otherwise known as Bushmen, Hottentots or Cape Malay – must reside in their own group areas, among their own people, subject to their own culture, where they can separately develop in peace and harmony, enjoying their own rights and duties. Our hard-working race classification officials, however, have found that *skelms* from the non-white groups, those with light skins, have been attempting to pass themselves off as white people to falsely gain the white man's God-given privileges. In view of this, it is my sacred duty and responsibility therefore to grant the officials permission to use what we are calling "*die potlood toets* – the pencil test" to assist them in the performance of their duties in a reliable, objective and scientific way and prevent persons whose race classification is uncertain from deceiving our officials. In such circumstances the official in doubt may slide a pencil through the hair of such a person. If the pencil falls to the floor, he or she may be considered "white". If it sticks, it will be shown that the person's hair is too kinky to be white and the person will be classified as "coloured".

Nou luister, mense: since deceitful people exist who might deliberately shave their heads, thinking by so doing they can avoid the pencil test, there is a further requirement. In such a case they must be ordered to let their hair grow and report back to the inspectorate after three months. What of those who are naturally bald, you may ask? All contingencies are covered. Those who are naturally bald will have to undergo the dog test. As is well known, any dog owned by any white man can sniff out any non-white and bark like bloody hell. Bald people will have to undergo that test. If all else fails the dog will decide.

    Buy a donkey. *Asseblief tog.* I mean to say *Baie dankie. Goeie dag. Finish en klaar.*

There was an outburst of applause and imitation of barking dogs and braying donkeys as the audience cheered. And a wag yelling '*Jou ma se poes, Verwoerd!*' The company and camaraderie, dagga fumes and booze, the pure pitch of the flute to throbbing drumbeats, the flirting and fornicating on the sea-sand, grunting of waves hitting the shoreline, sing-song and debates around the campfire held us all spellbound in a delicate infinite embrace. We were the centre of the Milky Way, children of the universe; the ugliness of apartheid had passed like an ill wind. I felt with all my heart and mind that I was sipping from the Holy Grail.

CHAPTER 21

Hidden Persuaders

Johannesburg, March 1959

THE FEW MONTHS PATSY AND I had in the Cape together were the best in our relationship. I suggested to her it was time we got back to Johannesburg where I needed to find a job; Larry was headed that way as well. She was agreeable and we jumped into Larry's Volkswagen Beetle and set out in the middle of the night to avoid the traffic and the daytime heat of the Karoo. There was a fourth passenger who came along with us. She was a friend of the landlord's at Water's Edge and they had asked Larry to give her a lift. She had bright staring eyes, hair dyed red, rouged cheeks, a cheap necklace of orange baubles, wore a green velvet gown and spoke in a hushed voice.

She and Patsy sat in the rear of the car and at some point I caught the gist of her prattling on about the occult. I was not happy about that because as much as Patsy showed a diffidence to people in politics she had no such suspicion of people who dabbled in such dubious beliefs. It was impossible in the small car to turn around and engage them or even change the subject. I grew even more concerned when I heard this interloper, who had just met Patsy a few hours earlier, advising her to exorcise the torment within her. From Patsy's response I realised she had been totally drawn into the nonsense the woman was preaching. It was midnight in the depths of the Karoo and I suggested to Larry that we pull off the road and take a coffee break.

Stepping out of the confines of the vehicle into the vast silence of a deep black sky afire with the firmament of stars was mesmerising. The dryness of the great arid landscape had cooled to a pleasant temperature. It took some time coming down to earth – for some of us at any rate. Just as we were beginning to relax with Patsy organising coffee from a thermos flask with some deliciously sweet *koeksisters* and spicy samoosas prepared by Miriam as *padkos* (food for the road), the woman we had given a lift to let out an excited squawk: 'Look!' she cried triumphantly. 'Did you see it? A flying saucer!'

'That's a falling star,' I retorted. 'Look – there's another one. It's common to see shooting stars in the countryside on a clear night and especially in a place like the Karoo.'

'No! No!' she insisted. 'You've been indoctrinated. There is a conspiracy to prevent us being at one with our universal brethren. The governments make people like you deny what's obvious to the true believer.'

'My god we've got a nutter here,' I said to Larry and Patsy, hoping that Patsy would now see through the lady. But Patsy seemed doubtful. I told her that I couldn't believe that she thought flying saucers were real things. Why would aliens not switch off the lights if they were secretly visiting earth? She accepted that what we had seen were in fact falling stars but was not inclined to be as dismissive as me and Larry were about the woman's spiritualism.

Almost on cue as we were finishing coffee the lady brought up the issue of reincarnation. She told Patsy that she could see that in a previous life she had been a Roman slave. 'A Christian convert,' she suddenly added, and I noted how she held Patsy's interest. She told me that I had been a gladiator and that Larry was from the patrician class.

'And what about you?' I asked her.

'Oh, me?' she replied. 'I was a slave like Patsy and we were both fed to the lions going to our deaths hand in hand, stoic in our common belief.'

What else could Larry and I do but turn all this into a joke. Even Patsy, initially mesmerised, now found it most amusing and we got back into the Beetle and continued the journey. It was a relief to drop the

TOP: *Patsy Rushton and friend Tertia, Retief's Kloof, near Rustenburg, 1959 (photo Larry Salomon)*

BOTTOM LEFT: *Kasrils rolling a joint, False Bay, Cape Town, 1958 (photo courtesy Larry Salomon)*

BOTTOM RIGHT: *Larry Salomon and Kasrils, Clifton, Cape Town, 1958*

TOP: *The Salomon family, Germany, 1938, Larry's parents and his twin sister*
BOTTOM: *Partying near Cape Point. 1958, foreground: Alf von Loggenberg, Patsy Rushton, Zoot Mohammed; background: Kasrils centre with friends. (photo courtesy Larry Salomon)*

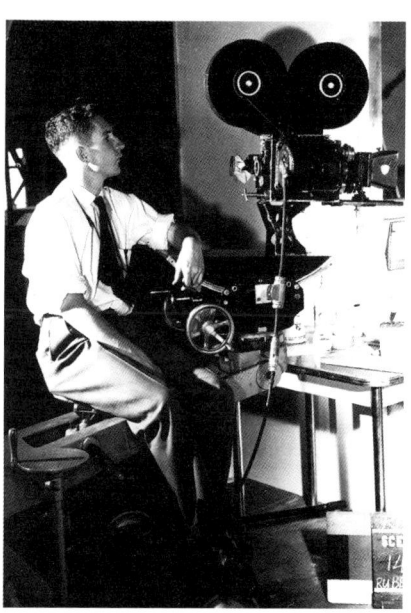

TOP LEFT: *Kasrils performing Mike Holt sketch, Cape Town, 1958*

TOP RIGHT: *A typical party in full swing, Kasrils on the left*

BOTTOM LEFT: *Grenville Middleton, KES old boy, and Kasrils's workmate at a camera shoot, Alpha Film Studios, 1959*

BOTTOM RIGHT: *Madeleine Anderson, fellow script writer, Alpha Film Studios, Johannesburg 1959 (photo courtesy Grenville Middleton)*

TOP: *René's cousin, Jacqueline Arenstein at left, with fellow treason trialists Yetta Barenblatt and Julius Busa, Johannesburg, 1957*

BOTTOM LEFT: *Rowley Arenstein, being chaired by women he successfully defended, Durban, 1959*

BOTTOM RIGHT: *Kasrils's wife of short duration, Patsy Rushton with banned communist Vera Ponnen, Durban, 1960; segregated beach for Indians, Kasrils in background*

TOP: *Ronnie and Patsy, Clifton Beach, Cape Town, 1958 (photo courtesy Larry Salomon)*
BOTTOM RIGHT: *Wolfie Kodesh who painted the slogan "An Attack on Communism is an Attack on You" on the Yeoville Wall, 1950. (Photo: London 1976*

TOP: *Johannesburg Reunion, 1990. Judy Feinberg née Cohen, Eleanor Kasrils, Uncle Solly Cohen, Andrew Kasrils, René, Aunt Esther Cohen, Kasrils at rear*

BOTTOM: *Ronnie Kasrils reuniting with sister Hilary Jaffe after years in exile, 1990*

TOP: *Kasrils with wife Eleanor, sons Andrew and Christopher, London, 1970*
BOTTOM: *Amina Frense, Ronnie's wife, 2019*

Kasril's with granddaughter Leilani, Johannesburg, 2019

lady off within a few hours because her destination was the Karoo dorp of Colesberg. I was left with a worrying feeling, however, about how vulnerable Patsy had been about the woman's posturing. Sometimes such imaginative flights of fantasy can beckon. I liked the thought of having once been a gladiator in a former life myself. She made sure to give Patsy her contact details if she ever wanted to get in touch and insisted that she felt destiny would determine that their paths would cross in the future or in another life. She repeated the words: 'in the future or in another life'. She never even bothered to thank Larry or acknowledge me as she turned her back on us outside a small railway cottage. The way Patsy had so intently scribbled down her contact details had me worried.

It was 1959, the year I would be turning 21. I was happy to be back in Johannesburg, city of my birth, with its exciting vibe and energy and the opportunity of a creative job. Patsy seemed quite upbeat too. I immediately arranged rooms for all of us along the passage with Norman Seeff at Rydal Mount. While not ideal for Patsy, we would hunt for a better apartment.

I arranged a small welcome home party for Patsy and the opportunity to introduce Larry to the crowd. We lit up the basement with candles and festooned the place with ribbons. The party proceeded at a subdued pace with relaxed music. There was a good vibe and convivial conversation. Then Gloria was suddenly at my side in an agitated state. She hurried me to the bathroom. Patsy had slashed her wrists and the blood was draining into a basin filled with water. She stood there as though in a trance with Rosemary trying to stop the bleeding with a towel. Gloria had the good sense to enlist assistance from Norman, who had commenced his studies at medical school, and he managed to staunch the flow. Luckily the cuts were superficial and soon he had tightly wrapped the wounds in bandages. He and I helped Patsy to his car and rushed her to hospital while Gloria and Rosemary had the task of closing down the party.

Patsy's wrists were stitched and we picked up painkillers so that she could get a good night's rest. The young medic on duty recommended that she see a psychiatrist as soon as possible. It was very hard getting her to communicate over the next days. She simply wanted to sleep all the time. In due course she did see a psychiatrist who was a friend of

Gloria's. He said Patsy was deeply depressed over being rejected by her past lover (which was what we all knew) and he doubted whether she had the confidence at present to retain a firm relationship. She was terrified, he said, of being forsaken again. He put her on a course of tranquillisers, which was the automatic remedy of the time. I wanted to find a quiet place well away from the bustle of Hillbrow but while I was out being interviewed for a job Patsy found a small apartment above the Montparnasse Café. When I got back that afternoon and found her in such a chirpy mood over the accommodation she had secured I fell in with the plan. It was a pleasant enough place with a lot going for it. The outer door above a flight of steps was very solid and secure and was kept locked at night. There were a few small apartments along the short corridor and what was so convenient was that an artist friend, Wendy Beckwith, a prominent lesbian, and her lover occupied one.

Within the month Patsy had acquired a job as an assistant in an art gallery and appeared satisfied. The pay wasn't bad and meant she had a fair amount of economic independence. Time and again I strove to get her to explain why she had attempted suicide but I was inadequate for the task and she would brush me off by either changing the subject or just falling into my arms and asking me to hug her as hard as I could. I heard somewhere that people who superficially cut their wrists or take an inadequate dosage of pills do not intend suicide but are crying out for attention. It sounded as though she fitted that category and I determined to pay more attention to her.

As for me I had found the job of my dreams. I started work at a film studio half an hour's bus ride along Louis Botha Avenue to Balfour Park. This was Alpha Film Studios where I was taken on as a scriptwriter after an interview with a bohemian type from London by the name of John Goldblatt. I had given him my portfolio of short stories and poetry compiled in my spare time over the two years since I had left school. The subject matter was an expression of revulsion of the apartheid system and racism. As I was not in any political organisation, my form of expression was not propagandist, which would probably have spelled doom regarding the result of the interview. I was taking a chance because I had no idea whether the person interviewing would be sympathetic to my views or opposed to them. I simply hoped they would detect some writing talent. As it happened John Goldblatt was vehemently opposed to racism and, as I was to discover, most of his friends were black. The monthly salary to start was £40 a month, five times what I'd been getting at Marks and Kaplan. Alpha mainly produced commercials for the cinema, which required an exacting, concentrated skill. The challenge was to reduce the content and punchline into a format which could be 30, 60 or 90 seconds. This was demanding and required much thought and skill. I soon got the hang of the technique, however, and enjoyed the work despite the fact that it was so heavily commercialised. I regarded this as a step towards serious film-making and had no insight whatsoever at that naïve point in my life into the malevolent role of advertising in duping the consumer. That was until I got my hands on a book entitled *The Hidden Persuaders* by Vance Packard. His aim was to alert the American public to the psychoanalytical techniques used by the advertising industry and its impact on society. Over time, the techniques have served to infiltrate the hearts, minds and bodies of the people of the world, inducing the masses, to crave commodities they do not need and cannot afford. Consumerism has become an addiction and intrinsic to capitalism.

I learned a great deal about the art of film-making from the senior scriptwriter, Lee Marcus, who was also a playwright, and a French-Canadian named Madeleine Anderson, who soon became a friend. She was funky and cool and wore a large pair of dark glasses day and night, indoors and out, even, as I was to discover, in Hillbrow's numerous clubs. She painted her fingernails black, 40 years ahead of her time. I got such a shock – it was as though beetles were sitting on her nails. She used to pull my leg about my looks and said I would make a good poster boy for Israel tourism. I told her I was not sure about Israel's intentions and that I was not a Zionist. She said she had an inclination to support Quebec independence from Canada and had always thought that Israel had the right to its independence. What about the Palestinian rights, I asked her. Supposing native Americans had survived in Quebec as a national entity, having escaped with sufficient numbers from the original genocide, would she in the mid-20th century support their ethnic cleansing in favour of Quebecan settler rights? I was empowered with my argument owing to discussions I had with Larry Salomon, who graphically explained to me the process of genocide that had been launched against the native American nations as the continent was won from north to south by European conquistadors. I had also picked up a book by the American author Howard Fast who, apart from writing such outstanding novels as *Spartacus*, about the heroic slave rebellion against Roman rule, had produced *The Last Frontier*, which was about the desperate struggle for survival of the Cheyenne Indians. I loaned Madeleine the book and it changed her attitude.

I was soon regarded as a successful scriptwriter as many of my scenarios written on spec for sales staff hawking them to big and small commercial companies were snapped up and made into films, netting decent profits for the studio. There were several talented film directors on the staff from Europe. I watched them drinking coffee and cognac on cold winter mornings and working on the studio floor. In less than a year I was given the opportunity to direct films as well as script them. My friend from KES, Grenville Middleton, who I had introduced to Dorothy Masuka and the Hillbrow scene, was a cameraman at Alpha and we worked on films together. I was writer-director, he was cameraman and my main actor in comedy-style commercials was none other than my talented friend Kendrew Lascelles, who had us in stitches for the character parts I asked him to play.

In the process of work I gained the trust of the black labourers who lived close by in Alexandra township. Apart from the small emancipated group in the scriptwriting department, as well as Grenville, the rest of the staff treated them with indifference. It was a case of '*Bheka lapa, tata lapa*' (Come here, carry this, take that) as ordered by the white South African set designers, which was cold and humiliating. The labourers asked me to buy alcohol for them from the nearby store on Louis Botha Avenue and I became their main supplier, with some help from Grenville. The white artisans were quick to pick up my fraternisation with the blacks and passed what they thought were witty quips about me being a 'kaffir boetie', such as: 'Would you like your sister to marry a black man?' While not letting on that my sister was actually married to a white man, I affected a counter to their nonsense, answering: 'Yes indeed – we have been trying for years to get her married off without success.' This kind of tension-laden conversation could easily degenerate into a fist fight but I had got to a point in my life after my street fighting days not to descend to that level. Turning their animosity into a joke tended to work for they appreciated the banter and thought I was being macho. I'd noticed them gawking at the stunning black models we often filmed and would sidle up behind them with a warning that they'd better be careful because there were police spies about assessing who might be inclined to break the Immorality Act.

If ever Alpha Film Studios rocked with energy it was at that time when we were shooting an ambitious Coca-Cola commercial for the township market featuring some of the cast of *King Kong* in a song and dance routine from that sensational musical. Centre stage was none other than my lady friend Miriam Makeba. She did not hide her joy at meeting me on the film set in front of virtually the entire studio for those who weren't working on the advert were captivated spectators.

Madeleine Anderson's husband Al was a jazz musician and composer and his group appeared at the Montparnasse. I introduced her to Gloria which resulted in the break-up of two relationships: Gloria left Rosemary for Madeleine and Madeleine left her husband for Gloria – for a short time at any rate.

My resolution to avoid fist fights at all costs came to naught. Patsy and I were sauntering back to the apartment above the Montparnasse hand in hand one sultry night without a care in the world. At the foot of the stairs we encountered two young thugs molesting our neighbour Wendy and her lover Colette who were just returning home. I attempted to remonstrate with them but they turned on me, throwing punches. I knocked one down and turned on the other, who grabbed me and we fell to the ground together. The guy I had floored got up and kicked me across the bridge of my nose right between my eyes. I staggered to my feet, my shirt ripped off in the melee, and backed against the wall better to defend myself. One of the thugs pulled out a knife. Colette rushed upstairs, picked up a heavy vase and dropped it onto his head. Wendy, meanwhile, had run for help. Patsy stood by me screeching obscenities at my opponents. As Wendy reappeared with a musclebound professional wrestler in tow the two took to their heels. For a moment the wrestler thought I was the problem and advanced on me with deadly intent. Luckily Wendy stopped him in time. The blood was flowing from where I'd been kicked and I was rushed to a nearby hospital for attention. I needed stitches across the bridge of my nose and also learned it was broken – and not for the first time. I had double vision and was given an appointment with an optometrist. Painkillers were prescribed and I slept for two days. When I turned up for work wearing an eye-patch my boss John Goldblatt photographed me for his personal album.

Larry had befriended a psychology professor at Wits who was carrying out experiments with the mind-altering drug mescaline,[89] prompted by the work of Aldous Huxley. They wanted me in on the experimentation but apart from my work commitment I drew the line at messing around with drugs. Larry recounted his experience to me of seeing visual patterns in intensely illuminated colours and floating like a butterfly. Huxley was interested in drugs and experimented with them. He studied and wrote about psychopharmacology. Huxley's book *Brave New World* was a product of this. Mundy-Castle was attracted to Huxley's theories.

Huxley wrote in *Brave New World* about the production of a perfect drug to solve all of humanity's problems. For me that was ridiculous. I thought of opium addiction and the drug dens where users indulged in flights from reality. No way to solve humanity's problems through narcotics even if Huxley's perfect drug was invented. Take a holiday from reality? And if that reality was like South Africa? No way you could change it through a drug. It was a bit like Joseph Kibel's solipsist theory, that nothing exists which the individual is not conscious of in the world of his own. Just like the apple which he had placed in the box. Once out of sight it ceased to exist. I felt I was beginning to develop a healthy disrespect for mystical philosophy.

Through Larry I became friends of Mundy-Castle and his equally unconventional wife Heather. They believed in free love and were frequently changing partners, especially across the colour line. In this way I met a leader of the ANC, Robert Resha, who was said to be a firebrand. He was a very busy man, organising the revolution around the clock, and when he popped in to see her in private it was usually a case of – as Heather put it – *Wam! Bam! Thank you Mam!*

While Heather dallied with various menfolk, including a very suave man who owned the Lyric Cinema in the mixed-race area of Fordsburg, his cousin Dolly Hassim was enjoying the attention of Mundy. On one occasion during a party I was called on by Mundy to bring them a couple of beers while they were together in a bath and remarked as a matter of fact what fine breasts she had. From that time I became her best friend. Dolly Hassim was one of the rare woman writers at *Drum* magazine. Among other things she ran the Agony Aunt column with verve and wit and was always cheekily provocative about racism. She and Mundy ultimately ran off to Ghana together.

I had the opportunity of talking to Robert Resha and he explained to me the ANC's policy and objective of a non-racial South Africa based on the Freedom Charter. He was among the 156 members of all races charged with treason in December 1956 which had included my cousin Jackie Arenstein. He knew Jackie and respected her. He was among the batch of 30 of the top leaders still on trial in 1959 when I met him at the Mundy-Castles and that trial would last until 1961 when the state's case collapsed and they were all acquitted alongside Chief Luthuli and Nelson Mandela.[90]

Resha was a fearless activist who had worked on the mines and been blacklisted because of his role in agitating for better wages. He was regarded by the regime and the media as one of the most dangerous and aggressive ANC leaders because in addressing volunteers for the Defiance Campaign in 1953 he had stated that if they were called on to murder then they would have to murder. Much was made of this statement by the state in the Treason Trial but the defence argued that it was a turn of phrase, albeit unfortunate, calling on volunteers to be obedient and disciplined for the ANC was non-violent and did not advocate such action at that time.

He informed me that the ANC had launched an economic boycott of certain products to create pressure for change. He had just launched the campaign in Durban. Products from cigarettes to potato crisps to fruit were on the list. He gave me some stickers calling on people to boycott such brand products. I put them up on lampposts and shopfronts during nocturnal walks around Hillbrow and other parts of the city. That was my first political act and I didn't think it was very significant or could make much of a difference. I carried out Resha's request more out of politeness than any real commitment. It would have been embarrassing to refuse to take the stickers and once I had them I thought I should at least get rid of them and not by throwing them into a dustbin. That would be an utterly dishonest thing to do. I must've kept the stickers for over a week before remembering to get rid of them.

I did not join any organisation at that time. There were other visitors who attended parties at Mundy-Castle's home which was near Alexandra township and these included Resha's fellow ANC friends, Duma Nokwe, the first black advocate in South Africa's history, and Joe Matlou.

They came with their wives to a formal party and out of respect for them the evening was rather quiet and well behaved. Certainly no wife-swapping or risqué behaviour. They were rather tense for at that time the Pan Africanist Congress (PAC) led by Robert Sobukwe had broken from the ANC who they contemptuously called Charterists. Nokwe explained that the PAC rejected the Freedom Charter's call for all South Africans, black and white, to unite together to change the system. The PAC was anti-communist, he said, but were more opposed to the non-racism of the Freedom Charter because they were racists. Africa for Africans and sweep whites into the sea. 'Guests' such as the Indians should go back home. He told us that the ANC was organising a national pass-burning campaign for 1960 because those 'badges of slavery' controlled every aspect of black people's lives. The passbook was a pillar of apartheid. The next step on the road to revolution required that passes should be abolished.

Nokwe said that there was a place in their ranks for all South Africans. There might be things that only Africans could do, like burning passes, but then there were things only whites could do since they could move freely where blacks were prohibited to go. There might be different tasks but also many tasks in common. He was very clear in this respect and I discerned that there were shades of difference between him and Resha regarding how each viewed the role of whites. In Nokwe's case they should be equal members. In Resha's case they provided support. The nuance of this difference as I thought of it did not bother me. Little did I understand how qualitatively different the two positions were and how in later years serious decisions and in fact historic actions would be formed around them. At the time I was equally impressed by both men.

Robert Resha pulled me aside and in a quiet voice asked me to consider assisting the Movement. 'Just give us an hour of your time once a week,' he suggested. 'We need you to give us assistance. We meet at a place called Chancellor House near the Johannesburg magistrate's court.' I knew the building because when I was at Marks and Kaplan July Marishane had pointed the building out to me. The ground floor was the legal offices of Mandela and Tambo. The legal practice was virtually defunct, Resha said, because Mandela and Tambo had been preoccupied with the Treason Trial and nationwide political activity. Robert could be located in rooms off an alleyway to the rear of the building, for which he gave detailed directions on how to find him. I felt impressed that he should show such trust in me.

Robert Resha's friends thought well of Larry, who was on the point of returning to America. They encouraged him to explain to fellow students what he had seen and learned in South Africa and said that they hoped the boycott which had been launched in South Africa would become an international campaign.[91] Nokwe was very pointed in emphasising internationalism. He said it was not just about assisting another people but was the bedrock of solidarity of all people mutually struggling for a better world against a common adversary which he termed imperialism. I asked him to elaborate on the meaning of the term. I had in mind the image of Imperial Rome and I couldn't make sense of that. He was very patient and explained in very simple terms that he was referring to powerful modern states like Britain, America and France extending their power and influence initially through colonial conquest and military force followed by a system of financial exploitation and control. A spiderweb of inter-linking financial control across the entire globe. It differed from early forms of colonialism and the rule of ancient empires. In modern times international financial institutions and corporations had emerged to dominate the global economy. Modern imperialism, he said, quoting Lenin without me knowing it, was the highest stage of capitalism. I was both flattered and impressed. Flattered because I discerned that this celebrated advocate was finding time to clarify key points of communist theory for me.

I realised I was extremely fortunate to have access to African leaders like Robert Resha and Duma Nokwe. These were struggle leaders who knew what they were talking about. They were exceptionally impressive and affected me more than anyone I had encountered. Over the past year the time of my discussions with cousin Joel in Cape Town through to the direct struggle engagement with Resha and Nokwe I had begun to question my own integrity and belief that an existentialist choice could make me free. I might have been misconstruing Sartre's philosophy for in fact he was a man who had come to choose public action, as had become very clear in his support for Algeria's armed liberation struggle against France. It also appeared that he was attempting to reconcile existentialism with Marxism.[92] Yet to me it seemed he was content to be an onlooker and not a participant. Did one have to be a participant? How could Sartre be a participant in an armed struggle in Algeria? As a white could I be a participant in the South Africa struggle which, after all, was fundamentally the arena of black emancipation? Nokwe in particular held out the possibility of those like me being accepted as an equal in the struggle and not simply as a supporter. I noted this distinction between his view of the role whites could play with that of Resha's which was less inclusive. In turn I came to realise that this was the difference between a communist and a black nationalist, which had repercussions for the ANC in later years.[93]

There was a crop of young African and Indian students at the university with whom I was fleetingly coming into contact, particularly at some of the jazz events. Among them was a very young Thabo Mbeki, who was always very neatly dressed in grey slacks and a black blazer with a Lenin button on the lapel. He was particularly articulate and very impressive in a quietly-spoken manner. A group of university students formed the Africa Society, of which Essop Pahad was one of the combative elements. Ronnie Leader, who was studying at Wits, seemed to know a number of people who he said were not only ANC but wore red vests under their shirts. He seemed in awe of Pahad. 'One day,' he said to me, 'that guy will be a leader of the Communist Party.'[94]

I was going to miss Larry because he was an important sounding-board for my inner debate and doubts, which revolved around whether I could be satisfied with my white identity even though I refused to follow the conventions required of white South Africans. As my guru of the time Jean-Paul Sartre would put it: was I creating meaning in my life and therefore was mine and honest existence? The crux of the question for me or anyone who wished to oppose the system and break with it, or so I believed, was to understand the meaning of 'identity' within the social setting of the time which did not allow for a free individual identity to be formed. Then there was the question of whether it was possible to be both free as an individual and equal with others? Particularly those who were not at all free. like the black people, whether uneducated farm labourers or an educated elite like Mandela, Nokwe and company? And what system was called for? How did capitalism and communism answer that? Was it possible for the systems to provide both freedom and equality? The liberal or democratic capitalist countries might allow for individual liberty not found in communist countries, as my reading was suggesting. It was clear on the other hand, not only in racist South Africa but in the USA, that African-Americans and industrial workers suffered from massive economic inequalities. Never mind that Harry Pollitt was a communist, his description of the life and working conditions of the British labouring class illustrated the enormous gap between the wealth of the bosses in the struggle to survive of the workers. These questions challenged me for I did not know how to provide complete and satisfactory answers. One question led to another but I was not afraid of questions; questions are the only path to answers. I ploughed on and persevered.

Even more perplexing at the basic human level – could I freely choose for myself and were my answers and the ideology I was searching for necessarily what I could live up to? I had read enough to understand that people might be sanctimonious about their ideology, but contradicted their beliefs in their personal behaviour.

I considered my love and responsibility towards Patsy. Could I live up to that responsibility? Would I fail as I had come to perceive so many men and women I read about had in their personal relationships? I was none too impressed by Resha's obvious philandering with Heather Mundy-Castle virtually under his wife's nose. Did that undermine his moral conviction to the freedom struggle? I was not at all sure. Free love might be acceptable in the behaviour of people like the Mundy-Castles but so what? They did not have the responsibility of leadership like Robert Resha.

Sexual attraction and gratification which had possessed me as a teenager could not remotely assist. It was not free love that provided the preferred existential state of life as I observed with the Mundy-Castles. I could not discern love in that marriage, nor was theirs the kind of relationship I would ever want.

Could what we describe as love be sufficient basis for happiness? Could personal happiness be attained in such a perverse society as South Africa under apartheid, even if one kept one's distance from its corrupting power and asserted one's independence as I had been attempting to do? And if the country surmounted that problem, could such happiness be attained under capitalism – a system of inequality even if it provided the democratic basis for freedom? So many questions.

CHAPTER 22

Sharpeville
March 21st, 1960

WHILE I WAS BUSY GRAPPLING WITH philosophical questions about the individual, 21 January 1960 witnessed a dramatic outburst of violence in the Durban township of Cato Manor. The police were on a campaign to destroy the home-made beer production of African women, which provided some income for them. In the course of a brutal raid angry women and their menfolk in support rose up and nine policemen were hacked to death. In the subsequent trial of those involved in the attack the advocates for the defence stated that you can have your foot stamped on 999 times without reacting but the 1 000th time can result in a deadly outburst.

Within three days a horrific mining disaster at Coalbrook in which 435 miners perished illustrated the appalling safety conditions in the mining industry and the huge profits made on the bones of exploited black miners. The miners were suffocated by methane gas and crushed to death by rockfall. Many miners had attempted to leave the mine at the first sign of trouble but had been ordered back to work.

Two apparently diverse incidents within three days of one another were illustrative of the calamitous situation in South Africa. More epic drama was soon to unfold. The country was a powder-keg with a short fuse. The mood among South Africa's oppressed was reaching an explosive moment.

The rising tension did not reach the white suburbs other than in newspaper reports, which sparsely covered an ANC-organised strike at the end of 1959; news of the PAC's breakaway at the time; a call by both organisations for mass action against the pass laws with the PAC attempting to outdo the ANC, which believed in proper preparation before action. White South Africa, as ever, was in a state of soporific denial.

There was some tension at Alpha Film Studios when policemen arrived to arrest one of the labourers who it was said had been involved in fermenting riotous behaviour in the nearby township. When I spoke to the workers I learned that the situation was worsening, with police raids becoming more brutal. They showed me some ANC leaflets which had been distributed calling on the people to prepare for the pass-burning campaign. Discussions at drinking sessions and parties with friends from the black media such as writers Lewis Nkosi, Nat Nakasa, Bloke Modisane and Can Themba were becoming increasingly frenetic. The central debate revolved around the rivalry between the ANC and PAC and impending resistance which they explained was responsible for the increased police repression as the authorities sought to pre-empt action. The police were becoming increasingly trigger-happy and were particularly nervous following the Cato Manor killings. A peasant rebellion in Pondoland erupted against government-imposed Bantu chiefs and guns were used by the resistance. The British Prime Minister, Harold Macmillan, addressing South Africa's parliament, warned of the 'wind of change' blowing through Africa and said his country could not support South Africa's racist laws.

I was becoming more and more impatient with my circle of friends, black and white, because while everybody decried the state of affairs no one seemed to have any interest in becoming involved in the anticipated storm. The white media, fearing a revolution, felt that the answer was to remove the architect of apartheid, and that was the country's Prime Minister, Dr Verwoerd. The main mouthpieces of business, *The Rand Daily Mail*, the *Star* and *The Sunday Times*, kept up a concerted campaign under the banner headline: Verwoerd Must Go! It seemed something had to give. Verwoerd survived an attempted assassination when he was wounded by David Pratt, a white farmer, early in April but, like most individual acts, the system survived.[95]

Sharpeville

March 21, 1960 started off as a quiet day at Alpha. Nothing spectacular was happening. Then Lee Marcus entered my office, looking pale and drawn.

'Have you heard about the shootings?' she asked me, her eyes troubled.

'No-o-o?' I replied, sensing something awful.

'I've just heard on my car radio. Dozens of Africans have been shot by the police at Sharpeville...' Before I could ask, 'Where is that?' she added, 'It's a township near Vereeniging.'

'*Merde*!' Madeleine Anderson interjected in French which she seldom used. 'Those trigger-happy bastards.'

I wandered around in a state of rage and shock. We tuned into the BBC for more reliable news. Africans had been demonstrating against the pass laws outside the Sharpeville police station and had been shot down without provocation. The final count was 69 dead and 179 wounded. The victims were men, women and children – all unarmed. Many had been shot in the back as they fled. We could hear and see military spotter planes buzzing about the sky, and this added to my fury. The black workers were standing around, talking earnestly among themselves. I went to commiserate. They told me: 'This is South Africa. *Amapoyisa yi'zinja*' (the police are dogs).

The white studio technicians, English- and Afrikaans-speaking artisans, were all gathered together to keep up the spirit. It was as though everyone realised that we were in the middle of a national crisis and uncertain of the consequences. They grinned inanely at me and jeered: '*Moenie worry, boetie*. You will be in the trenches with the rest of us. *Ons wit ous* have to sink or swim together.'

In the following days my mood turned impatient. One intense argument followed another with family, friends and colleagues. Although my Hillbrow friends, from Norman to Gloria and Madeleine, were disturbed, I sensed they felt I was going overboard. My friend Vic Katz said I frightened him with all my talk and he didn't want to get into such discussions. After all, what could be done? Outside my immediate circle, few whites showed any sensitivity – the general view being: 'We should machine-gun the lot of them.'

The African workers at Alpha struggled to hide their anger. It was some consolation for my sense of frustration when they showed me ANC leaflets denouncing the shootings and calling for nation-wide protests and pass burnings. There were photographs of Chief Luthuli and Nelson Mandela burning their passes. This made me feel part of some cause aimed at challenging the injustice, but I felt the impotence of the spectator. A march of 30,000 Africans on Parliament in Cape Town, apparently inspired by the PAC, resulted in the government announcing the temporary suspension of the pass laws. Lee Marcus interpreted this as a panic-stricken measure and for the first time I had the glimmer of what mass protest could achieve. However, within a day, as though to compensate for the sign of weakness, a state of emergency was declared, followed by the banning of the ANC and PAC. Robert Sobukwe, the PAC leader, and 30 of his followers were arrested and soon thereafter leading ANC people were pounced on. I watched British-made Saracen armoured cars racing through the streets to nearby Alexandra township while aeroplanes continued to buzz overhead.

What could be done? I was dismayed to discover that there were no answers forthcoming from my circle. The one change was that the drinking got heavier. I accused my friends of 'fiddling while Sharpeville and Alex burned'. I realised I had been fooling myself. It was not possible to live life as a free and independent agent within a system that produced atrocities like Sharpeville. I felt I'd been basking in self-indulgent luxury. I cursed myself for not having responded to Robert Resha and Duma Nokwe to give the ANC some of my spare time. The newspapers spoke of thousands of arrests throughout the country, including leading members of the ANC-led liberation movement. What could be done? What could *I* do? Even if it was the small task of sticking up posters which I had previously thought made no difference? Now with the country burning and people in jail any act of defiance, no matter how small, had some meaning.

From the time I had left Marks and Kaplan I don't think I had donned a suit and tie once. Now I stood outside the magistrate's courts in formal business attire carrying my old briefcase. From a safe distance I was eyeing Chancellor House, the offices of Mandela and Tambo. The news had reported that the latter had slipped abroad on ANC orders to mobilise support from abroad and that the former had been detained. But no news, as far as I could tell, about Robert Resha. I had decided therefore to seek him out at the address he had given me.

To my dismay there was huge activity outside Chancellor House. There must have been six police cars parked outside the building. A large crowd had gathered and at least a score of policemen, some in plain clothes, were keeping onlookers at a suitable distance. Cars were being prohibited from using the street. But there were no police in the vicinity of the alleyway to the rear of the building which led to the back rooms that Resha had directed me to. Should I risk going around the block and enter from that direction? Then I saw the policeman who had arrested me outside the cinema after the Bill Hayley movie – Van Schalkwyk. To me that seemed to have taken place ages ago. I opted for boldness and walked confidently in his direction. He recognised me immediately, clearly thinking I was now an attorney. He was effusive in his greeting and asked how I was getting along. I told him fine though very busy indeed. He told me I couldn't be as busy as they were with all the nonsense that the '*ANCees*' were up to. He pronounced the word as though the '*ANCees*' were a collective noun for persons.

'And what's going on here?' I asked him.

He puffed out his chest and, giving me a broad wink, explained that they had escorted 'the top *oke*' of the ANC from *die tronk* in Pretoria to wind up his office.

'Which *oke* is that?' I asked.

'The Agitator-in Chief – the *bliksem* Nelson Mandela,' he replied.

'And what happens after that?' I asked.

'Back to the cozy cells of Pretoria where the rest of his crowd are being entertained courtesy of the state.'

That was all I needed to know. For sure Resha and Nokwe must have been detained as well. In fact that was the case and although they were being held under the emergency regulations, they were also the last remaining group still facing trial for treason.

I couldn't help noticing a huge, bull-necked policeman smirking with his cronies. Not the kind of man you would like to get stuck in a lift with. His close-cropped red hair was as distinctive as his girth. Van Schalkwyk noticed me looking at him and remarked: 'That's our secret weapon to smash the communists. Rooi Rus Swanepoel. The *oke* knows all about the Russians. He can knock down an ox with a single blow.'

The brute loped over, sizing me up and down. Van Schaikwyk told him I was an attorney. He looked at me with cold eyes, nodded, and left us, an unsmiling psychopath. Shelley's lines from his 'The Mask of Anarchy',[96] about Lord Castlereagh, the perpetrator of the Peterloo massacre, ran through my mind:

I met murder on the way –
He had a mask like Castlereagh –
Very smooth he looked yet grim;
Seven blood hounds followed him.

The man became the most vicious interrogator as the liberation struggle intensified. I personally knew comrades who died at his hands.[97]

As I was leaving Van Schalkwyk asked whether I was still rock and rolling. I said no, but that anyway the new dance craze in America was the Twist. I told him it would probably take a year before it reached South Africa. He showed a surprising sense of humour. 'Whatever the case, Mr Kasrils, don't twist too much,' he advised with another huge wink. 'Best to keep to the straight and narrow.'[98]

CHAPTER 23

Crossroads

March–April 1960

JUST AS THE SHARPEVILLE MOMENT of 21 March 1960 saw South Africa at the crossroads, I found myself at a crucial point in my life. While the massacre hit me with shock force, like being struck by a mighty electric bolt, I was desperate to channel my anger into some form of action. The bolt did not turn me into a Captain Marvel of my youth but I certainly had reached a major turning point in my life.

Sharpeville sparked me into realising the limitations of existentialism and individual pursuit of freedom. I decided that I must make a clean break and go in search of practical action in co-operation with others. Philosophical readings can be difficult, dense and complex. I found when I was isolated from people actively trying to change things it was easy to descend into depression and despair and be overwhelmed by complex detail. I came to see existentialism as highly individualistic and negative, in contrast with my short interaction with the members of the ANC, which had the opposite effect. The thought of involvement in an organisation of like-minded people striving against the most difficult of odds for change had an alluring impact on my mood. Art and literature, rather than dry philosophical treatises, can hit the mark. I had been reading all of Samuel Beckett's novels, and attended a public reading of his *Waiting for Godot*, a classic of existentialist theatre.[99] It is about a couple of tramps awaiting the arrival of a mysterious person called Godot. They wait and wait but whoever they are waiting for never materialises. Their fate is to be trapped in their helpless and hopeless existence.

The reading took place at the Montparnasse Café, with a formal discussion of the play afterwards – which was when I got into a huge row. Virtually everybody saw in the play a reflection of the human condition. I vehemently disagreed and goaded them with reference to what had happened to the people of Sharpeville waiting outside the police station. Life – and Death – presented for those people a very different Godot. At the mere mention of the word Sharpeville an irate voice shrieked out, 'My God! What the hell's Sharpeville got to do with this event?' That opened the floodgates. I was scoffed at. Didn't the fate of the people at Sharpeville prove Beckett's outlook? No, I responded. African people were rising up all over the country to change their conditions. They might face death but they were quite aware of the circumstance.

Another person, in a very supercilious tone, argued that if one wished to use a political perspective, the blacks were in fact waiting for their leader as represented by Godot, but their deliverance never materialised because all leaders everywhere in the world were either unreliable or downright imposters and couldn't be trusted. The blacks would go on and on awaiting deliverance which would never come.

I contested that and said history had shown otherwise, from the French Revolution to the way the Russians had defeated Hitler, that people could bring about radical change. That brought out more jeers about the Robespierres and the Stalins who consign millions to their deaths and 'even consume their own children', as someone put it – meaning that they go to the guillotine or get purged.[100] I accepted that leaders could betray the people but countered by claiming that it was the people who drove history. That solicited another derisory response with someone jeering, 'The people, the people, who are the people?' I tried to respond to that but my voice was drowned out. No use trying to argue that all of us present were pale faces who benefited from the system whether we voted for Verwoerd or not and that the people I was referring to were the oppressed Africans. Only they had the potential to fundamentally change things.

Debate within my inner circle continued afterwards. Gloria and Madeleine remarked in a not-unfriendly way that I sounded like a communist. But I didn't even know what communism was, I retorted, lamenting that when one spoke out against tyranny everyone interpreted that as communism. The Montparnasse debate was heated and emotional but it helped to clarify my thoughts and confirmed my realisation of the immense gulf between myself and even fairly liberal-minded people. That was the first time I had spoken in public, although it was a small audience of a few score. I was rather nervous when I first raised my voice in the debate but I discovered that when you argue from the heart your confidence rises and you find your voice.

My emotions were in turmoil and that night I could not sleep. One of the books Larry had left me was the collected plays of an American playwright named Clifford Odets. I had noticed that one of the plays, written in 1935 – well before Beckett had written his *Waiting for Godot* – was entitled *Waiting for Lefty* and I raced through it.[101] It is about workers engaged in a debate about whether to strike or not, being misdirected by crooked union leaders secretly in league with the bosses intent to subvert a 'yes' vote. The workers insist on waiting until Lefty, a leader who champions their rights, arrives. As with the Godot play the would-be saviour fails to appear and it is only learned at the end that he had been assassinated on his way to the meeting. The workers had in any event decided they would not wait for him any longer and decided to take charge of their destiny by opting to strike.

That play gave me the encouragement I required. It enabled me to see the contrast between existentialism and political activism – Marxism, if you like. The one based on individualism and despair about human destiny; the other a belief in people's power and the possibility of change. If I needed theory to persuade me rather than simply my gut feeling, *Waiting for Lefty* was further motivation.[102]

It was Easter, just over a week after the Sharpeville massacre, and I was able to take a short break from work. Patsy readily agreed to my proposal that we travel to Durban where we arranged to stay with our friend Wendy Beckworth, who had been jilted by her partner and had changed jobs and abode.

My aim was to connect with my mother's cousin Jacqueline Arenstein who would surely be able to put me in contact with the ANC. I could still be diverted by other interests. Wendy announced that the Royal Ballet company from London was in town and owing to her connections she could get tickets for us to attend a performance that very evening, after which there would be a party at the home of Durban's leading art fundi Neil Sac. We accepted the offer with alacrity, adored the performance and had a heady time interacting with the dancers afterwards. I am ashamed to say that with all that revelry the pain of the country was a million miles away. The ANC would have to wait until the following day.

Cousin Jackie, an impressive woman, cool and thoughtful, was relieved to receive me. We met in the Indian area of town at the apartment of a close friend of hers, Vera Ponnen, a tough British communist from London's working-class East End who had settled in South Africa, marrying a prominent trade unionist, George Ponnen. Jackie had a subversive sense of humour but seldom smiled, reminding me of the Parisian beauties in Norman Seeff's book. She soon put me in touch with her husband Rowley, a people's attorney, who was immensely popular with his black clients, from whom he hardly took a penny. Rowley was a leading Marxist theoretician and activist, outwardly an extremely gentle person but intellectually as tough as iron bolts. He was in hiding from the police. Since I had not been politically active, I was an unknown entity to the security police who were hunting him and others, and could safely act as his and Jackie's go-between.[103] I arranged safe accommodation for Rowley with my former boss John Goldblatt, who was working in Durban. I borrowed a car to drive Rowley around. He was a great teacher and answered many of the questions I had been grappling with, reinforcing my determination.

Patsy appeared content to spend time with Wendy and some fun-loving hedonists from the Royal Ballet who remained in Durban for a holiday break. We accompanied Rowley to Johannesburg where he reconnected with the Communist Party's underground leadership. It was a real-life adventure being with him as I suddenly found myself in the deep end of clandestine life, from the disguises an artistic Patsy fashioned for him to the remote rendezvous points and secret meetings I delivered him to. One such venue straight out of an Alfred Hitchcock film was a Persian carpet emporium in Johannesburg replete with a solemn-looking custodian not unlike Sydney Greenstreet. Another was being picked up by a short man with dark glasses, hat and raincoat who thought he had mistakenly allowed two tramps from the library gardens into his vehicle at the pre-arranged rendezvous point. He became a lifelong friend and was one of those who had painted up the AN ATTACK ON COMMUNISM IS AN ATTACK ON YOU slogan in Yeoville ten years previously – Wolfie Kodesh.

No sooner were we back in Joburg than Patsy and my relationship broke down and we did not see each other for several months. Then I was offered a job in Durban by Lever Brothers' Film and TV division, with an executive title no less, and I jumped at the opportunity because I had enjoyed the clandestine political activity in that city. This intended move brought about a resumption of the relationship with Patsy for neither of us could bear the thought of conclusively breaking things off and were drawn back into one another's arms again. The heightened emotion pitched us into passionate declarations of love, leading to an impulsive tying of the matrimonial knot at the magistrate's court in Johannesburg in July 1960. In something of a gamble, I hoped that marriage would provide the security Patsy lacked and hopefully stabilise her.

My parents initially took this development very badly. They tried to talk me out of my decision, mortified that I was marrying a non-Jew. When they saw I would not budge they accepted the inevitable. They hoped that Patsy would convert and she had no problem with that suggestion, but I insisted that we wait and see how things worked out. Before we departed for Durban my father presented me with a cheque for 100 guineas as a wedding gift. The value of one guinea was one pound and one shilling. Prize money for most of the prestigious horseraces was in guineas so I saw this as a warm gesture by my father. When my decision to marry had been bitterly contested by my parents an interfering relative, trying to curry favour with me, told me to spit in their faces. I was utterly shocked and told him to mind his own business. I said that I understood my parents' concern, respected them and would not wish to break ties with them.

Unfortunately, the tensions and differences that arose between Patsy and myself during a brief marriage of only six months saw us arriving at a mutual decision to go our separate ways at the end of 1960. What went wrong during the few months we lived as a married couple in Durban? I was settling into my new job at Lever Brothers and it was not as though I neglected her, or so I chose to believe. She had a job as a receptionist in a motorcar salesroom.

The state of emergency lasted through to September and although I attended discussion groups and participated in the clandestine distribution of leaflets, I was not involved in active public politics, which were only revived at the end of the year. Patsy was borrowing money without telling me to fund a dependence on medication which I had not been aware of. It is possible that she was feeling insecure because of my increasing interest in politics and perhaps believed that she was being neglected. I regret that. By the beginning of December, she left me to return to Johannesburg. I arranged for her to stay with my sister and said I would be in Joburg for Christmas and that we should review our relationship then. Within a week my sister was phoning me to plead that I should give up my interest in politics because that was what was terrifying Patsy, or so she thought. At that point she was clearly on Patsy's side. By the time I arrived in Johannesburg the two of them were barely on speaking terms. Patsy was out most nights, returning intoxicated, if at all.

That kind of behaviour was anathema to my family and to friends like Vic Katz and Ronnie Leader.[104] They felt it their duty to report that Patsy was being unfaithful to me. I could have ignored that if I felt she was prepared to make a genuine go of our relationship. She was a woman I really had loved and I had been prepared to put up with her problems. I felt I understood the reason for her instability, which I was not prepared to be judgemental about because I knew she was a decent person. It was clear, however, that we were making each other miserable. It was Patsy who initiated the final break by disappearing from my sister's home and really leaving me in the lurch. I never saw her again.

Patsy was a very attractive woman who had much loving to give. She paid no attention to the colour of a person's skin, whether they were from high society or down and outs. She was perfectly at ease with the upper crust and with what some would call riff-raff. She was kind and generous but life had not been kind to her. She was sad and vulnerable owing to an unhappy family background but particularly the betrayal she suffered at the hands of a man who clearly had been the one real love of her life. I caught her on the rebound and perhaps if I had not got so deeply involved in the political struggle, which frightened her, we might have had a better chance of success. She was in a bad way for about a year. I received letters of demand from her creditors whom she was obviously dodging. I was sad about that because I knew she was not a dishonest person so she must have really been desperate to make the purchases she did, although I winced when I saw some of the needless luxury items. I realise those had been purchased in a desperate attempt for gratification. The amount of debt continued to rise without her contacting me at all. I could see that some of the items were for men's clothing – that really irritated me. I could not let things drift so in the end I closed all my accounts, changed my bank and sued for divorce.

Patsy had several relationships after me, one with the Rydal Mount landlady's son and another with a budding young poet, and as far as I know gave birth to a baby girl as a result of her relationship with the latter. I heard that within a few years she lost her daughter to a court order claiming she was not a suitable mother which gave custody to the father's parents. That must have been a devastating blow for her, poor woman. It was rumoured that she had retreated to a Karoo town and, if true, I wondered whether she had formed a bond with the strange occult lady Larry had given a lift from Cape Town to Colesberg on our way to Johannesburg in 1958. Then all information concerning Patsy dried up.

Soon after Mandela formed the first democratic government in South Africa in 1994 and I became Deputy Minister of Defence, Patsy attempted to reach me by phoning my office. I was abroad at that time and the call was referred to my wife Eleanor, who had met Patsy in Durban in 1960. Eleanor asked if she could do anything but Patsy was abrupt and said she wanted to speak to me about a personal matter. She refused to leave a contact number and was supposed to phone again. Would that number have caused embarrassment? An institution of some kind (which, without malice, I thought possible)? That was the last I ever heard of her. I have attempted to get in touch but the trail has long gone cold.

Afterword

2018 – My 80th Year

The Child is Father of the Man.

– William Wordsworth

In recording my story leading to 1960 and particularly the earliest recollections I have had to rely on, a search for the maddeningly elusive tadpoles has, seemingly – and I would hope seamlessly – transmuted into a connectivity revealing the meaning of my life in my early years and reflecting a wider social arena and the lives of others. As I consider those 'tadpole moments' which have been invoked by my thoughts during many a lengthy swim, I have found insight into myself and the answers as to what awoke, impelled and motivated me to act.

My grandmother Clara, when talking to me about the tadpoles and memory, would put the question to me: 'If I am not for me, who is for me? And if I am only for myself, what am I?' She would tell me to know myself if I wished to do good in the world. From her and my mother the golden rule of morality was often quoted: *Do unto others as you would have them do unto you.* That, they would tell me, was what my Jewish heritage really amounted to.[105] In my own time I came to discover that it meant a universal human heritage far beyond my ethnic origin. It also answers a question that is invariably put to me by so-called 'born frees' – black and white youngsters who never knew apartheid – but also an older generation, who want to understand why I gave up white privileges for a life of danger and sacrifice.

The tadpoles I caught were revealing. Apparent random happenings can constitute a coherent narrative of a life. I hope that as I have demonstrated my personal process in this book it will help others to understand the complex metamorphosis we all go through in life – change over time that can be as dramatic as the tadpole becoming a frog and the caterpillar becoming a butterfly; the infant becoming an adult.

The golden rule of a universal morality was passed on to me by my grandmother and my mother, but uppermost was the compassion and tolerance I imbibed from my mother's milk; exemplified in her response to my questions about the beating of an African man by white thugs in the centre of Johannesburg when I was seven years old, which kept my heart and mind open to suffering.

Catching childhood phantoms is like trying to trap tadpoles with your hands. Who hasn't been fascinated by those quirky ink dots and blots with flickering tails darting around the tepid pond of the inner skull? You snatch at them and miss by fathoms. You wise up. Daydreams can be caught if you thread together grey cells like a fine fishing net sweeping up the emotions. Tadpoles might be insignificant and without a backbone, but they metamorphose into an amphibian indispensable to a healthy planet.

As I swam and swam, length after length, tumble-turning or floating gently on my back, hands pushing at the water that slipped through my fingers, fractures and fragments came to me from the past. Some were crystal clear and vivid; others murky and as yet undefined. All were important in forming the shape of the man I would become.

The struggle of my immigrant grandparents and the working life of both my parents, and especially my father, played their part. The pride it gave me when I observed the humane relationship between my father and his largely Asian customers in his work as a travelling commercial

Afterword

salesman was a factor in the natural way I sought friendship between all people, irrespective of colour, creed and background.

The love of my childhood nanny Poppy meant I was not afraid of differences in 'colour' and precipitated my love affair with Africa from a tender age.

A significant moment took place in a Durban playground on a summer holiday, when a little boy told his mother he wanted to go back to their hotel and not play anymore because he had noticed an African father and his son peering through the fence, the expressions on their faces revealing so much. That others could be locked out from such enjoyment affected the boy profoundly. He couldn't bear the idea of enjoying privilege and happiness while others were excluded.

Three sisters teaching me how to dance explained the horrors of the atomic bomb, the execution of a couple on the framed-up charge of spying for Russia, and alerted me to the threat of apartheid rule in 1948, and the need to be wary of Zionism.

My rebelliousness at school contributed to giving me the guts to stand up for my rights. The senseless punishment sensitised me to a comparative brutality – by no means as severe – that black people were suffering from. The teachers who helped build character and backbone – including a crazy Scottish physical training teacher who strengthened my resolve to be brave – and my schoolmates who helped forge my personality and taught me to appreciate teamwork all played their part. An addiction for sports and particularly running strengthened my stamina, not only the physical side but the mental, too, allowing me to survive many testing times and to persevere against all odds.

The major turning point during my high school years was undoubtedly the creative teaching of Teddy Gordon, who opened my mind to the reality of the South African situation and, more importantly, the belief that it could be changed. Simultaneously, the appetite for poetry and literature which I developed at school aroused and inspired me to change the world.

A photograph of a Jewish family destroyed by the Nazis made me rage against barbarism. The surviving son became a best friend of mine and something of a mentor.

A mother, despite the alarming atmosphere of the Holocaust, reminding me that not all Germans were bad Germans, taught me tolerance.

A slogan on a Yeoville wall – AN ATTACK ON COMMUNISM IS AN ATTACK ON YOU – helped inoculate me against the worst forms of red-baiting. Instead of repelling me against relatives who had joined the Communist Party, I actively sought them out and the ANC connection at the same time.

Learning from a simple rural messenger in an attorney's office how to assess the behaviour of others.

Learning respect for other human beings which helped me avoid the trap of racism, homophobia, male chauvinism, the ill-treatment of women and gender discrimination.

Learning from good friends such as my cousin Joel Tobias, Norman and Larry, Gloria and Patsy, Zoot and Miriam and so many others in my early adult life about the finer things in life.

Learning from my first contacts with the ANC, people like Duma Nokwe and Robert Resha, about the organised struggle for liberation against white domination and that whites could play a role in it.

Learning through the women of my early adulthood, I was fortunate to have relationships which helped me through my sexual awakening and developed within me a healthy attitude to humanity's essential needs based on the desire to love and be loved, for it is not only satisfying the need for food, clothing and shelter that enables us to survive and reproduce.

And then came Sharpeville: 21 March 1960.

Carpe diem? Would I seize the day or not? I do not claim that at that point I was taking a decision in a calculated and measured way to make a decisive choice that would change my life irrevocably. I am a hot-blooded person not unknown for acting in a spontancous and impulsive manner. There is no doubt many of my comrades would criticise me for this, not to mention school chums from my rebellious teenage years. To many a school pal I was regarded as a traitor during the anti-apartheid struggle, although several congratulated me after apartheid had fallen and were pleased to relate to me, foremost among them Ali Bacher the cricketer.

Afterword

A second category became even more hostile when it became apparent that I was as opposed to Israel's treatment of the Palestinians as I had been to apartheid brutality. I would claim that the action I threw myself into stemmed from a strongly felt conviction in what was right and what was wrong; what was just and unjust. I am fortified by the saying I heard when undergoing military training in the Soviet Union in 1964: *He who makes no mistakes does nothing.*

In the Easter of 1960 sticking to the straight and narrow, refraining from being bold, was the last thing on my mind. In old age now, as then, I will not follow the path most trod but will do as Dylan Thomas penned, *'Do not go gentle into that good night, rage, rage against the dying of the light'.*[106]

I have written a lengthy memoir, *Armed and Dangerous: From Undercover Struggle to Freedom*, which thoroughly deals with the period from Sharpeville and beyond which has its roots in my early life – from childhood to the onset of adulthood.[107] The time spent in Rowley Arenstein's company at the onset of 1960 gave me my initial grounding in Marxism, the South African struggle and international events. In lengthy discussions with him he helped sort out all the problematic questions I had been wrestling with over a year or more. When we discussed the issue of existentialism versus Marxism and I mentioned the two plays I had read, he found that extremely amusing and took great pleasure in unpacking all the negative features of the Godot play, which he did with ease. I was intrigued to hear his views of Jean-Paul Sartre and existentialism. Although he felt that Sartre had exonerated himself by supporting the Algerians in the struggle for national independence and courageously exposing France's colonial brutality and criminal use of torture, he criticised Sartre's world view. He did concede that his philosophy was more progressive than the obscurantism of the central school of existentialists bogged down in the search for the elusive 'meaning of life' and their ultimate pessimism, owing to their fear of the masses. He debunked my former guru's appropriation of Marxism. He termed this 'fancy sophistry' which led people down a *cul-de-sac*. He called it 'an appropriation of Marxism' which emptied it of its core, which was class struggle, with the working class the leading class at the helm. He termed Sartre a liberal which, as I came to know Rowley, was a term he used to describe any theory or individual whose position was devoid of class content. In the final analysis all such philosophies propped up bourgeois class rule, he explained. In my brief meetings with his wife Jackie I gained from her a need to be sceptical of all things and that inherent to Marxism was never to stop raising questions.

I cannot say that I developed a refined understanding of Marxism at that stage but Rowley strove to make sure that I grasped the full meaning of what is referred to as Marx's key proposition: 'The philosophers have hitherto attempted to interpret the world. The point, however, is to change it.'[108]

Was that the answer to all the fuss and bother of my adolescent years? Was that what my search for the elusive 'meaning of life' was all about? Some say the answer lies in the path to God and the hereafter. As we have seen, the existentialists focus on the individual who must exercise his or her will. Not to say that there is no overlapping. The hedonists are fixated by the pursuit of pleasure; narcissists are pathologically in love with themselves and devoid of feeling for others; pessimists say that life has no meaning so don't even bother to ask why we are here.

Followers of Monty Python will laugh in agreement and add that life's just a bad joke, as depicted in *The Life of Brian*. Ditto the nihilists, without the humour. Marxists will inform you of a reality that focuses on the material productive condition and necessities of life. Unless reasonably satisfied, all other pursuits and the prospect of happiness is severely limited. When such conditions develop those in a position to benefit are able to lead meaningful lives. If you do not have the material means to sustain life – the necessary food, shelter, health care, clothing, employment, education – there's not much quality of life to enjoy. And the only point to your life is a struggle to survive. Scant happiness or a meaningful life for the slave under the Romans, serf under the aristocracy, mine worker at Coalbrook, the forced labourer on the Bethal potato fields. The question which bothered me from my formative years was the wish for such happiness to be shared in the initial moment of seeing a black child prohibited from enjoying playground activities alongside the likes of me. My conscience and the circumstances I encountered led me to make the choice of joining with others to make that better life happen for all.

Afterword

My political choice was consistent with that childhood wish. I was able to participate for over 30 years in the liberation struggle against apartheid South Africa with the support of my late wife Eleanor and live to see the unjust system collapse in 1990 when we returned from 27 years' exile working for the ANC and Communist Party abroad. In all that time I worked voluntarily, like so many others, and received an allowance that couldn't even rival what had been paid at M&J Marks and Kaplan. Eleanor put the bread on the family table in all those years and raised my sons. This was followed by serving in the new democratic government from 1994 to 2008 in various cabinet portfolios. There were sacrifices of a personal nature, long periods when I lived apart from my London-based family and problems this created in their lives, and the pain of seeing scores of comrades in arms perish in the struggle. If I was given the opportunity to start my life afresh I would make the same choice again and hopefully avoid some of the errors and the wounds I unconsciously created.

My father died within a few months of my going into exile towards the end of 1963 with the police hot on my trail. I had a secret meeting with him and my mother in Johannesburg just prior to my slipping out of the country. They were greatly relieved that I had not been captured and did not admonish me for becoming a political outlaw. Izzy showed a quiet pride in the fact that I had stood up to the government. I understood this as his approval of the choice I had made. After my departure he became fatally ill with the sudden onset of pancreatic cancer. I learned from my mother that he was relieved to hear that I had arrived safely in Tanzania.

My grandfather Abe Cohen died the following year after being admitted to hospital with a diabetic condition that resulted in the amputation of a leg. Whenever he received visitors, he would ask them if they had seen a leg running around. He died soon after the operation from a heart attack. In my old age I struggle with his physical legacy for it is his genes that appear to be enforcing a portly physique on me. When I last saw him he had all of three teeth in his head. At the age of 80 I have all my teeth save for a single extraction – the advantage of my more privileged upbringing as a child. He was never happy with my involvement in liberation politics and in that biting way he often used appended some lines to a letter my mother wrote informing me of my father's death:

Dear boy, I am happy you made good your escape thanks to God. These meshuganas would have strung you up. Oy gevalt. God forbid. One thing you always did was run fast. Sometimes you reminded me of Cocky Feldman. What a mensch. A Jew to be proud of. I must admit you also had his chutzpah. Your late Dad said that. May he rest in peace. My considered advice is stop being meshuga yourself. Get out of politics. Find an honest career. Like in that movie business you did. I believe that pay's better and you get a lot of free popcorn. It will help you settle down and raise a family. Politics is a dirty game. These ANC people you are helping won't thank you in the end. Last piece of advice and I won't bother you anymore. Get out of Africa. Go to America. Make your fortune there.

I wanted to be able to tell my grandfather that what I was doing was not about seeking appreciation. It was not about personal interests. But I didn't realise how tough and disappointing things could get after freedom had been achieved. I know he would be telling me in the South Africa of today: 'Well, didn't I tell you a thing or two?' 'Come on, Gramps,' I would respond, 'did you ever think we would overthrow apartheid?'

My mother lived to the ripe old age of 94, remaining steadfastly loyal to me. She was very proud that I had become a government minister and was always reassuring me that my father would have felt the same way. She voted ANC in the two national elections that took place before her death. I am constantly aware of the debt of gratitude I owe my parents.

While accepting Stuart Hall's point of view (that it is generally difficult to distinguish between 'the philosophies through which people understand the world, and the practices through which they operate in it'), I have come to see that many a respected revolutionary can certainly deviate in personal behaviour from the finest moral principles emanating from his or her philosophy. Human development has a long way to go to achieve that moral credo. Human foibles, ego and greed, do not negate that philosophy. We all have our personal weaknesses and few of us can be regarded as paragons of virtue. This of course does not exonerate the immoral and the corrupt. We are ultimately judged by history and the extent of the contribution that is made in the course of life and struggle. As Rusty Bernstein discusses in his review of *Armed and Dangerous* (see Appendix), history asks not only what happened, but why. Was the course chosen justified by the situation, and its conduct vindicated by the outcome? Could it have been done differently, better, and with different endings? Was it necessary?[109]

I leave history to be my judge – should history think I'm that important. This memoir, *Catching Tadpoles*, covers the first score years of my life. In the course of writing and of engaging with my memories of the past I have been amazed at the extent of the impact of my formative years on my later adult development. Three other memoirs cover the following 60 years in which I had much to learn, all played out within an epic historic context, and I am but a pebble in the sand. Had I not been born or had I made a different choice, to be uninvolved, what remote difference would there have been in the final outcome? I don't believe freedom for South Africa would have come a minute earlier or later. To individual lives affected by me, yes, there would have been an impact – but not to the grander picture.

Another way of looking at it is the extent to which one's involvement positively affected or influenced others as a link in a human chain. Countless numbers of actions, interactions and reactions build up to a critical mass over many years of human activity and endeavour. The actions of many ordinary people transform into enormous energy, energy which can move mountains and in fact did.

To have participated even in a small way helped to make a difference. Was the course I chose justified by the situation I found myself in? Were my decisions and actions vindicated by the outcome? Could those have been done differently, better and with different endings? Was it necessary? Those rigorous questions can only be answered by a critique of an entire life but I can answer the last question in the affirmative.

Yes! in the final reckoning it was necessary for me to stand up and be counted, to act against the unjust apartheid system instead of upholding it.

Yes! it was necessary to act rather than retreat into a shell out of fear, opting to be safe and docile or neutral and sitting on the fence or going to live safely in another country.

Yes! to confront the terrible reality rather than being in denial as though nothing was wrong.

Yes! it was necessary for me to be true to myself and therefore to a common struggle with others. In so doing I found meaning and purpose in life; I came to understand the world better and I believe I helped to change it.

I did discover the power of Captain Marvel of my boyhood. But not as an individual masculine superhero of the comics. There was a bolt from the heavens, if I am to speak metaphorically, that charged me with energy and transformed me. That was the spirit of the masses that moved through me as it did countless others, creating a concrete force of millions upon millions that changed history with the potential to finally end selfishness and greed where power and wealth is vested in the few at the expense of the many. For me it follows that the meaning and purpose of life is found through joining hands with others to make the world a better place to live in. By the time I reached 20 the meaning of life was no longer an enigmatic problem to solve, but a reality to experience.[110] Striving to help make that reality a better life for all, by changing the world for the better for all of humanity, became a mantra to motivate and propel me in my actions. There is that saying, 'the child is father of the man'. Was the starting point of my journey the soft heart of a little boy who could not abide seeing black children shut out from the enjoyment of the playground – a privilege he enjoyed?

At 80 I am a bullfrog swimming in an ocean of hope. For the greater part of my life I have been swimming with dolphins.

Notes

1. Bill Briggs, *Body Odd*, 24 August 2012:
   'Our first palpable recollections – from vital, early mileposts to seemingly random snapshots of our toddler years – stick for good, on average, when we reach 3½ years old, according to numerous past studies. At that age, the hippocampus, a portion of the brain used to store memories, has adequately matured to handle that task, experts say.

   'In fact, a fleet of neural-engines are simultaneously revving to life at roughly that same age, including our verbal abilities and the revelation that we are each our own entities, says Julie Gurner, a Philadelphia-based doctor of clinical psychology.

   '"We know that having language can be very important to memories because in having words for our experiences, we can talk about them, repeat them, and structure them," says Gurner, who lectures on the brain's anatomy and functions as assistant professor of psychology at the Community College of Philadelphia. "Around the age of three, we are also developing a distinct sense of self that allows you to distinguish who you are from the outside world."

   'For whatever reason, one lone moment has been selected and stamped in our brains as the first day our life experiences became worthy of mentally filing away and cataloguing. In a sense, they're our cognitive birthday.'

   For further on Gurner and others, see endnote 26.
2. https://memoriesofatime.blog/tag/julie-gurner/
3. The generation born in South Africa after its transition to democracy.
4. https://memoriesofatime.blog/tag/julie-gurner/
5. Within four years from 1886 and the discovery of gold, the initial mining camp became the city of Johannesburg, dominated by mining magnates, with a well laid-

out city centre and immediate suburbs of the white working class and the affluent, surrounded by various shanty towns and slums housing black labour. The population was estimated as 100,000 – divided equally between white and black inhabitants. The population by 1905, following the Anglo-Boer War (The South African War), when thousands fled the city, saw the reinstatement of that number. Approximately 10% of whites were Jewish immigrants from Lithuania and Latvia, which means that when my grandparents came to settle, there would have been approximately 5000 Jews. By 1938, the year of my birth, the population was approximately half a million and the Jewish population had grown to some 25,000. The black population – a mix of indigenous Africans, Indians and the mixed-race coloured people, including some of Chinese and Malay extraction – were of comparable number but began to increase dramatically after the Second World War, and considerably outnumbered the white population. For an excellent account, see Luli Callinicos, *Gold and Workers*, Ravan Press, 1981.

The pogroms in Russia became more acute in the latter half of the 19th century up to the 1905 Revolution, when many Jews left for the West: 100,000 went to Britain; 2 million to the USA; 10,000 to South Africa. Most were seeking to get to the USA and few to Palestine. – https://en.wikipedia.org/wiki/History_of_Johannesburg

6. *Gauteng maboneng*: Sesotho and Setswana languages; *eGoli*: literally 'place of gold' – the Zulu-Xhosa term for Johannesburg
7. List from Yad Vashem, Holocaust memorial centre in Israel. Courtesy of my nephew Ian Jaffe.
8. Andrew Ezergailis. *The Holocaust in Latvia 1941–1944 The Missing Center*. Riga: Historical Institute of Latvia in association with USHMM, 1996. See also Wikipedia – Massacre of Jews, Libau (Liepaja), Latvia, 1941.
9. Long after my grandfather Abe Cohen's death an American relative who had worked on a family tree contacted my mother and her brother, Solly Cohen, and verified the Zaga-Kahn name.
10. 'Oh! Susanna' is a minstrel song by Stephen Foster (1826–1864), first published in 1848. – https://en.wikipedia.org/wiki/
11. Chandrea Serebro. *This Much Loved South African Shtetl*, www.jewishlife.com.
12. Bar mitzvah is the rite of passage for young Jewish boys who, on turning 13, read from the Torah in the synagogue and are considered to have reached adulthood.
13. Turffontein, one of the most prestigious racetracks in South Africa, was the site of a British concentration camp for Boer women and children during the South African War (1899–1902). Over 27,000 women and children died from diseases which were rife in the camps. Several thousand Africans who sided with the Boers died as well in separate camps reserved for them. According to the *Encyclopaedia Britannica* nearly 100,000 lives were lost, including those of more than 20,000 British troops and 14,000 Boer troops. Non-combatant deaths include the more than 27,000 Boer women and children estimated to have died in the concentration camps from malnutrition and disease; the total number of African deaths in the concentration camps was not recorded, but estimates range from 13,000 to 20,000.

Notes

Undisclosed numbers of Africans died in combat on both sides. – https://www.geni.com/projects/Anglo-Boere...Boer-War-1899...Boer-Casualties

14. Popular Irish ballad written in 1910. – https://www.thetabernaclechoir.org/articles/the-history-of-danny-boy.html
15. A bridge-style card game, Dutch and Hungarian in origin, popular with Jewish immigrants and beloved by my grandfather, Abe Cohen. He appeared to play it every night with his customers, generally Jewish and Afrikaaners, on his travels in the countryside.
16. Non-Jews
17. The Battle of Blood River is the name given for the battle fought between 470 Voortrekkers, led by Andries Pretorius, and an estimated '10,000 to 15,000' Zulus on the bank of the Ncome River on 16 December 1838. Once commonly known as Dingaan's Day, in today's democratic South Africa it is known as The Day of Reconciliation.
18. National Horseracing Authority, Turffontein, Johannesburg
19. 'Do unto others as you would have them do unto you' – from the Jewish sage Hillel. See Mike Marqusee, *If I Am Not for Myself – Journey of an Anti-Zionist* Jew, Verso, 2008; and Israel Shahak, *Jewish History, Jewish Religion – The Weight of 3000 Years*, Pluto Press, 1994.
20. *Armed and Dangerous – From Undercover Struggle to Freedom*. Jacana Media, 4th edn, 2013. First published by Heinemann in 1993.
21. '... a wagon loaded with sacks drove into the prison. The cargo was piled so high that the buffaloes could not make it over the threshold of the gateway. The attending soldier, a brutal character, began to beat away at the animals with the heavy end of his whip so savagely that the overseer indignantly called him to account. "Don't you have any pity for the animals?" "No one has any pity for us people either!" he answered with an evil laugh, and fell upon them even more forcefully .... Finally, the animals started up and got over the hump, but one of them was bleeding ...

    'Then, during the unloading, the animals stood completely still, exhausted, and one ... that was bleeding, all the while looked ahead with an expression on its black face and in its soft black eyes like that of a weeping child. It is exactly the expression of a child who has been severely punished and who does not know why, what for, who does not know how to escape the torment and brutality ....

    '"We both," Rosa added, "stand here so powerless and spiritless and are united only in pain, in powerlessness and in longing ..."

    'Meanwhile, the prisoners bustled busily about the wagon, unloading the heavy sacks and carrying them into the building. The soldier, however, stuck both hands into his pockets, strolled across the yard with great strides, smiled and softly whistled a popular song.' – from Stephen Eric Bronner (ed), *The Letters of Rosa Luxemburg*, Humanities Press, 1993.
22. William Foster and his wife Peggy died together in the cave. They are buried in the same grave, next to the 1922 miners' strike graves in the Braamfontein cemetery. Two other members of the gang died with them. The grave of my grandfather, Nathan Kasrils, is in the same cemetery.

23. The abortive attempt took place at the Rand Easter Show, Johannesburg. Pratt shot Verwoerd in the head with a .22 calibre pistol. The deed was an individualistic one. Pratt was not committed to any political party but was a liberal-minded man who loathed apartheid. He was incarcerated in prison for mental observation but soon died. The authorities claimed he had committed suicide by hanging himself. The police questioned employees at Crispettes Candy, including my father, in their enquiries concerning possible cohorts of Pratt.
24. See Chapter 20: Water's Edge for more on my introduction to Sonia Bunting.
25. A highly toxic home-made township brew
26. 'Our first palpable recollections — from vital, early mileposts to seemingly random snapshots of our toddler years – stick for good, on average, when we reach 3½ years old, according to numerous past studies. At that age, the hippocampus, a portion of the brain used to store memories, has adequately matured to handle that task, experts say. In fact, a fleet of neural-engines are simultaneously revving to life at roughly that same age, including our verbal abilities and the revelation that we are each our own entities, says Julie Gurner, a Philadelphia-based doctor of clinical psychology.

'"We know that having language can be very important to memories because in having words for our experiences, we can talk about them, repeat them, and structure them," says Gurner, who lectures on the brain's anatomy and functions as assistant professor of psychology at the Community College of Philadelphia. "Around the age of three, we are also developing a distinct sense of self that allows you to distinguish who you are from the outside world."

'Gurner's own first memory was notched, she says, at about age 2, taking place on the farm where she grew up. She is standing in her playpen, gazing out the window at a creature in the pasture. As she soaks in the image, her brain is flooded with questions and feelings of amazement because it is the largest single thing the girl has ever seen. The object: a horse.

'"That sense of wonder and curiosity has never left me," Gurner says. "I believe that sharing a first memory is meaningful because it reveals something uniquely personal about us to others. It allows us to share a moment in time from a vantage point of a younger version of ourselves, and gain insight into the younger versions of someone else.

'"First memories get beyond the presentations of everyday life – of clothing, career and status – and reveal something distinctly personal and unique about you ... something about our families or environment," she adds. "But all of it has something that has been so resilient that it has withstood many years of other memories and experiences without erasure. For some it will be fun, for others, very painful – but for everyone, it's personal." – From Bill Briggs, *Body Odd*, 2012.

Other researchers contest Gurner's dating of first memory recollection, placing that at around five years of age, and yet others as between six to seven years.
Dr Shazia Akhtar, senior research associate at the University of Bradford, and co-author Martin Conway, a professor at City, University of London, believe on the basis of that recollection only goes back to about the age of five. '[This is] partly

Notes

due to the fact that the systems that allow us to remember things are very complex, and it's not until we're five or six that we form adult-like memories due to the way that the brain develops and due to our maturing understanding of the world ...' – From https://www.researchgate.net › University of Bradford › Department of Psychology.

'The magic age for having memories that can last into adulthood is around 3.5 years,' Julia Shaw, psychological researcher London South Bank University, contends.

27. To sum up: Nathan Kasrils received a naturalisation certificate from the Colonial Secretary of the Cape Colony on 25 November 1889, granting him the same rights and obligations of a natural- born British subject in the colony; he received his discharge papers from the Kimberley Rifles Command on 25 January 1893, having enrolled on 26 January 1890 – his conduct was held to have been 'very good for the whole period', the remark that he was attentive to duty; on 20 September 1902 he received a document from the Dock Command, office of the Royal Navy, Cape Town, to the effect that 'he has been employed in the intelligence department of this office from December 20, 1901 up to this date, during which time he has performed his duties to my entire satisfaction'. Signed by the Commander, Royal Navy.

28. In *Jews on Commando* by David Saks, 2005: 'Antipathy to British imperialism was occasionally a motive for Jews joining the Boers. Nathan Kasrils, grandfather of the current Deputy Defence Minister Ronnie Kasrils, was hotly opposed to British imperialism in general and to Cecil Rhodes in particular. He evidently fought on the Boer side at some stage as his nephew, Joel Tobias, recalled seeing a certificate to him from General de la Rey describing him as a "sharpshooter and spy" ("skerpskutter en spioen"). Interestingly, Kasrils was also at some stage a member of the Kimberley Mounted Rifles. Although it is not known if this was during the war or not, it does raise the intriguing possibility that he served in the regiment as a Boer agent.' – http://www.jewishgen.org/SAfrica/commando.htm Sourced 9 January 2005

The source of this information was from my cousin Joel Tobias who wrote to me after reading the Heinemann edition of my memoir *Armed and Dangerous* which did not mention Nathan Kasrils' connection with the Boers.

29. The bout took place on 15 November 1952, my 14th birthday.
30. The original Captain Marvel was created in 1939 by Bill Parker and C.C. Beck for Fawcett Publications. The boy was named Billy Batson and he had the power to turn into Captain Marvel, the World's Mightiest Mortal, by saying the magic word 'SHAZAM!', which was also the name of the ancient wizard who gave him that power, and an acronym for the source of those powers.
31. 'Comic books went to war before the United States did [published from 1939]. No villain was up to Superman. Kryptonite, in a way, is a substitute for Hitler, because Hitler was the ultimate villain. They fought the Japanese and demonised them, but this was what superheroes were made for. Comic book covers from the period are superheroes punching out U-boats and tying anti-aircraft guns into knots ... There was something about ... the superhero figure, the messianic figure who would redeem the suffering and helpless of the world. There was a Jewish element to all that, and the creators of all these golden age comic books, many of them were Jewish

kids.' – Pulitzer Prize-winning author Michael Chabon, interviewed by Alexander Jurgs, 'Superman was Anti-Fascist', *SCHIRN* magazine, 11 September 2016.

32. Communist Party members Wolfie Kodesh and Percy Cohen (no relation to my grandparents) had painted the slogan on the wall in Yeoville when the Nats began announcing their intention to outlaw the party, which they did in 1950. I met Wolfie in 1960 in Johannesburg when I became involved in underground work against the government after the Sharpeville massacre. I met Percy in 1966 in London where we were in exile and he became my dentist as well as friend.

33. Among the leaders that organised the Springbok Legion during wartime were Jack Hodgson, Brian Bunting, Rusty Bernstein, Wolfie Kodesh, Joe Slovo and Cecil Williams, who taught at King Edward's. All were leading members of the Communist Party of South Africa. The legion had pressed for the return of the servicemen from the time the war ended when there were tremendous delays in organising transport home. The Springbok Legion played a leading role in mobilising servicemen against the National Party in the 1948 elections. It continued to mobilise against the repressive racist legislation that brought into being the apartheid system in the early 1950s before the legion became defunct as most white ex-servicemen became complacent and, with the privileges of apartheid, came to accept the regime.

34. Abridged note on the Jewish National Fund (JNF) received by the author from Dr Uri Davis, Palestinian-born Jew based in Ramallah, West Bank, who has made a life-long study of the organisation (March 2019): 'The Jewish.National Fund/JNF (Keren Kayemet le-Yisrael/KKL) was established by the Fifth Zionist Congress convened in the Swiss city of Basel in 1901 as the primary organ of the World Zionist Organizations/WZO designated to purchase lands in Palestine and beyond on behalf of the "Jewish" people for "Jews" only. The registration of the JNF in London under English law in 1907 as an "association limited by guarantee and not having capital divided into shares" endowed the JNF the legal standing of a not-for-profit organization, thus enabling the JNF to register as a Charity in numerous member States in the UN. Having appropriated inter alia approximately 2 million dunams/500,000 acres of lands owned by some approximately 500 Palestinian rural and other localities ethnically cleansed by political Zionist militias (e.g., Deir Yasin) and since May 1948 by the Israeli army under the cover of the 1948 war (e.g., Lubiya/South Africa Forest) the JNF now owns approximately 15–16 percent of the total land holdings of pre-1967 "Israel proper". Furthermore, having signed in 1961 a Covenant with the Government of Israel – the JNF apartheid Constitutional stipulation (for "Jews" only) is effectively applied also to State owned lands (approximately 75–77 percent of the said total) – resulting in approximately 90–93 percent of the said "Israel proper" being reserved in law for development and settlement of "Jews" only. Ethnic cleansing is a crime-against-humanity under international law. The ruins of many of the said 1948 ethnically cleansed (almost completely razed to the ground) Palestinian localities (e.g., Lubiya/South Africa Forest) and now including some Palestinian localities inside the 1967 Israeli occupied territories (e.g., 'Imwas, Yalu and Beit Nuba/Canada Park) are now covered by JNF-planted forests speckled with recreational facilities. Thereby the JNF is rendered a

Charity complicity with crimes-against-humanity and therefore ought to without delay be struck off the list of tax-exempt Charities in every State that allowed it be so registered.' – (http://www.uridavis-official-website.info).

35. The other version to the Israeli one was that the five Arab armies advanced into that part of the British-mandated territory which the United Nations had decided should be reserved for a Palestinian homeland.
36. Lubya, the Palestinian village, was destroyed in 1948 and its inhabitants driven into exile. The forest that was planted in its place was called the South African Forest because the donations had been collected from South Africa by the JNF. Attempts by the South African Zionists to have it renamed The Mandela Forest after 1994 were foiled. A documentary made by Heidi Grunebaum in 2013, *The Village Under the Forest*, recounts this tragedy.
37. The name Betar (ר"תיב) refers to both the last Jewish fort to fall in the Bar Kokhba revolt (136 CE) and to the altered Hebrew name of 'Brit Yosef Trumpeldor' (תיר יסוי רודלפמורת). Although Trumpeldor's name is properly spelled with tet (ט), it was written with taf (ת) so as to produce the acronym. (Ref: Wikipedia) Jabotinsky became its most prominent leader. He died soon after his visit to South Africa in 1941. Menachem Begin was another prominent leader and one of his prime successors.
38. Avi Shlaim, *The Iron Wall*, Penguin Books, 2000, pp 11–16.
39. Letter signed by Albert Einstein, Hannah Arendt and other prominent Jews, published in the *New York Times*, 4 December 1948, denouncing Menachem Begin, a prominent leader of the Irgun terrorist group, visiting America on a fund-raising drive for his newly formed political party Herut (later Likud) emerging from the Irgun Zvai Leumi (National Military Organisation). Einstein and his fellow signatories wrote:

'Among the most disturbing political phenomena of our times is the emergence in the newly created state of Israel of the "Freedom Party" (Tnuat Haherut), a political party closely akin in its organization, methods, political philosophy and social appeal to the Nazi and Fascist parties. It was formed out of the membership and following of the former Irgun Zvai Leumi, a terrorist, right-wing, chauvinist organization in Palestine.

'The current visit of Menachem Begin, leader of this party, to the United States is obviously calculated to give the impression of American support for his party in the coming Israeli elections, and to cement political ties with conservative Zionist elements in the United States. Several Americans of national repute have lent their names to welcome his visit. It is inconceivable that those who oppose fascism throughout the world, if correctly informed as to Mr. Begin's political record and perspectives, could add their names and support to the movement he represents.

'Before irreparable damage is done by way of financial contributions, public manifestations in Begin's behalf, and the creation in Palestine of the impression that a large segment of America supports Fascist elements in Israel, the American public must be informed as to the record and objectives of Mr. Begin and his movement ...'
– Dr. Albert Einstein and Michael R. Burch Global Research, 10 September 2018,

New York Times and hypertexts.com
40. Prime Ministers of Israel 1948 to 2019.
41. See the works of Ilan Pappe, *Britain and the Arab-Israeli Conflict* Macmillan, 1988; *The Ethnic Cleansing of Palestine*, One World Oxford, 1988; *The Making of the Arab-Israeli Conflict, 1947-51*, Tauris, 1992; *The Israel/Palestine Question*, Routledge, 1999; Avi Shlaim, *The Iron Wall*, Penguin, 2000; John Rose, *The Myths of Zionism*, Pluto Press, 2004; Nur Masalha, 'Expulsion of the Palestinians', Institute for Palestinian Studies, Washington, 1992; Edward Said, *From Oslo to Iraq – and The Road Map*, Vintage Books, 2004; Karma Nabulsi, *Traditions of War*, Oxford University Press, 1999; Suraya Dadoo & Firoz Osman, *Why Israel?* Media Review Network, 2013.
42. Bubbles Schroeder's body was discovered on 12 August 1949 in the Birdhaven plantation, a short drive from the posh Illovo home of David Polliak, aged 21, where she had been partying with him and a second accused, Morris Bilchik, aged 19. Hymie Liebman, aged 20, had given her a lift home after a minor altercation over her drinking, the three claimed. He explained that he had dropped her off without taking her home because they had a disagreement in the car. See Bubbles Schroeder - Crimes & Mysteries of South Africa, www.africacrimemystery.co.za/books/fsac/chp10.htm
43. Joe Slovo and Harold Wolpe were childhood friends from Yeoville. Slovo arrived in South Africa from Lithuania at the age of ten. Wolpe was born in South Africa of Lithuanian ancestry. They both became members of the Communist Party of South Africa and rose to prominence. Joe Slovo became the leader of the SACP, ANC and MK, the armed wing of the ANC.
44. In a review of *The Boer War* by Thomas Pakenham *(New York Times Review of Books*, 6 December 1979) Neal Acherson writes:
'The Boer War of 1899–1902 was Alfred Milner's war, as surely as the Second World War was Hitler's. He himself said to Lord Roberts, the British commanding officer, "I precipitated the crisis, which was inevitable, before it was too late." As Britain's proconsul at Cape Town, ruling the British colonies of the Cape and Natal, Milner was determined to provoke a war with the two independent Afrikaner republics to the north, the Orange Free State and the Transvaal ... South Africa would become a component of a Greater Britain of the white race – by which he meant the "English" race. There would arise a supreme federal world state, in which Canada, Australia, New Zealand, Britain, and the new South Africa would send their representatives to an Imperial Parliament in London ... In this vast structure, the black and brown millions would be no more than "justly governed" servants.'
45. The school war-cry was largely based on the war-cry of the first South African Infantry Brigade in France during the First World War. Many of the words are onomatopoeic gibberish describing the range of fire power.
46. David Mackenzie (Mac) was the first KES Old Boy to contact me after I returned from exile in 1992. He invited me to the school's 50th anniversary celebrations that year. I meet him and Bobby Fussell for occasional lunches to this day, as part of the 'over 80 year old club of survivors'. I met up with Grenville Middleton after school

when both of us worked for Alpha Film Studios in 1958-59 and we knocked around Hillbrow's bohemian set together. Later in Britain he and his wife Juliet founded a famous puppet theatre, the Movingstage Marionette Company, based at Little Venice, London. (See his memoir, *Like a Dead Bird Flying*, Mule Publishing, 2014)

47. Gary Player had been fervently patriotic during the apartheid years; was publicised as South Africa's sporting ambassador by the regime; and played golf with the racist prime minister B.J. Vorster, who was regarded as a hard-line extremist even by apartheid standards. At Mandela's inauguration as president in 1994, prominent South Africans such as he were invited, although in a tiny minority; they could scarcely hide their discomfort.

48. Cadets was a pre-military service training in all-white schools going back well before the apartheid government was voted into power by a white electorate in 1948. Connected to this was firearms training at well-endowed schools such as KES, which boasted its own firing range.

49. For an excellent treatise on this subject see 'Corporal Punishment and Bullying: The Rights of Learners' by Salim Vally, Education Rights Project, EPU Wits, vallys@epu.wits.ac.za and 'Alternatives to Corporal Punishments – Growing Discipline and Respect in our Classrooms' by Kimberley Porteus, Salim Vally and Tamar Ruth, WIts Education Policy Unit, Heinemann, 2001.

50. White farmers were being secretly supplied by the police and magistrates with victims of the pass laws. Those without adequate documents swept up in the pass raids were processed through the courts and distributed by the police to farmers in areas like Bethal in the then Eastern Transvaal, now part of Mpumalanga.

51. An ANC stalwart, Gert Sibande, who grew up in the Bethal area, reported to Ruth First and Joe Qabe of the left-wing *New Age* journal and after investigating the atrocious conditions reported the story of beatings and deaths in the potato fields. Journalist Henry Nxumalo and photographer Jürgen Schadeberg provided graphic testimony in *Drum* magazine. Nxumalo had gotten himself arrested to report conditions from within the system. These exposés prompted an ANC-led boycott of potato products in 1959 which became the forerunner of the international boycott movement. https://en.wikipedia.org/wiki/South_African_potato_boycott; https://www.iol.co.za/news/south-africa/digging-up-the-past-in-bethal.

52. For a brilliant book on the revolutionary Shelley, see Paul Foot, *Red Shelley*, Bookmarks, 1984.

53. Percy Bysshe Shelley's 'The Mask of Anarchy' was written in 1819 following the Peterloo massacre in Manchester that year. In his call for freedom, it is perhaps the first modern statement of the principle of non-violent resistance. The poem was not published during Shelley's lifetime and only appeared in print in 1832 when published by Edward Moxon in London with a preface by Leigh Hunt, who had withheld it from publication because he 'thought that the public at large had not become sufficiently discerning to do justice to the sincerity and kind-heartedness of the spirit that walked in this flaming robe of verse'. (Extracts from Wikipedia)

54. Tennessee Ernie Ford Sings 16 Tons – YouTube https://www.youtube.com/watch?v=Joo90ZWrUkU. Writer/s: Merle Travis. Publisher: Warner/Chappell Music,

Inc.

55. On 25 June 1955 in Kliptown, Johannesburg, 3,000 delegates from grass-roots committees from all over South Africa came together to co-ordinate their demands. South Africans representative of all races and class positions, from doctors, ministers, shopkeepers to labourers, domestic servants, peasants, students and teachers attended this historic meeting which gave birth to the Freedom Charter. The charter and the organisational work around it was deemed by the apartheid regime to be treasonable. Charges were drawn up and an indictment of High Treason served on 156 leaders and activists, who were arrested in a mass round-up in December 1956.
56. The Treason Trial, 1956-61: The state's case collapsed in March 1961 when the final 30 accused were discharged. The other 126 had been previously discharged in batches from as early as 1958. Jackie Arenstein was released with the first batch.
57. See Pappe's and Shlaim's works in note 41.
58. As quoted in the document 'Generals Balck and Von Mellenthin on Tactics: Implications for NATO military doctrine'; from 19 December 1980 presentation; Office of the Secretary of Defense, USA, Unclassified report. Von Mellenthin became an executive of Lufthansa Airways in South Africa and the author of numerous articles and books, among them *Panzer Battles* and *German Generals of World War II*.
59. Putco – Public Utility Transport Corporation
60. Nicknames for Transvaalers and Natalians
61. I was working for Lintas, Lever Brothers' advertising agency, as a film director between 1960–62. See *Armed and Dangerous*, Jacana Media, p 16.
62. Wolpe was a member of the Communist Party and was arrested with other Rivonia trialists but managed to escape with Arthur Goldreich. In a vindictive act of revenge the police then detained his partner and brother-in-law James Kantor and put him on trial with Mandela and the Rivonia accused. Kantor was one of those subsequently acquitted but his legal practice was ruined and he left the country. He wrote a book about the experience: *A Healthy Grave*, Hamish Hamilton, 1967.
63. Charles Dickens, *David Copperfield*
64. Dr J.G. Strijdom was the successor to Dr Malan. His Afrikaans praise-name, the 'the Lion of the North', denoted both his strength among his fervent followers and the fact that he came from the former Northern Transvaal (now Limpopo province). It was about this time in 1957 that the women of South Africa, 20,000 strong, organised by the South African Women's Federation and led by Helen Joseph, Lillian Ngoyi and Sophie de Bruin-Williams, marched on Strijdom's office at the Union Buildings in Pretoria protesting at the move to extend the carrying of passes to African women.
65. It was only when South Africa left the Commonwealth in 1961 that court cases would be prosecuted in the name of the state and not the English monarch.
66. Statistic of the South Africa One in Nine campaign. The British statistic: *The Guardian*, London, 27 July 2019.
67. The meaning of rock and roll was quite explicit if you studied its history. The

African-American diva Trixie Smith was already singing a great song: 'My Man Rocks Me With Some Steady Roll'.
68. *State vs Marks 1965*; Wits Local Division, before Hill J. See note 69.
69. Despite considerable research and attempts at tracing the characters described in this case, I have found it impossible to discover their fate other than the *State vs Marks* court finding as per the previous endnote.

   This letter to me from a leading Johannesburg firm of attorneys whom I sought assistance from indicates just how problematic that is: 'As stated in my previous email, a consultant at our firm who is the [former] Chairperson of the Law Society and a former senior partner is assisting us with your request. I consulted with him this morning and he informed me that this case forms part of the pre-law society, namely the Incorporated Law Society of the Transvaal; of which he doubts there are any records left. He has a contact who has just retired from the Law Society who may be able to assist us with your query. However, he is the only person who our consultant feels would be appropriate to assist in this regard. Therefore, if he cannot provide us with any further information then unfortunately we cannot provide you precisely with what you are looking for. I will keep you updated once I receive word from our consultant if his colleague is able to assist us or not.' – Jessica Ferreira, Webber Wentzel, Johannesburg, 29 April 2019.
70. Norman Seeff, born in Yeoville, was a fellow pupil at KES and we were in the athletics team together. After studying art in Johannesburg, he became a medical student and graduated as a doctor. In 1969 he visited me in London where I was living in exile. He was on his way to the USA where he wanted to work as a professional photographer. He settled in Los Angeles and became highly successful, possessing one of the world's best collections of portraits that he had taken over the years of actors and musicians.
71. Lionel Abrahams, whose parents were immigrants from Lithuania, was one of South Africa's outstanding writers, poets and literary critics. For *Purple Renoster*, see 'The Purple Renoster: An Adolescence' by Lionel Abrahams, *English in Africa*, Vol 7, No 2 (Sept 1980), pp 32–49.
72. Chris McGregor (1935–90) was born in the Eastern Cape and after studying music in Cape Town founded the Blue Notes in the 1950s and later, in England, the Brotherhood of Breath in the 1960s.
73. Dollar Brand (who changed his name to Abdullah Ibrahim), born Cape Town 1934, Kippie Moketsie (1925–83) and Hugh Masekela (1939–2018) from Johannesburg all became world-famous in their own right.
74. Careers of Dolly Rathebe (1928–2004); Miriam Makeba (1932–2009); Dorothy Masuka (1935–2019) can be found at https://www.sahistory.org.za.
75. The trio were among the foremost divas of the 1940s–50s. Their careers started in similar fashion – singing in the Sophiatown shebeens, graduating as elite singers in the big bands of the time such as The Manhattan Brothers. They featured regularly as 'cover girls' in *Drum* magazine and starred in films and big-time in the 1959 performance of *King Kong* before pursuing their careers overseas to re-emerge post-1994 in a democratic South Africa where they were fêted.

76. They ended up in Dar es Salaam but soon parted. Joe Lowe went to America and worked as a journalist. Pam was linked to the ANC and became the romantic partner of the Mozambican Frelimo leader Marcelino dos Santos. He became vice-president of an independent Mozambique and Pam supported the ANC operating from the capital Maputo between 1975 and South Africa's independence in 1990.
77. The word *kwela* was township slang for a police pick-up van.
78. Tixie Smith – Wikipedia; https://en.wikipedia.org/wiki/Trixie_Smith
    Trixie Smith (c.1885/1895–September 21, 1943) was an African-American blues singer, recording artist ... making her first recordings for Black Swan Records in 1922, among which was *My Man Rocks Me (With One Steady Roll)*.
79. Barry Feinberg, *Time to Tell – An Activist's Story*, STE Publishers, 2001.
80. Isaac Witkin, born in Johannesburg in 1936, matriculated KES and studied sculpture in London; he became apprenticed to Henry Moore and then became one of his most trusted assistants. He earned the reputation as one of the most original and masterful sculptors in the modern era. By 1985, *The New York Times* wrote that Isaac Witkin 'long ago worked his way out of aesthetic debt to such mentors as Anthony Caro and David Smith and into a powerful lyrical expression of his own'.
81. Years later when I was a father and my son Andrew was in a dilemma about remaining on in a secure job with the Foreign Affairs department of the South African government or throw it up in favour of following a musical career I was clear that I would not stand in his way. I had every reason to understand from my own experience as a 20-year-old that the worst thing to do was stifle a healthy ambition. I told Andrew at that point that I would never wish to be in a situation when years later he might blame me for having dissuaded him from making his own choice.
82. Harry Pollitt, *Serving My Time: An Apprenticeship in Politics*, Lawrence & Wishart, 1940. He was both leader and founding member of the Communist Party of Great Britain from 1920 to 1959 and served as a member of Parliament.
83. Leo Huberman, *Man's Worldly Goods: The Story of the Wealth of Nations*, Victor Gollancz Ltd, 1937.
84. Cecil Williams was being chauffeured by Nelson Mandela in August 1962 when the car was stopped by police near Howick, in then Natal, and Mandela arrested.
85. Also known as khalifah or ratib, ratiep is an expression of Sufi mysticism. Ratiep made its first appearance in Cape Town in the 17th century, brought by slaves from Indonesia. As members of the group or *jummah* recite prayers and sing religious songs to the accompaniment of drums, others enter a mystical state which allows them to strike themselves with swords and daggers without causing harm, thereby demonstrating the power of faith.
86. See Larry Salomon's database of images illustrative of African and South African history at https://www.youtube.com/my_videos?ar=2&o=U. These include a 12-part video, *History of South Africa*.
87. My nephew Ian Jaffe has downloaded the list from the Yad Vashe, Holocaust memorial centre in Israel.
88. Edward Roux, *Time Longer Than Rope – A history of the black man's struggle for freedom in South Africa*, University of Wisconsin Press, 1964. First published in

Notes

South Africa in 1948. Roux had been a long-time member of the Communist Party of South Africa before it was banned in 1950.

89. Mescaline is a psychedelic drug that occurs naturally in the peyote cactus found in Mexico and used in religious ceremonies by native Americans – it induces a psychedelic state similar to that produced by LSD, but with unique characteristics. Subjective effects may include altered thinking processes, an altered sense of time and self-awareness, and closed- and open-eye visual phenomena.

    Prominence of colour is distinctive, appearing brilliant and intense. Recurring visual patterns observed during the mescaline experience include stripes, checkerboards, angular spikes, multicolour dots, and very simple fractals that turn very complex. Aldous Huxley described these self-transforming amorphous shapes as like animated stained glass illuminated from light coming through the eyelids. Like LSD, mescaline induces distortions of form and kaleidoscopic experiences but they manifest more clearly with eyes closed and under low lighting conditions.

90. For more on the Treason Trial, see Helen Joseph, *If This Be Treason*, Kwagga Publishers, 1963; Anthony Sampson, *The Treason Cage: The Opposition on Trial in South Africa*, Heinemann, 1958; Nelson Mandela, *Long Walk to Freedom: The Autobiography of Nelson Mandela*, Little, Brown, 1995; Elinor Sisulu, *Walter & Albertina Sisulu*, New Africa Books, 2011.

91. The boycott campaign went international with tremendous success. Both Nokwe and Resha were among ANC representatives who, under Oliver Tambo's leadership, made the case for South Africa's isolation to the United Nations. But even before they left the country to join Tambo, the latter, with Yusuf Dadoo, was already mobilising international support reflected in the first United Nations resolution leading to boycott, sanctions and divestment against apartheid South Africa. On 1 April 1960 the United Nations Security Council adopted Resolution 134 which called upon the South African government to abandon its apartheid policies and general discrimination. The resolution was passed with nine in favour and France and the United Kingdom abstaining.

92. From the late 1950s on, Sartre tried to marry his existentialist philosophy with the revolutionary doctrine of Marxism. In his 1960 philosophical treatise 'The Critique of Dialectical Reason', for example, Sartre declared that existentialism was a subordinate branch of Marxism which aspired to 'renew' and 'enrich' it. See Jean-Paul Sartre, Existentialism and Marxism at https://www.marxists.org/archive/novack/works/history/ch17.htm.

93. Resha became critical of the ANC's incorporation of whites at leadership level at the Morogoro Conference of 1969 and was expelled with a group of eight in 1975 for factional activities.

94. The prediction was accurate. Essop Pahad became a leader of both the SACP and ANC and a minister in Thabo Mbeki's government.

95. The attempt took place at the Rand Easter Show in Johannesburg April 1960. Verwoerd survived a small wound to the head fired by David Pratt with a .22 calibre pistol. Six years later Verwoerd was fatally knifed to death by a parliamentary court messenger, Dimitri Tsafendas, on 6 September 1966. – Harris Dousemetzis, *The*

Man Who Killed Apartheid – The Life of Dimitri Tsafendas, Jacana Media, 2018.

96. See note 53 for more on this poem.
97. Swanepoel was one of the most vicious of the security police and tortured many political detainees as well as certainly being responsible for the deaths in detention of, among others, Babla Saloojee, whom he claimed had jumped to his death from Swanepoel's seventh-storey office in 1964. Saloojee was one of 164 political detainees who died in detention under suspicious circumstances between 1963 and 1990.
98. *The Twist* was an American pop song written and originally released in early 1959 (having been recorded on 11 November 1958) by Hank Ballard and the Midnighters as a B-side to *Teardrops on Your Letter*. Ballard's version was a moderate 1960 hit, peaking at number 28 on the Billboard Hot 100.
99. The play was published and premiered in 1952.
100. 'The revolution like Saturn devours its own children'. It was a common saying during the French Revolution (1789) and was most famously uttered by Danton during his trial.
101. Clifford Odets (1906–1963), *Waiting for Lefty*, 1935. This one-act agitprop play was first performed by New York's Group Theatre in 1935.
102. Years later in London, exile Robert Resha's growing antagonism to the South African Communist Party led him to sarcastically refer to Joe Slovo, who had become prominent in the ANC, as Lefty.
103. This has been extensively described in my memoir *Armed and Dangerous*.
104. I was in exile and devastated to learn that both my friends had died under tragic circumstances while they were still young – Vic Katz in an accidental shooting and Ronnie Leader by suicide.
105. That was the teaching of the Jewish Rabbi Hillel. He said that everything else in the Torah was merely commentary.
106. Dylan Thomas, *Collected Poems, 1934–1952*, Dent, 1952.
107. *Armed and Dangerous: From Undercover Struggle to Freedom*, Jacana Media, 2013.
108. Rowley Arenstein became a critic of the move to armed struggle at the end of 1961 and this soon led to his disengagement from the SACP. He served four years' imprisonment for his political opposition to the government, was prevented from practising as an attorney, and became an adviser to Nkosi Buthelezi of the Inkatha Freedom Party. For further information and the story of my relationship with him, see my three books, *Armed and Dangerous*; *The Unlikely Secret Agent*; and *A Simple Man*. The last in that series has an interesting account of my friendship with his youngest daughter, Jenny Friedman, who became my attorney from 2016.
109. Lionel 'Rusty' Bernstein, 'At Home in the Underground', A review of *Armed and Dangerous*, 26 November 1993
110. Quote by Frank Herbert, American author of the novel *Dune*.

Appendix

LIONEL 'RUSTY' BERNSTEIN. (26 November 1993) 'Armed and Dangerous – At home in the underground'. Unpublished and abridged review of Ronnie Kasrils' memoir *Armed and Dangerous: From Undercover Struggle to Freedom*, Jacana Media, 4th edition, 2013. First published by Heinemann, 1993. Source: Lionel & Hilda Bernstein Papers, Wits Historic Archives, Willam Cullen Library, University of the Witwatersrand, Johannesburg.

At home in the underground

You can cover the whole history of Umkhonto we Sizwe (MK) in the life and adult adventures of Ronnie Kasrils. When it was formed in 1961 he was in the ranks of its first Durban unit. When it consolidated and began its campaign of sabotage he was in the Natal Regional Command. When it suffered virtual suppression in the post-Rivonia period, he was wanted and on the run into exile. He became an essential cog in the slow reconstruction directed from London, Dar es Salaam, Lusaka and Maputo.

He was amongst the first guerrillas to be trained in Angola and in

Eastern Europe; planned and promoted the first attempts at armed guerrilla incursions into South Africa; became a key organiser of the MK infiltrations from the Front Line states which re-established an armed MK presence inside South Africa. He crossed and re-crossed borders, legally, in disguise and illegally; and finally returned the MK and ANC exiles from abroad after the de Klerk reforms. He was one of the leaders of MK's last stand, Operation Vula, when MK and the ANC were already legal but Vula's Maharaj and Kasrils remained at the head of the police 'Wanted' list.

Or, to put it another way, the story of Ronnie Kasrils post 1961 is the story of MK, and of the clandestine cloak-and-dagger side of the South African liberation struggle. It starts at the very beginning of armed and violent struggle by the ANC and its allies, and ends appropriately in the negotiating team at the CODESA talks when a new South African constitution and state is being born.

He was in the very centre of the underground, in the hub of the terror with its raids, ambushes and assassinations by the South African security Services, police and military. He bore a charmed life, surviving to observe all - and now to tell all - while hundreds around him fell into the hands of the jailers, assassins and torturers, and others were 'turned' by the enemy through a combination of bribery and physical pressure. Inevitably as his exploits became known, Kasrils the survivor was nicknamed by the South African press and public as 'The Red Pimpernel'. ...

Kasrils tells his tale simply, straightforwardly and well ... He is the authentic 'cheeky chappie', shown characteristically ... with both arms raised aloft in triumphant salute, with ... grin a mile wide across his face. And well he might grin, for he and his colleagues and their cause came out triumphant from a thirty-year battle against the vastly larger, better equipped and better resourced enemies in the state security battalions. Though those were thirty years of constant threat, constantly hunted and in dire peril, it seems to have been a life he revelled in; at least in retrospect ...

Kasrils, I think, loved all the clandestinity, the daring-do, and all the physical and psychological challenge of confronting Goliath armed only with a sling. Perhaps more importantly, he loved the comrades of all colours and races who joined him in his peripatetic life in the underground. Over the years, as many of them fell in the struggle, he must often have felt 'there but for the grace of God'. Deep dedication to their cause made it possible for the survivors to carry on without losing that feeling of excitement and adventure

Armed and Dangerous is his account of high adventure accompanied by suffering, sacrifice and endurance. It never dramatises the negative sides of violent political activity, but it underplays the tensions and perils, and concentrates on the dramatic events. It is an adventure story of a real life, of real skulduggery, of espionage and counter-espionage, told with no holds barred.

... Kasrils conceals nothing of his own operations or of those with which he was associated. Some have been reported before in less detail; from court hearings and security briefings. Some have been the stuff of unconfirmed rumour; and some have never before even been rumoured. Together they add up to a classic true-life thriller, which it is impossible to put down, told by a somewhat larger-than-life revolutionary who it was; and is impossible to keep down ... Unlike fiction, his story has no gratuitous account of violence, no glorification of the power that comes 'Through the barrel of a gun', and no voyeuristic lingering over injuries or pain or death. His main concern is for the life of his comrades and for their concerns with families and communities and nation. His story is concerned with the cause they all upheld; rather than with a desire to shock.

Other titles by Ronnie Kasrils

First published in 1993, Armed and Dangerous was one of the earliest struggle memoirs to deal from a personal perspective with the formation and development of Umkhonto weSizwe, and the remarkable role it played in helping to bring about the downfall of apartheid. Kasrils gives an insider's account of the workings of Umkhonto weSizwe, the armed wing of the ANC, during the underground years.

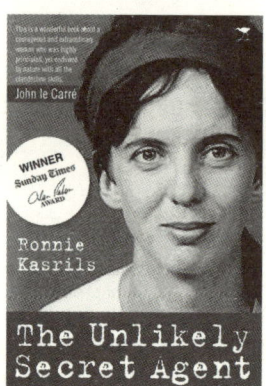

This remarkable story of a young woman's courage and daring at a time of increasing repression in apartheid South Africa is told here for the first time with great verve and élan by Eleanor's husband, Ronnie Kasrils, who eventually became South Africa's Minister of Intelligence Services in 2004. He is the author of a bestselling autobiography, *Armed and Dangerous*.

Ronnie Kasrils's insights into Jacob Zuma in *A Simple Man*, both shocking and revelatory, are vividly illuminated through this story, from their shared history in the underground to Kasrils's time as minister of intelligence and his views on South Africa now. Our understanding of Zuma the struggle hero, now perceived as having sold his soul to the devil, becomes clearer through this narrative.

Index

A

20th Century Fox, Johannesburg 22
Abdullah Ibrahim, *see* Dollar Brand
Abrahams, Lionel 183, 218, 283
African National Congress (ANC) 223
Albyn Court Courier 68
Albyn Court, Raymond Street 3–15, 23, 24, 34, 51, 54, 62, 66, 67, 75, 78, 103, 104, 106–108, 110, 133
Alexandra, Johannesburg 112, 141, 156, 157, 160, 165, 235, 240, 248
All Blacks rugby team 61
Alpha Film Studies xvi, 234–7, 246, 247
American Depression 21
Anderson, Madeleine 235–6, 237, 247, 253
Andrew Sisters, The 23
Anglo-Boer War (South African War) 60
Anglo-French Sweetworks 29
Animal Farm 73, 80
Apollo Café, Yeoville 182
Archie comics 50
Arenstein, Jacqueline (Jackie) 71, 113, 134, 239, 254, 264
Arenstein, Rowley 254, 263, 264
Armed and Dangerous xii, 25, 263, 267
Athlone School 64, 91

B

Bacher, Ali 49, 58, 262
Bacher, Yudel 58
Bales, Graham 58, 59, 85
Bantry Bay, Cape Town 216
Barkman, Betty (née Cohen) 35–6, 50, 211
Barkman, Harry 36
Barkman, Mervyn 18
Barkman, Stan 75
Batman 50
Battle of Ncome 16
Bechuanaland 110
Beckett, Samuel 251
Beckwith, Wendy 234, 237–8, 253–4
Beethoven 184
Begin, Menachem 82, 86
Beira, Pamela 196
Belgravia, Johannesburg 7
Bellevue-Yeoville, Johannesburg 4
Benjamin, Mr 'Dumbo' 102
Berea, Johannesburg 41, 138
Berman and Chimes 175, 177, 179
Betar Zionist group 80–84
Bethal, Eastern Transvaal 123, 132, 213, 264
Bicycle Thieves 186
Biggles 50

Bill Haley & His Comets 130
Black Beauty 212
Blood River 11, 16, 22
Bloom, Tony 124, 126, 128, 137
Blue Notes 193
Blyton, Enid 50
Boer War 3, 27–28, 37, 56, 66, 67
Boorany, Cassim xvii
Boy Scouts 80
Braamfontein, Johannesburg 6
Bradman, Don 61, 77
Brave New World 238
Bree Street, Johannesburg 137, 146
Brener, Jasper 145, 198
Brideshead Revisited 201
Briggs, Bill xii
British Boys' Own 50
British Kimberley Rifles 37
British Protectorate 79
Brittain, Victoria xvi
Brubeck, Dave 184
Bunting, Sonia 29, 226

C
Camus, Albert 196, 207
Captain Marvel 50, 51, 251, 268
Carruthers, Jimmy 46
Cato Manor killings 246
Cato Manor, Durban 245
Chancellor House, Johannesburg 241, 248–249
Cheetahs South African Squadron 74
Chevrah Kadisha 52
Chimes, Mr 175, 177–180, 182, 211
Churchill, Winston 74
Clarendon Cinema, Hillbrow 146
Classic Comic series 51
Coalbrook, Clydesdale 245, 264
Cohen, Abe (Kepkela) 4, 5, 6, 8, 10, 12, 13, 14, 19, 38, 112, 189, 265
Cohen, Clara xix, 3, 4, 5, 6, 8, 17, 22, 35, 55, 79, 133, 190, 259
Cohen, Solly 6, 7, 18, 33, 86
Colbert, Claudette 36–37
Cold War 65, 69, 73, 74, 80
Coleridge, Samuel Taylor 124
Colesberg, Karoo 233, 257
Colosseum, Johannesburg 22
Coloured People's Congress 225
Commercial Travellers Union (CTU) 31

Commissioner Street, Johannesburg 147, 152
Communist Party 71, 75, 91, 95, 126, 213, 222, 226, 242, 254, 262, 265
Community of the Resurrection 128
Congress of Democrats 126
Conrad, Joseph 125
Count Basie 184
Coyan, Gerald 24, 62, 64–65, 72–73, 76
Credit Control 149, 150, 151, 153–154, 170, 189, 206
Crispettes Candy 28–29
Crosby, Bing 12

D
Dagwood 50
Danny Boy xv, 12, 13, 15, 18–19, 30, 69
Darryl's, Johannesburg 214–215
DC Comics 50
De Beauvoir, Simone 196
De la Rey, General Koos 27
Dean, James 130, 184, 194
Decline and Fall 201
Defiance Campaign (1953) 239
Deir Yassin, Palestine 82
Devil's Peak, Cape Town 223
District Six, Cape Town 223–224
Doll House, Johannesburg 191
Dollar Brand (Abdullah Ibrahim) 193
Don Quixote 51
Doornfontein, Johannesburg 6, 9, 60, 178
Dostoyevsky 207
Dr Zhivago 212
Drill Hall, Johannesburg 133
Drum magazine 194, 239
Duke Ellington 184
Dyne, Marlen xv

E
Eagle Star House 147
East Rand, Johannesburg 28
Edwards, Professor Ian xvi
Einstein, Albert 81–82
Ellish, Megan xvi
Emil and the Detectives 50
Empire, Johannesburg 22

F
Famous Five, The 50
Fast, Howard 236

Index

Feinberg, Barry 197–198
Feinberg, Hymie xvi
Feinberg, Judy (née Cohen) xv, 6
Feldman, Cocky 13–15, 19–20, 80, 155, 266
Ferreira, Jessica xvi
Fingleton, J.H. 61
First, Ruth 123
First World War 25, 27, 176, 219
Fischer, Bram 95
Florence Nightingale Maternity Home 4
Florian, The, Johannesburg 201, 204
For Whom the Bell Tolls 212
Ford Foundation 219
Fort, The 4
Foster gang 27
Frances Street, Johannesburg 67
Freedom Charter (1955) 133, 239–240
Freidman, Jack 41, 88
French Resistance 114
Fugard, Athol 183
Fussell, Bobby xvi, 116

G

Geffen, Okey 60, 80
Germiston 19, 167, 168, 172
Germiston Hotel 168, 172
Gloria (Rosemary Taylor's partner) 195, 196, 204, 213, 237
Glory That Nearly Was Greece, The 86
Goldblatt, John 234, 235, 238, 254
Golden City Post 227
Golden Ray Café, Johannesburg 183, 198–199, 202–204
Goldstein, Abe 19
Goldstein, Ezra 19
Goldstein, Jumbo 19–20
Goldstein, Warren 19
Goldstone, Richard 118, 124
Gordon, Teddy 113, 120, 121–128, 134, 141, 156, 200, 226, 261
Gould, Shirley 148, 171, 177, 180
Gqabi, Joe 123
Grapes of Wrath, The 186
Greenstreet, Sydney 255
Guilty or Not Guilty? 21
Gurion, Ben 82, 86

H

Habonim (The Builders) 82–84

Hamburger, Hillary xvi
Hamburger, Tony xvi
Handful of Dust, A 201
Hardy Boys' adventures 50
Hashomer Hatzair 80, 82
Hassim, Dolly 239
Hathorn, Moray xvi
Hayley, Bill 187, 249
Headley, George 77
Henning, Brian 58, 59
Henning, Dan 119, 125
Herman, Kasril 46
Herzl, Theodor 86
Hidden Persuaders, The 235
Highlands North High School 131
Hillbrow, Johannesburg xvi, 4, 6, 146, 171, 182, 183, 185, 186, 190, 192, 195, 197, 198, 199, 212, 215, 234, 235, 236, 240, 247
His Majesty's, Johannesburg 22
History of South Africa xvi
Hitler, Adolf 24, 50, 51, 62, 63, 64, 69, 70, 81, 252
Holocaust 220, 262
Holt, Mike 184, 229
Hope, Bob 23
Hopkins, Berty 59
Huberman, Leo 212, 213
Huddleston, Trevor 127–128, 226
Hutton, Leonard 77
Huxley, Aldous 238

I

Inanda, Durban 202
Irgun Zvei Leumi (National Military Organisation) 82, 86, 113
Iron Curtain 73
Isreali Defence Force 79

J

Jaffe, Hilary (nee Kasrils) xvii, 5, 21, 33, 35, 74
Jaffe, Ian xv
Jaffe, Michelle xv
Jenny Friedman Attorneys xvi
Jeppe Boys High 27, 97
Jeppe, Zelide 184
Jewish Board of Deputies 133
Jewish Government School 6
Jewish National Fund 78

Jewish Passover 123
Johannesburg Stock Exchange 179
Johannesburg Zoo 6
Johnson, Hewlett 213
Jordan River 81

K
Kaplan, Izzy 'Kappie' 148, 152, 156, 160, 161, 162, 168, 177, 179, 189
Karlin, Sammy 182
Kasrils, Amina xvii
Kasrils, Andrew xvii
Kasrils, Eleanor xvii, 257, 265
Kasrils, Isadore (Izzy) 4, 7, 15, 27, 28, 30, 31, 36, 265
Kasrils, Nathan xvi, 27, 36–39
Kasrils, René 3, 6, 7–8, 15, 18, 20, 25, 34, 36, 136
Kasrils, Sarah 35, 36, 38
Katz and Lurie, Johannesburg 182
Katz, Vic 141, 146, 189, 247, 256
Kensington, Johannesburg 27, 37
Kerouac, Jack 219
KES *see* King Edward VII School
Kibel, Carmen 220
Kibel, Joseph 220–221, 227, 238
Kibel, Wolf 220
Kierkegard 207
Kimberley diamond fields 36
Kimberley Train 213
King David Hotel, Jerusalem 113
King Edward Education Trust xvi
King Edward VII School (KES) xvi, 18, 91–92, 94, 97, 100, 102, 103, 107, 113, 114, 125–126, 128, 129, 130, 131–132, 141, 153, 156, 157, 172, 183, 194, 203, 213, 236
King Farouk 74
King George 56
King Kong 194, 237
Kodesh, Wolfie 255
Korean War 74
Kubeka, Kollie Moffat 156, 157, 160, 162, 164, 166

L
La Strada 186
Lascelles, Kendrew 184–185, 229, 236
Last Frontier, The 236
Last of the Mohicans, The 51

Lazerson, Fay 34
Lazerson, Ivor 14, 25, 54, 55, 58, 60, 61, 63–64, 73, 76, 80, 81, 82, 84, 93, 95, 113, 124, 128
Lazerson, Sam (Six Finger Sam) 11, 12, 14, 32, 34, 128
Leader, Ronnie 187, 189, 198, 242, 256
Leister, Lynne xv
Leitch, Mr 55
Lennon, John xii
Les Miserables 51
Lever Brothers 255, 256
Libau, Lithuania 4, 220
Liebman, Hymie 88
Life of Brian, The 264
Likud Party 82
Lindwall, Ray 61, 77
Louis Botha Avenue, Johannesburg 28, 56, 122, 141, 156, 191, 234, 236
Louise, Peter xvi, 145
Lovatt, David xvi
Loved Ones, The 201
Lowe, Joe 196
Lowenstein, Charlotte 71, 134
Lubya, Palestine 80
Luthuli, Chief Albert 133, 223
Luton Town, England 224
Luxemburg, Rosa 25
Lyric Cinema, Fordsburg 239

M
M&J Marks and Kaplan 147, 155, 167, 175, 179, 195, 206, 235, 241, 248, 265
Mackenzie, David (Mac) xvi, 94, 102
Macmillan, Harold 246
Magid, David 57
Main Reef Road, Johannesburg 28
Makeba, Miriam 194–197, 237
Malan, Dr D.F. 70–71, 72, 75
Maloi, Morris 151
Man's Worldly Goods 212, 213
Mandela, Nelson 86, 126, 166, 239, 248
Manhattans, The 196
Mapam labour movement 82
Maphilas, Angelo 182, 214, 215, 217
Maphilas, George 182, 214, 215, 217
March of Time, The 74
Marishane, July 149, 152, 153, 158, 160, 180, 241
Mark of Zorro, The 67

Marks, Joe 148, 175, 177, 179
Marks, Lynne xv
Marks, Morris 177
Marks, Theodore Isaac 177, 179, 180
Marshall Square, Johannesburg 188, 189
Marxism 212, 214, 220, 242, 253, 263–264
Masekela, Hugh 193
Masuka, Dorothy 194, 195, 197, 236
Mathis, Johnny 139–140
Matlou, Joe 240
May, Fred 12, 13, 15, 64, 65, 70
Mayfair, Johannesburg 27, 30, 84, 178
McGlew, Jackie 77
McGregor, Chris 193
McLean, Roy 77
Metro, Johannesburg 22
Middleton, Grenville xvi, 94, 194, 236
Miller, Keith 61, 77
Milner, Lord Alfred 92, 103
Miranda, Carmen 8
Modisane, Bloke 246
Moeketsi, Kippie 193
Mohale, Gabriele xvi
Mohammed, Miriam 223–228, 232, 262
Mohammed, Zoot 223–228, 262
Molefe, Nanny Poppy 17, 34, 35, 40, 66, 103, 104, 106–111, 194, 261
Montparnasse Café, Hillbrow 186, 192, 198, 204, 206, 234, 237, 252, 253
Mossadegh, Mohammad 74
Movietone News 74
Muller, Jock 95
Mundy-Castle, Professor 238–240, 243–244
Munro Drive, Johannesburg 117–118
Mussolini, Benito 81

N
Nakasa, Nat 246
Nancy Drew 50
Nasser, Gamal 74
National Horseracing Authority xv
National Party 70, 80
Naught for Your Comfort 127, 226
Netanyahu, Benjamin 82, 86
New Age 123, 225
Nietzsche 207
Nitch, St John B. 99, 101, 102, 114, 117, 119, 126, 127, 131, 161
Nkosi, Lewis 246

Nokwe, Duma 240, 242, 248, 262
Norwood Primary 58
Nugget Hill, Johannesburg 183

O
O'Reilly, Tony 60
Odets, Clifford 253
Olawumi, Stella xvii
Olmert, Ehud 82
On the Road 219
Orwell, George 80

P
Packard, Vance 235
Pahad, Essop 242
Pan African Congress 240
Pasternak, Boris 212
Pather Panchali 186
Patterson Park, Johannesburg 58
Pearls, Stephen 62, 64, 65, 68, 85
Pickup on South Street 73
Pimville, Johannesburg 157, 160
Player, Gary 94, 98, 126
Plaza Cinema, Johannesburg 187
Pollitt, Harry 211, 213, 243
Pondoland 246
Ponnen, George 254
Ponnen, Vera 254
Population Registration Act 229
Pratt, David 246
Pratt, Stewart 29
Presley, Elvis 130, 131, 140, 200, 222
Princess Elizabeth 56
Princess Margaret 56
Purple Renoster, The 186
Python, Monty 264

Q
Queen Elizabeth 56

R
Rand Daily Mail, The 246
Rand Revolt, The (1922) 6
Rangers football team 59–60, 130
Rathebe, Dolly 194
Raymond Street, Johannesburg 4–15, 39, 62, 68, 77, 107
Rebel Without a Cause 130
Red Army 31, 69, 74
Regina v. James and Five Others 167

Regina v. Kollie Moffat Kubeka 162
Resha, Robert 238, 239, 241–242, 244, 248, 249, 262
Resnik, Isaac 9
Retief, Piet 16
Revolt, The 86
Rhodes, Cecil John 37
Riga, Lithuania 4, 81, 220
Rissik Street post office, Johannesburg 22
Road to Rio 23
Rock Around the Clock 187
Rockey Street, Yeoville 22, 33, 39
Roeland Street, Cape Town 224
Rosenberg, Ethel 74
Rosenberg, Julius 74
Roux, Eddie 222
Royal Ballet 254
Royal Naval Dock Command 37
Royal Navy 121
Rushton, Patsy 198–199, 200–207, 212, 214–217, 218, 220–223, 226–228, 231–234, 237, 243, 253, 254–257, 262
Russian Revolution 31
Rydal Mount, Johannesburg 183–184, 190, 202, 218, 233, 257

S

Sachs, Bella 68–69, 72, 74, 87, 91
Sachs, Faygie 68–69, 91
Sachs, Minky 68
Sachs, Solomon 68, 74, 82
Salant, Lithuania 4
Salomon, Larry xvi, 219–224, 227, 231–233, 236, 238, 241, 243, 253, 257, 262
Sartre, Jean-Paul 4, 196, 206, 207, 212, 221, 242, 243, 263
Saxonwold, Johannesburg 187
Schroeder, Bubbles 87–88, 139
Scotland Yard mysteries 50
Second World War 4, 73, 121, 179
Seeff, Norman 183–186, 196, 198–199, 202–203, 212, 233, 247, 254, 262
Sekoto, Gerard 4
Serebro, Chandrea 9
Serving My Time 211
Seven Steps, Cape Town 224
Shakespeare, William 125, 185
Sharon, Ariel 82, 86
Sharpeville massacre 29, 245–250, 251–252, 253, 262, 263
Shelley, Byron 124, 129, 250
Sher, Joe xv, 18
Shostakovich 182
Shubin, Vladimir xvi
Sieve, Mrs 54–55, 85–86
Silver, Jock 'the shnoz' 9, 12–14, 16, 19, 109
Simonson, Karina xvi
Skylarks, The 196
Slovo, Joe 91, 128, 149
Smith, Trixie 197
Smugglers Den, Johannesburg 214, 215
Smuts, General Jan 6, 11, 13, 53, 64, 70, 92, 95
Sobukwe, Robert 240, 248
Socialist Sixth of the World, The 213
Sonik, Izzy 190
Sonik, Michelle 190
Sonik, Roz 190
Sophiatown, Johannesburg 35, 109, 157, 158, 160, 161, 185, 194
South African Armed Forces 64
South African Derby 12
South African Parliament 75
South African War *see* Anglo-Boer War (South African War)
Spartacus 236
Special, Lemmy 197
Splendour That Was Egypt, The 86
Springbok Legion 75, 213
Springboks rugby team 60–61, 114
St John's Old Boys 92
Stalin, Joseph 65, 69, 212, 252
Star 31, 36, 76, 119, 246
Stein, Brian 224
Stein, Isaiah 224
Stein, Mark 224
Steinbeck, John 186
Strijdom, Dr J.G. 156
Suez Canal 74
Sunday Times, The 246
Superman 50
Swanepoel, Rooi Rus 250

T

Table Mountain, Cape Town 211, 222, 223
Tale of Two Cities, A 51, 122
Tambo, Oliver 241, 248

Index

Taylor, Jeremy 184
Taylor, Rosemary 186, 195, 196, 204, 213, 237
Themba, Can 246
Thomas, Dylan 186, 263
Three Stooges, The 51
Time Longer Then Rope 222
Tito, Marshall 182
Tiyo, Dottie 194
Tobias, George xv, 36
Tobias, Joel xv, 38, 211–214, 262
Tobias, Minnie (née Cohen) 18, 35–36, 38, 39
Tobias, Sylvia 211, 213
Tom and Jerry cartoons 51
Tom Brown's School Days 50
Toweel, Vic 45–46
Transkei 224
Transvaal Education Department 125
Tshabalala, Baba Ngomezulu 106–111
Turffontein, Johannesburg 12, 59, 97
Twist Street, Johannesburg 183

U
Uncle Tom's Cabin 51

V
Valli, Salim xvi
Van der Riet, 'Boetie' 96, 98–99
Van Ghent, Henk 9–10, 13
Van Schalkwyk, Captain 189, 249–50
Verwoerd, Hendrik 29, 70, 95, 225, 229, 230, 246, 252
Vilna Gaon Jewish State Museum, Lithuania xvi
Von Loggerenberg, Alf 224
Von Mellenthin, General 136
Von Mellenthin, Gisela 136

W
Waiting for Godot 252, 253
Waiting for Lefty 253
Walcott, Clyde 77
Water's Edge, Cape Town 216, 218–230
Waugh, Evelyn 201, 204, 205, 206, 222
Webber Wentzel Attorneys xvi
Weekes, Everton 77
Weinberg, Eli 31
Weinberg, Violet 31
Wessels, Jacobus 153–154
Western Main Reef xvi, 178, 179, 180
Whyte, Derby 114, 115, 118
Williams, Cecil 126, 213
Witkin, Aaron 199, 203, 227–228
Witkin, Jacob (Jacko) 203–204
Wits Historical Papers Research Archive xvi
Wolpe, Harold 91, 149
Wonder Woman 50
Wordsworth, William 124, 126
Worrell, Frank 77
Wright, Tiger 20
Wynberg police station 156

Y
Yeoville Boys Primary xvi, 45–46, 71, 73, 77, 78, 84, 91–93, 107, 110, 129
Yeoville, Johannesburg xvi, 9, 14, 23, 24, 39, 41, 66, 67, 71, 72, 86, 94, 114, 126, 128, 134, 141, 182, 196, 255, 253

Z
Zaga-Kahn family name 6
Zedong, Mao 74
Zionist Federation of South Africa 133, 136
Zionist movement 78–88, 113, 135